Outcasting Armenians

Modern Intellectual and Political History of the Middle East
Fred H. Lawson, *Series Editor*

Select Titles in Modern Intellectual and Political History of the Middle East

The Autocratic Parliament: Power and Legitimacy in Egypt, 1866–2011
Irene Weipert-Fenner

Everyday Politics in the Libyan Arab Jamahiriya
Matteo Capasso

Figures That Speak: The Vocabulary of Turkish Nationalism
Matthew deTar

Iran's Experiment with Parliamentary Governance: The Second Majles, 1909–1911
Mangol Bayat

Killing Contention: Demobilization in Morocco during the Arab Spring
Sammy Zeyad Badran

The Politics of Public Memory in Turkey
Esra Özyürek

Sayyid Qutb: An Intellectual Biography
Giedrė Šabasevičiūtė

Watermelon Democracy: Egypt's Turbulent Transition
Joshua Stacher

For a full list of titles in this series,
visit https://press.syr.edu/supressbook-series/modern-intellectual-and-political-history-of-the-middle-east/.

Outcasting Armenians

Tanzimat of the Provinces

Talin Suciyan

Syracuse University Press

All images including the cover photo are scanned and reprinted with permission of the Bibliotheque Nubar de l'UGAB, Paris.

First Edition 2023

23 24 25 26 27 28 6 5 4 3 2 1

∞ The paper used in this publication meets the minimum requirements of the American National Standard for Information Sciences—Permanence of Paper for Printed Library Materials, ANSI Z39.48-1992.

For a listing of books published and distributed by Syracuse University Press, visit https://press.syr.edu.

ISBN: 978-0-8156-3819-3 (hardcover)
978-0-8156-3812-4 (paperback)
978-0-8156-5694-4 (e-book)

Library of Congress Control Number: 2023933985

Manufactured in the United States of America

In memory of my female maternal ancestors from Garin/Erzurum.
Disappeared, converted, survived, and remained nameless.

Contents

Acknowledgments

This book is the revised and extended version of my *habilitation*, which was accepted by the Ludwig-Maximilian University of Munich in November 2019.

It was not an easy task to work with primary sources on which there was no secondary literature when I started my research for this book in 2014. Particularly in the field of Turkish studies, I was alone with an extremely rich corpus that I was expected to make sense of. For this difficult task, it was a rare opportunity to have such an exceptional Turcologist as Dimitri Theodoridis with whom to discuss the content and context of these archival materials. A brilliant intellectual who has served as one of my most valuable mentors, his support and friendship throughout the past fourteen years of my research and teaching in Munich have been a real privilege. I cannot thank Mr. Theodoridis enough for all I learned from him.

Another blessing was the encounter with one of the leading Marxian historians of our times, Harry Harootunian, who invested his precious time and energy discussing the revisions I have been making on the book, introducing me to the new perspectives of temporality, enhancing my understanding of peasantry, and encouraging me to combine temporality with territoriality. I thank Professor Harootunian for his patience, knowledge, and enthusiasm and for always being there for me when I needed his guidance.

I thank Christoph K. Neumann (Munich), Hans-Lukas Kieser (New Castle/Zürich), Martin Sökefeld (Munich), Bedross Der Matossian (Nebraska), and Martin Schulze-Wessel (Munich), who each wrote detailed reports on my *habilitation*, giving me important feedback to better develop my ideas in this book. I am also thankful to the editors of Syracuse University Press, especially to Margaret A. Solic and Laura K. Fish, who did their best to guide me throughout the process of preparing the book for the publication. In the same vein I would like to thank the book's peer reviewers for reading the manuscript carefully and making some very valuable suggestions.

I cannot thank enough Paul Vartan Sookiasian for his patience with me as he copyedited and proofread this book throughout the entire publication process. Sticking to *σοφόν το σαφές* (the wisdom is embedded in the clarity), his work in fostering greater precision in the text helped develop what is hopefully a more understandable book out of quite complex historical contexts and concepts. During the marathon of proofreading and preparing the manuscript to print, Sesil Artuç's meticulous work was an enormous help, for which she has my deep gratitude.

One of the biggest challenges that a researcher faces while working with Armenian sources is their worldwide dispersion. The first library I visited in order to review its Armenian periodical collection was Istanbul's Atatürk Kitaplığı in 2013. Its small collection of newspapers from the nineteenth century was a good start. I then worked in the library of the Armenian Patriarchate in Istanbul, where I mainly scanned the publications of the Armenian provincial administrations. The library of Surp Pirgiç Armenian Hospital in Istanbul has a special place in my academic career as it was organized into a library through the publication of my doctoral dissertation. A considerable portion of the primary and secondary sources of my first book, *The Armenians in Modern Turkey: Post-genocide Society, Politics and History*, were predominantly found in a storage room there, which later became a full-fledged library. I am thankful to librarian Azad Kurtlukaya, who was always ready to help me whenever I needed something.

If the Armenian Hospital's library was a discovery for me at home, the Armenian General Benevolent Union (AGBU) Nubar Library in Paris was one abroad, when in 2014 I first realized the existence of the patriarchate's nineteenth-century archive in the middle of Europe. I extend my thanks to Boris Adjemian and Megerditch Basma for making my stay in Paris a fruitful one as they made archival documents available and scanned them for me. Nubar Library is definitely one of most important places to research nineteenth- and twentieth-century Ottoman history and Turkey. Working in this historic place is an extraordinary opportunity for a researcher. The main corpus of this study was collected during my research visits to Nubar Library in 2014 and 2017.

The newspaper collection of the Armenian State Library is a very rich one where the librarians as well as then director Tigran Zargaryan were always ready to help and digitize the sources I needed. I thank them wholeheartedly.

My research conducted at the Armenian Research Centre at the University of Michigan–Dearborn and at the library of the National Association for Armenian Studies and Research in Boston were both very productive. Ara Sanjian and Gerald Ottenbreit from the Armenian Research Centre and Marc Mamigonian from NAASR were always ready to provide me the materials I needed. My research at the Library of the Mechitarist Congregation in Venice in 2018 was similarly very productive. I am thankful to all of those who supported my research at every stage.

Special thanks goes to Helmut Thiess from the Bavarian State Library who, as always, located sources and made some very rare finds available to me. An example is the collection of the *Zhamanag Hantēs Hayrenanuēr* newspaper. Published biweekly in Istanbul during the mid-nineteenth century, this newspaper included exceptionally detailed articles on Armenians in the provinces.

There are a number of people to whom I feel indebted a heartfelt gratitude, first and foremost a group of female friends with whom each of us has been privileged to share a life, regardless of where we are. Words fall short of expressing their exceptional emotional support throughout the writing and publication of this book. In addition, the women of Parrhesia Collective, consisting mostly of Armenian women living in diaspora, have been of immense importance over the past two years. We shared our experiences, realized the historic contexts of these experiences, and learned to think and produce together, which in turn created a deeply connected network of autochthonous women during a time of quarantine and loneliness. I should also name some of the friends and colleagues who read and commented extensively on the chapters during the preparation of this book: Ani Garmiryan, Ayşe Günaysu, Chrisa Lazariotou, Ertuğrul İnanç, Gülhan Balsoy, Jörg Heinemann, Katia Zamarian, Nazan Maksudyan, Sibel Türker Heinemann, Vartan Halis Yıldırım, and Yeliz Soytemel. I extend my gratitude to them for their support and generously devoting their time.

My first book has a lengthy chapter on the Armenians living in Turkey's provinces, yet this book is specifically about the Ottoman provinces. Within a century, life has changed dramatically and drastically for all inhabitants of the provinces. It's been a privilege to be disciplined and generously taught by the archival material that not only revealed to me villages, districts, locations, peoples, words, dialects, and expressions that are no longer known today, but also introduced me to a completely different world, a way of life that no longer exists. Reading, thinking, and reflecting upon this material was more than anything else an extremely empowering experience, as it reestablished a connection with that which had been lost long ago.

Munich, November 2022

Note on Transliteration, Translation, and Calendars

The transliteration follows the Library of Congress's transliteration table found at https://www.loc.gov/catdir/cpso/romanization/armenian.pdf. I have used the Western Armenian transliteration system throughout this book.

I did not transliterate names that already had an established orthography, such as Arshag Alboyadjian, Ghugas Injijian, or Zabel Yesayan. I used *-yan* for Armenian surnames instead of transliterating them as *-ean* in the main body of the book, in order to facilitate the reading.

Throughout this book, the terms *Nizamname* and *Constitution* are used interchangeably, without giving preference to one or the other. Similarly, both *Constantinople* and *Istanbul* are used, depending on context.

While the titles of the official publications of the patriarchate are translated, their transliterations can be found in the endnotes and bibliography.

Whenever city or village names appeared in Armenian, I included their contemporary Turkish names.

While preparing the book for publication, it occurred to me that many of the concepts and institutional names mentioned in the archival material do not have a standardized English translation. It was a challenging task to find appropriate translations to Ottoman bureaucratic institutions and regulations such as Tahrir-i Emlâk Nezareti or Tahrir-i Nüfus ve Emlâka Dair Nizamname, and at times in the cases of taxes such as *şahnalık* and *ölçek hakkı*, it was not possible to find an equivalent term.

All Armenian publications including newspapers and official publications were principally dated in the Julian calendar during the nineteenth century. Many also included the dates in the Hijri calendar and in some cases even the Gregorian calendar. The correspondence files of the Archive of the Patriarchate of Constantinople carry the Julian date. However, regardless of the language, in the main body of the Armenian archival documents, references to specific years are usually written in Arabic Hijri calendar.

Outcasting Armenians

Introduction

It is not coincidental but structural that some periods in history enjoy more scholarly attention than others. Usually, these are the periods that have come to be celebrated for such distinctions as being the start of "modernity," having paved the way for "reform movements," leading to "technological and/or industrial developments," or heralding "progress" that created "revolutionary and fundamental changes" in people's lives. By the same token, however, it mainly goes unsaid that also embedded in those periods are the most painful, brutal aspects of many people's histories. Hence, "progressive developments" take place at the expense of those whose contributions, agency, and even very existence are denied. In other words, following Johannes Fabian's terminology, in such cases, the coevalness of the "reformer" or sovereign and that of the "reformed" or oppressed is denied.[1] Over time, governance means to decide whose time has come to an end, and, therefore, whose histories and temporalities ought to be consigned to oblivion. Time means place; if we do not have time for something or someone in our lives, we do not have a place for them either. The decision to give time and therefore space is a structural one, as is the bringing of someone's time to an end.

The era of Tanzimat is often demarcated as starting with the reading of the Imperial Edict in 1839 and ending with the proclamation of the first Ottoman Constitution (*Kanun-ı Esasi*) in 1876. It is undoubtedly one of those eras of "reform and progress" lauded in the historical literature, whose ideals were promulgated in the Sultan's promise of "benevolent (re)organization" (*Tanzimat-ı Hayriye*), continued with the Reform Edict of 1856 and culminated in the constitutional period of December 1876–February 1878.[2] However, since the Russo-Ottoman War was the reason for the suspension of the Constitution, it would be more appropriate, as rightly suggested by Dzovinar Derderian, to consider the outbreak of war as the end of Tanzimat, if time periods in history can even be said to start and end in such a fashion.[3] Despite varying approaches, there is a near consensus that Tanzimat was a period of reform, and conversely that the reign of Abdulhamit II was a very bloody one. While these two periods are often represented in opposition to each other, the historiographic discrepancy created between Tanzimat and the Hamidian eras hides the many links connecting them from the 1830s to the end of the empire. This study considers historical processes in continuities akin to geological formations,[4] allowing us to think of them not in terms of a linear past and present but as a cumulative one, as suggested by Massimiliano Tomba. Thus, one of the most important markers of history in the twentieth century, the Ottoman state's decision to annihilate its Armenian population, cannot be understood without looking at the formative structural, institutional, social, and political layers that shaped the time, place, and experiences throughout the nineteenth century that permitted such a crime to be committed.

"Security of life, safety of chastity, honor, and property" (*Emniyet-i can, mahfuziyet-i ırz ve namus ve mal*)[5] is an emblematic expression stemming from the original text of the *Gülhane Hatt-ı Hümayunu*, which was often referenced by Armenians and Armenian sources. Indeed, the security of life, honor, and property was what Armenians needed and most hoped for from Tanzimat. Security and equality before the law were aspirations not just of the Armenians but of all those who were hierarchically inferior in relation to the sovereign. Therefore, the promises of Tanzimat were a call for a new era, an era of egalitarianism in which all subjects of the empire aspired to share in not only the mechanisms of equality before the sovereign but more importantly the ambitious yet ultimately impossible attainment of coevalness with the sovereign.

One of the main aims of this study is to unearth and analyze nineteenth-century archival documents of the Archive of the Patriarchate of Constantinople (APC)[6] from both the capital and the provinces. Although the archival material has been available for the past hundred years, it remains an understudied corpus. While the multiethnic and multicultural character of the Ottoman Empire is often underscored in the historiography, sources of non-Turkish or non-Muslim populations like those of Armenians, Alevis, Assyrians, Chaldeans, Catholic communities, Greeks, Jews, Nestorians, Romas, and others are rarely used, if not outright omitted. Similarly, while the secondary literature more often than not mentions that the *millets* had their own administration according to their religious traditions, the scarcity or even nonexistence of literature on their functioning, their interactions with other *millets*, and their relations vis-à-vis the Ottoman administration reflect a lack of interest in this area, to say the least. In the same vein, as seen in Avner Wishnitzer's book on Ottoman temporality, though the reader is reminded about the existence of different calendars for peasants and different *millets*, the chosen or preferred temporality remains singularly that of the sovereign and the capital.[7] This preference or prioritization in turn excludes the challenges of simultaneously existing temporalities, making their repercussions invisible and decreasing the chances of integrated and comprehensive readings of the Ottoman state and society. Most important, excluding the temporalities of others by default is destined to reproduce the perspective of the sovereign in the writing of history. The subjects were aware and alert to the time and temporality of the sovereign. However, attentiveness that stems from subordination is a unidirectional one.[8]

This book follows the guidance of Massimiliano Tomba, who, inspired by Walter Benjamin, suggests working with the paths that have been repressed or not taken.[9] By unblocking the ruptures of historiography and intervening against its claim of completeness, this book follows the Benjaminian approach of not only facing the dark side of history but also pointing out its incompleteness. As expressed in his "On the Concept of History," understanding the tradition of the oppressed is the key to revealing the rule(s) of the sovereign.[10] To that aim, I will discuss here the meaning of there having existed multiple Ottoman temporalities and combine it with the concept of Ottoman territoriality. Provinces that have a central place in this research are not considered merely as geographic, spatial, or administrative units, but first and foremost as sites of different temporalities as well as subjects of different methods of temporal governance. In this sense, it is the provinces that are not only geographically or administratively "outside of the center,"[11] but more important temporally and territorially outside of it. Institutional and structural changes undertaken during Tanzimat included violent methods of synchronization to the center, combined with the creation of new regimes of territorialities "affecting, influencing, controlling people and their relationships by delimiting [and] asserting control over" reconquered areas.[12] Utilizing Robert David Sack's definition of territoriality in combining time and space, I will elucidate the impact of temporal and territorial methods of governance created and reproduced by the center and what they meant for the *millets* living in the provinces.

Tanzimat of the Provinces and the Tanzimat Literature

Growing scholarly interest in the provinces of the Ottoman Empire has led to a discussion on the concepts of center-periphery as well as the term *province*. Having noted this point, scholars agree on the fact that those Ottoman provinces or peripheries densely inhabited by Armenians and Kurds have not enjoyed the same attention from scholars as the Northern African, Syrian, or Balkan provinces do.[13] Even the vocabulary I came across in the literature on the Ottoman provinces showed a difference in perceptions and adjectives used to define various provinces. For instance, Ali Yaycıoğlu refers to Crimea as a strategic and prestigious province,[14] and Jun Akiba draws our attention to how the "privileged provinces" (*eyalat-ı mümtaze*) such as Egypt, Crete, and Mount Lebanon enjoyed special administrative arrangements, especially after the Treaty of Berlin in 1878.[15] It can be argued that these are the provinces that have attracted more scholarly interest, while the eastern provinces have been considered neither privileged nor prestigious, and in fact are described in much different terms. For example, when referring to the notables of the eastern provinces, Uğur Bayraktar mentions that they were regarded as untrustworthy allies.[16] This untrustworthiness must have stemmed from their demographic profile, that is, local Christians, such as Armenians, Assyrians, Chaldeans, Nestorians, and Sunni and Alevi Kurds, a profile that can be traced to the formation of the provinces during the nineteenth century via an important strategy that Akiba pointed out: "Thus, geographical Macedonia and Albania, inhabited by Slav, Greek, Albanian, and Turkish populations, was divided into five provinces, whereas Eastern Anatolia, inhabited by Armenians, Kurds, and Turks, was composed of five provinces, increased from three in the 1870s."[17] Consequently, it can be argued that the size and demographic profile of the population lay at the heart of Ottoman territoriality, which clearly affected the people living in a given province.

As for the concepts of center-periphery in the Ottoman context, Yaycıoğlu draws our attention to their use in the Deed of Alliance (*Sened-i İttifak*) that is considered the precursor to Tanzimat. He shows that the deed often juxtaposes the inner and outer, the inner being the central state, *devlet-i aliyye*, and the rest as *taşra*, outside of the center.[18] In her doctoral dissertation on the southern Balkans, Anna Vakalis pointed out Ottoman historiography's strong state-centered approach, which turned the provinces into far-away local societies.[19] Vakalis rightly criticizes the mainstream approach of considering the center to be the only meaningful unit of analysis. This state-centered approach has its roots in the early generations of Ottoman historians like Roderic Davison and Ömer Lütfi Barkan. Davison referred to "farther provinces,"[20] whereas Barkan imagined a center that seems to have its reference in post-1923 Turkey, defining Syrian provinces as being "far away from the homeland/fatherland" (*ana vatandan uzak*).[21] Similarly, Musa Çadırcı also attributes importance to a locality's distance from the center in terms of the applicability of the structural and administrative changes through the newly introduced institutions.[22] This book will instead argue that even long before the establishment of Tuna Vilayeti as the first model province based on the Provincial Regulations of 1864, the "demographically uneasy" regions mentioned by Akiba such as the eastern provinces were already a testing ground for the new Ottoman territorial regimes and methods of governance in development.

A particularly clear hint at the empire's determination to establish Ottoman sovereignty via its methods of governance even before the adoption of the Provincial Regulations is the process by which the Vilayet of Kurdistan was formed in 1847, with its constantly changing borders.[23] In their article on the establishment of the Vilayet of Kürdistan, Sezen Bilir and Alişan Akpınar point out the province's original borders included the

Vilayet of Diyarbekir, Van, Muş, Hakkari, Cizre, Bohtan, and Mardin. The borders were changed just two years later in 1849 to exclude Van, Mardin, and Cizre, which became part of the Vilayet of Hakkari and was later renamed the Vilayet of Van. That same year, Mustafa Pasha's dismissal from his position in Cizre (*kaimakam*)[24] must have been related to the division of the province in two. While the Provincial Regulations of 1864 have been almost exclusively discussed in terms of changing concepts of territorial governance units, such as *vilayet*, *liva*, *sancak*, and *kaza/köy*, this book will instead suggest discussing the regulations in terms of Ottoman territoriality, a process that had its roots in early Tanzimat. Robert David Sack argues that the greater the number of territorial hierarchies in an area, the more likely its boundaries are artificially imposed, the more administrators are rotated in and out, and the more distant and impersonal are the relations between governors and the governed.[25]

It is important to note that the Ottoman administration regarded the newly established Vilayet of Kurdistan as reconquered and therefore paid special attention to choosing *trustworthy* officers to serve there.[26] Their trustworthiness and effectiveness, however, were contested by the center's temporal policies through the constant rotation of officeholders. Karen Barkey's article on Ottoman temporal strategies of governance, which looks at policies of appointments and dismissals of the officeholders of the provinces, can help combine territorial and temporal methods of governance. Barkey argues that the rotation of officials was an important tool for reinforcing Ottoman rule in the sixteenth and seventeenth centuries.[27] Hence, the existence of this reservoir of knowledge has to be taken into consideration when looking at the developments of the nineteenth century. As mentioned with the changes in the Vilayet of Kurdistan's borders and the dismissal of Mustafa Pasha, here, too, paying special attention to the rotations, appointments, and dismissal of officers in the eastern provinces would enhance our knowledge on the temporal and territorial strategies of Ottoman governance.

In his book, Richard Antaramian also takes issue with the concept of center-periphery and proposes that the Ottoman Empire exercised its imperial sovereignty through overlapping and differentiated networks, which according to him consisted of fluid center-periphery relations rather than those of binary opposition often connoted by the term center-periphery. Antaramian suggests the image of a tapestry to best visualize these relations between networks of power,[28] a perception that resembles the mosaic or *ebru* model of Turkish society offered by Turkish liberal circles in the 1990s and 2000s.[29] Antaramian shows that the Armenian administration both in the capital and in the provinces took an active part in the process of restructuring and reordering the empire's institutions and local elites. As in Antaramian, this book will also argue that Armenians were excluded from the newly established power alliances and networks created at the height of Tanzimat.[30] While Antaramian's book offers a historiography of Tanzimat based on the networks of power at the level of the Armenian administration and its elites, in both the center and the provinces, this study will instead analyze the process of the centralization of the Armenian administration through a bottom-up historiography, with the extensive use of the provinces' correspondence with the patriarchate. Its primary sources include petitions and statements of Armenian peasants, the destitute, vulnerable Armenian women struggling against the odds to assert their agency, the disabled and imprisoned, along with the correspondence and speeches of patriarchs and prelates about the provincial oppressions and detailed reports of local village and city administrations. By investigating the territorial and temporal differences created between the capital and provinces through structural and institutional tools of governance, this study looks at documents written by provincial Armenians whose issues became the embodiment of the temporal as well as territorial differences between Istanbul and the provinces.

Methodology

The writing of this book was almost an obligation born out of the issues I discussed in the introduction of my first book, *The Armenians in Modern Turkey*. For me, in dealing with the history of the republic, and having been born into this context as an Armenian, the Armenian agency and participation in the functioning of alliances and power networks in Turkey were neither unknown nor unexpected. Similarly, as Armenians had a population of more than two million in the mid-nineteenth century, both in their autochthonous lands as well as scattered around the empire, it goes without saying that they were actively engaged in the Tanzimat process. Hence, if the Ottoman Empire was centralizing its administration during the first half of the nineteenth century, so was the Armenian administration. The ratified version of the Armenian Nizamname (Nizamname-i Ermeniyan, the Armenian Constitution as referred to in Armenian),[31] the comprehensive legal framework of the Armenian *millet*, guided the restructuring of the Armenian administration and centralized it at the capital with its civil and religious/spiritual councils.[32] Thus, as the Ottoman administration was violently synchronizing the provinces for its own centralization, so too was the Armenian administration bureaucratically synchronizing itself for its own centralization.

These centralization processes are mostly represented in the literature as privileges given to the non-Muslims in general, ascribing a special rhythm and direction to the period of Tanzimat for these subjects of the empire, in our case the Armenians.[33] However, this approach obscures the fact that the major beneficiary of centralization was actually the Ottoman administration. Through the newly established mechanisms of governance, participation, petitioning, local assemblies, and data gathering systems which were instrumentalized through taxation, the Ottoman administration gained access to an immense flow of data from the regions where Armenians lived that was crucial for governing them.

The term *centralization* appears almost without exception in all literature on Tanzimat and on the Ottoman nineteenth century. However, the administrative processes are more often than not described without referring to the violence inherent in that centralization, which includes temporal and territorial synchronization of the provincial administrations. Massacres, military operations, wars, and the policies that followed them are constitutive and indivisible parts of the state's violent synchronization of time that allowed for the centralization of its provincial administrations territorially.[34] Each act of mass violence targeting the autochthonous populations, irrespective of its geographical location, whether it be the April 1822 massacre at Chios by the Ottomans defined in the literature as the Ottomans' "reaction" or "response" to the Greek independence movement, or the 1840s massacre committed by Bedirhan and Nurullah Begs of Tiyari against Nestorians on the easternmost edges of the empire, each *brought to an end* the time of those who were annihilated. Each left the survivors and the newcomers clear as to the new set of rules in place as now synchronized subjects of the empire, taken under the sovereign's *complete* control via the centralization process.

This book argues that Tanzimat sealed the fate of the autochthonous populations and was not necessarily coupled with the most progressive and affirmative meanings of the concepts ascribed to it, such as reform and modernization. Masayuki Ueno argues that until 1840, *takrirs* submitted by the Armenian administration to the Ottoman one mostly related to its bureaucratic processes, such as the appointment or dismissal of clergymen, and that after the late 1840s the content of the *takrirs* was mostly about complaints, taxation, and violence.[35] The archival documents used in this book show the centrality of Ueno's argument that the Armenians were increasingly petitioning the Ottoman administration as a result of provincial oppressions. While centralization of the state seemingly made the Ottoman administration more accessible to the Armenians' struggle for the security of life, property, and honor, the methods of temporal governance used by the Ottoman administration were actually aimed at prolonging or leaving issues unresolved over time, and by doing so were actively contributing to the conflicts throughout the Empire. Therefore, Tanzimat should be regarded first and foremost as a process of implementing new territorial and temporal governance methods in which the security of life, property, and honor was constantly contested.

In an attempt to clarify and contextualize the above-mentioned processes, it was important to show the evolution and functioning of the Armenian administration, its temporalities both in the capital and in the provinces, their interactions with the Ottoman administration as well as with other *millets*, the changing societal orders and the constructions of power-relations, by putting at the center close readings of archival documents. While each case in the study examines different layers and levels of societal and administrative practices, they complement each other in revealing the similarities of practices across the empire, providing a better understanding of how the Ottoman societal fabric functioned. Hence, following Massimiliano Tomba's argument, this book aims to develop "a sensitivity towards the different temporal rhythms of the histories that are simultaneously present" in order to approach the history of the oppressed.[36]

Introduction to the Primary and Secondary Sources

A major resource of this study is the Archive of the Patriarchate of Constantinople, which found its way to Paris through a long and convoluted journey. Patriarch Zaven Der Yeghiayan was forced to leave Constantinople on a British ship in 1922 together with the head of the Armenian Relief Organisation and representative of the first Armenian state Madteos Eblighatyan, who had to depart his country incognito.[37] Before leaving, Patriarch Zaven sent twenty-two trunks of archival documents to the prelate of Manchester, Tokat-born Krikoris (Grigoris) Balakian.[38] A graduate of Sanasaryan College in Erzurum, Balakian was one of the intellectuals deported to Çankırı in the days after April 24, 1915, who managed to survive and reach Europe.[39] After being elected the Armenian bishop of Marseille in 1927, Balakian took the documents with him. Part of the archive was sent to Jerusalem in 1938 upon the request of Patriarch Zaven, who wanted to consult the documents to write his memoir.[40] Another portion was sent to the Nubar Library in Paris. Raymond Kevorkian utilized these archival materials in his book *The Armenian Genocide: A Complete History*, particularly the ones dating to the twentieth century.

The archival material consulted in this study is categorized according to the villages, cities, or administration units (*vijags*) with which the correspondences were held, 240 different locales in all. However, this doesn't mean that there are 240 separate files, as some villages or towns are categorized under their wider administrative units, as noted on the files. For my research I digitized documents from more than thirty-five correspondence files, choosing them according to their date, place, physical condition, and type. I paid special attention to have as many different locales as possible represented, especially those regions that are within the borders of present-day Turkey. One exception is the inclusion of Crete, as Crete was and even today remains under the jurisdiction of the Armenian patriarchate of Istanbul. I selected different types of documents in order to show the bureaucratic mechanism of the Armenian administration and its interaction with the Ottoman administration. By choosing the majority of documents from the provinces, giving priority to the smallest dwelling units, to be analyzed alongside the sociopolitical developments taking place in the capital, I aim to show the similarity of experiences of Armenians throughout the provinces and the deepening gap created between them and the capital. This choice was definitely not an easy one but proved to be very enriching in order to understand how and through which methods of governance the center reproduced itself across the empire.

Numerous languages and alphabets are employed in the APC. The majority of the documents are in Armenian. However, there are also a large number of Armeno-Turkish documents, and I also encountered other variations, including Turkish documents written in Ottoman, Greek, Greco-Turkish, French, and Armenian in the Roman alphabet. I have included in this study documents written in Armenian, Armeno-Turkish, Greco-Turkish, Greek, and Turkish in Ottoman script, all languages and language forms used by peasants, prisoners, and tradesmen, as well as by clerics and local administrations.[41] As Marc Aymes rightly argues, provincial history is a polygraphic history.[42]

I chose many types of documents from the early 1840s up to 1880 for this study, including personal petitions (*arz-ı hal*),[43] collective petitions (*arz-ı mahzar*),[44] interrogations (*istintak*), notarial attestations (*sened*),[45] records (*tahrir*),[46] medical reports, orders of the patriarchate, and regional reports of local administrations and clerics. A common characteristic of almost all of the documents introduced in this study is that they are very detailed and do not have formulaic expressions or long sentences at the beginning or end. Apart from *sened*, *istintak*, and regional reports, all documents have an *inscriptio* and a *salutatio*. Hence, the formulaic expressions are abbreviated and limited to addressing the office of the patriarch of Constantinople without mentioning his name. *İstintak* documents have the names of the people interrogated, their village of origin, and possibly the crime committed, and their signatures can be found under the text of the interrogation. *Seneds* very often have a signature and/or seal of the administrative unit or person, place, and date. They may also include the signatures or seals of witnesses, if need be. The majority of the documents have a date at either the beginning or the end of the narration, followed by the location. The majority of dates are in the Julian calendar, especially if the documents are addressed to the Armenian patriarchate. However, if the addressee is the imperial government, the documents mostly use the lunar Hijri calendar. On some documents, the rear includes a summary, information about the processing of the document, the decision taken, and even a file number, especially in later periods. Many of these documents are in the form of single-sheet mailers.

Rich and complementary primary sources also used in this study include official publications of the patriarchate, the orders and proceedings of the Armenian administration, regulations (starting in the 1860s), and memorandums. The issues mentioned in the archival materials could easily be traced through these proceedings. They are very illuminating in understanding the development of the Armenian administration throughout the Tanzimat period. The relations between the central Armenian administration and local ones, changing power relations, centralization efforts of the Armenian patriarchate in Constantinople, population data, possessions of the monasteries, unresolved cases of land and property, exile, famine, and other issues that needed to be presented to the Ottoman administration, as well as details about the provincial oppressions can all be found in these official publications.

This study also includes some of the periodicals of the time, both in Armenian and in Armeno-Turkish, not just from the capital but the provinces as well. Armenian periodicals used a number of calendars simultaneously. For instance, *Takvim-i Vekayi* (founded in 1831), which was considered the official newspaper of the Ottoman Empire and published in Armeno-Turkish, initially used the Hijri date. Later when it started to be published in Armenian only, the Julian date was added.[47] A wide variety of Armenian papers in this study used either the Julian or Hijri calendar, sometimes both, or even three including the Gregorian (*Alafranga*) calendar. This study consulted the weekly newspaper *Hayastan*, which began publication in Constantinople in 1846,[48] and provincial periodicals, including the daily *Hayrenasēr* (1843–46), published by Khachadur Melik' Selumyants' in Smyrna, and *Ardzuig Darōnoy* (1863–65) from the region of Muş, published by prominent intellectual, cleric, and close friend and colleague of Patriarch Khrimyan, Karekin Srvantsdyants‘ (1840–92). *Zhamanag: Hantes Hayrenanuēr* (1863–68) by Stepan Boghos Papazyan, one of the rare biweekly periodicals published in the capital, devoted long articles to developments taking place in the provinces, especially the eastern ones.[49] Also consulted were *Masis*, one of the longest-published Armenian-language newspapers in the Ottoman Empire (1852–1908); *Giligia*, published in Constantinople between 1861 and 1874;[50] *Manzume-i Efkâr*, one of the longest-lasting Armeno-Turkish newspapers (1866–1913);[51] and another Armeno-Turkish newspaper, *Ceride-i Şarkiye* (1885–1921).[52] There was an abundant number of periodicals published by the Armenians in the Ottoman Empire during the nineteenth century, 148 in Constantinople alone. There were 38 in other cities and towns, including Jerusalem, Aleppo, Erzurum, Tokat, Muş, Van, İzmit, Bardizag (Bahçecik), Marzvan (Merzifon), Antep, Kars, Harput, Sivas, and Hacın.[53] According to Hasmik Stepanyan's bibliographical work, there were 62 Armeno-Turkish publications in the nineteenth-century Ottoman Empire,[54] 13 of those in the provinces, including *Fr‘at‘* or *Fĕr‘at‘*, published in Aleppo between 1868 and 1869,[55] 4 in Varna, and 1 each in Cairo, Erzurum, Brusa, Adana, Bardizag (Bahçecik), Hacın, Sivas, and Antep.[56]

Another valuable historical source for this period is Avedis Bērbēryan's *Badmut‘iwn Hayots‘, 1772–1860*, published in 1871.[57] Bērbēryan was the former secretary-general of the patriarchate, which gave him access to the inner workings of the most important events and turning points of his time. Bērbēryan's book provides detailed accounts of diplomatic and political developments; executions and exiles of members of *Amira* families;[58] diplomatic crises between France, Britain, Russia, and the Ottoman Empire; wars and their consequences; important criminal cases; intercommunal issues; and other social, legal, and economic issues of the period.

Any research on Ottoman Armenians must consult Maghakia Ōrmanyan's three-volume *Azkabadum*, which is a great secondary source for historical developments, laws, and regulations; major political and administrative issues; and biographies of numerous prominent people, including the patriarchs.[59] Ōrmanyan himself was patriarch between 1896 and 1908.

As mentioned above, the primary sources of this study include a large body of administrative, legal, and bureaucratic texts. However, these documents from the nineteenth-century Archive of the Patriarchate of Constantinople have never been studied even in part to reveal and understand the most basic functions of the patriarchate. In the absence of secondary literature based on primary sources, it was a challenging engagement to understand which principles were followed by Ottoman-Armenian ecclesiastical law. A rare comprehensive source for the history of Armenian canonical law based on the manuscripts of the ecclesiastical councils over the millennia is the opus written by Nerses Melik'-T'ankyan.[60] Melik'-T'ankyan's 1,089-page book, published in two volumes in 1903 and 1905, is one of the most comprehensive studies on the subject.[61] My study makes extensive use of Melik'-T'ankyan in trying to compare and explain legal cases found in the primary sources from the patriarchate on the basis of ecclesiastical law.

While working with the patriarchate's archive, I consulted the available online sources of the Ottoman Archives in order to clarify and double-check the information provided in these documents. Such searching helped me to find several documents on the issues mentioned in the archival materials of the patriarchate. For instance, Ottoman documents on the yarn factory (*iplikhane*) are very useful in understanding the manifold functions of the institution. In the same vein, while looking for maps of the provinces from the period immediately after the Provincial Law (1864–71), the Ottoman Archives caused me to consider the significance of Ottoman mapping practices, which will be described in chapter 2. I also followed hints in the archives and prominent Ottoman statesman Ahmet Cevdet's[62] *Tezâkirs* (nos. 27–39) to trace the changes of administrative units within the Ottoman administration, which clarified the meaning of the petitions sent from Cilicia regarding the systematic exile and dispersion of Armenian villages. It was a very eye-opening experience. I consulted documents from several collections such as maps, Sıhhiye Nezareti, Zaptiye Nezareti, Hariciye Mektubi Kalemi (Foreign Ministry Correspondence), Yıldız Mütenevvi Maruzat Evrakı, Bab-ı Ali Evrak Odası, Dahiliye Nezareti Mektubi Kalemi, Dahiliye Tesri-i Muamelat ve Islahat Komisyonu, Yıldız Perakende Evrakı ve Mezahip

Nezareti Maruzatı, and others. During my research, I came across a great deal of correspondence between the Armenian and Ottoman administrations that has yet to be studied.

The Outline of the Chapters

The first chapter of this study analyzes and discusses the evolution of the Armenian administration and its mechanisms throughout the nineteenth century. I do not consider the Nizamname to be a final legislative and administrative text, but rather a point of reference with a constitutional essence and comprehensive administrative structure.[63] This chapter argues that throughout the Tanzimat period, the Armenian administration in the capital gradually became a centralized institution for resolving issues at the expense of other power centers, namely, the Catholicosates of Aghtamar and Sis along with the larger-sized monasteries. Furthermore, the centralization of power in the capital enabled the Ottoman government to interfere and create rivalries between the catholicosates. I traced these rivalries in Ahmet Cevdet Pasha's detailed report "Sis katoğikosluğu hakkında layiha" (1880–1/1298), which discusses internal power clashes and conflicts amongst Armenians, revealing the Ottoman administration's efforts to reproduce asynchronous relations upon them.[64] One of the questions that the first chapter deals with is whether the Nizamname was a result of pruning the authority of local powers, influential monasteries, and catholicosates. The first chapter also underlines the importance of data gathering in governance and administration. Through its councils and registration office, the Armenian administration gathered data on the Armenian population in the provinces, the assets of monasteries, and detailed information on local power relations. The research reveals that the Nizamname was not a static text of administration but an evolving one that created various challenges and contests both for the governors and the people it governed.

The second chapter demonstrates the unevenness and noncontemporaneity of the provinces and the capital based on the Armenian and Ottoman archives. The literature on Tanzimat and the borderlands, especially during the last quarter of the nineteenth century, covers in detail the conquests and administrative and structural changes of the western parts of the empire, namely, the Balkans and Arab *vilayets*.[65] While looking at the Arab provinces and their administrative structures, the link between conquest and reorganization is seen as an automatic outcome of the process. Yet this same connection is not considered in regard to the inner conquest of the eastern provinces. This chapter is central to understanding the functioning of temporal methods of governance as well as the changing territorialities in terms of wars, reconquests, and mass violence. From Cilicia to Dersim, the Ottoman reterritorialization process targeted the integrity of the Armenian villages by purposefully weakening their cohesiveness, if not completely dispersing them. In the same vein, land confiscations and other issues related to land ownership began in the 1850s and continued unabated until the annihilation of the Armenians in 1915. I consider the Ottoman government's refusal to resolve the issues faced by its Armenians for decades as one of its most effective methods of temporal governance, one in which time works *for* the state. It enabled the accumulation of all kinds of bureaucratic material such as petitions and correspondences. This allowed the state to achieve short-term solutions by making necessary alliances with local power holders and to constantly manipulate the course of action. By prolonging conflicts through making unjust interventions and decisions, the state ensured that none of the issues presented by the Armenians in the provinces could be meaningfully understood or even followed by the larger public.[66]

Rather than bringing equality, the administrative and institutional structures introduced during Tanzimat were instead utilized to perpetuate provincial oppressions, especially in areas where Armenians lived. Changes undertaken to administrative units by the 1860s as a result of the Provincial Law exposed Armenians to numerous oppressions, making them the targets of gangs or leaving them outnumbered by migrants purposely settled in their areas. By 1864 constant injustices had already turned the region of Daron/Muş into a disaster area.[67] The situations in two other major centers of the Armenian administration, Erzurum and Van, were not any better. Based on many cases from all over the empire, this chapter argues that the eastern provinces were not the only regions affected by the provincial oppressions. Furthermore, the provincial oppressions were not solely conflicts between the Kurdish and Armenian populations of the Empire but were embedded in the newly introduced regulations and structural changes. Thus, the Tanzimat regulations that promised equality and security came to mean *provincial oppressions* in the language of Armenian peasants and villagers. Tanzimat codified oppressions of every form into the daily lives of Armenians in the provinces while granting increased impunity for the perpetrators. Alongside the state's newly established alliances in those areas, it was the primary source for the insecurity of life, property, and honor that groups like the Armenians faced.

The third chapter discusses the relations between the two largest Christian groups, namely, the Armenian and Rum *millets.* Segregation and the production of hierarchical relations within society based on religious denomination was another tool of governance utilized by the Ottoman administration. For example, serious tensions existed between the Armenian Apostolic Church and smaller sects of Protestant and Catholic Armenians. The relations between the Armenian and Rum *millets* were no exception to these interconfessional tensions. By utilizing cases of conversion in Bandırma and Antalya, I show examples of power clashes between the two administrations. These two complex and detailed conversion cases are analyzed together with the existing literature, both in English and in Armenian, revealing daily life in villages south of the Marmara Sea and along the Mediterranean, while exposing the various levels of local power structures. In a state and society where life was primarily organized around religious confessions and the hierarchies created by them, conversion and apostasy meant a radical change in one's own rights and duties, marking the end of a period in one's life and the start of another.

Chapter 3 argues that the Ottoman administration and its interventions were aimed at keeping the empire's two most populous Christian *millets* in a constant state of conflict. Through the state's policies of offering unjust resolutions to the emerging and ongoing conflicts between the groups, or by not resolving them at all, it maintained and reproduced unevenness between Greeks and Armenians. Despite the fact that these groups were often locked in prolonged conflicts in most parts of the empire, cases in this chapter also show that the Armenian and Rum populations were more supportive of each other in important areas like Crete and Erzurum where one *millet* was considerably weaker than the other.

Chapter 4 aims to understand the principles and juridical processes within the Armenian administration throughout the empire, investigating its functioning within the larger context of Ottoman society. In particular, I consider the operation of family law to be an integral part of the Armenian and Ottoman societal regimes. My impetus for writing this chapter was my inability to find answers to the simplest questions in the secondary literature regarding the functioning of Armenian family law. The chapter reveals the interconnectedness of family law issues with the rest of the societal and political conditions in which Ottoman Armenians lived, thereby enriching our knowledge on a number of local rules and regulations that were previously unknown to us.

Family law issues did not exclusively take place behind closed doors, and thus every decision had to consider the wider political and social contexts of the state and society as well as reference points within Armenian ecclesiastical hierarchies and canonical law. In this quite complex institutional and structural field, I faced a number of challenges and had to find my way more or less in the dark. As there is no secondary literature on the functioning of the Armenian administration in regard to executing legal processes, it was necessary to read a considerable number of documents in order to make sense of one decision or to recognize the meaning of the terms utilized. Furthermore, there are a number of variables that must be taken into consideration, including the existence of multiple systems of seeking justice in Ottoman society which could work against each other. In cases where they did contradict, one must consider the implications for each individual who sought justice. Most important, the ongoing centralization process of the Ottoman as well as Armenian administrations and their repercussions at both the local and the empire-wide levels must be taken into account when approaching the materials.

Petitions, notarial attestations, interrogation protocols, and judicial investigations based on medical attestations are all very informative and enriching in terms of showing both the agency of Armenian women and that of the Armenian administration and its methods of finding solutions to problems, as well as outlining the limits of its authority. They also led me to discover interesting and unique aspects of Ottoman and Armenian imprisonment practices through the details they provide on punishing crimes of "improper behavior," as they are called in the documents, along with the meanings behind terms such as "violent passion," "sent from zaptiah to the hospital," and "sent to the yarn factory."

An Intervention into the Rhythm and Direction of Historiography

The focus of Ottoman historiography has generally defaulted to the history of the empire's dominant groups, using a singular temporality and preferred territoriality, that of the capital. This mainstream approach puts out of the realm of consideration alternative approaches such as bottom-up historiography with the Armenians of the provinces at its center. The discourse of progress and reform created a temporal regime around Tanzimat that remained untouched for a *very long time*. It governed the historiography with its discursive divisions and ruptures like the one created between Tanzimat and the Hamidian period; the former being one of progress and reform, while the latter was despotic and bloody. Through the portrayal of these periods as totally unique and opposite to each other, the many continuities between them were blurred. In addition, the same temporal regime utilized historiographic leaps backward and forward to further obscure the temporal and territorial policies applied throughout Tanzimat, hindering our understanding of the repercussions they had on Armenians.[68] This discursiveness can be traced through the repeated progressiveness attributed to the period of Tanzimat while not touching upon its darker side,[69] which left Armenians with forty long years of *waiting* and hoping for "progress" to *arrive* in the provinces.

The secondary literature more often than not reiterates the state's commitment to the principles of Tanzimat and regards the Reform Edict of 1856 to be an enhancement of it, with the aim of improving the empire's image in the eyes of its European counterparts after the Crimean War. The emphasis in mainstream historiography that the edict was enthusiastically embraced by the state apparatus distracts our attention from the rapid increase in petitions sent from the provinces by Armenians after 1856. The religious call to jihad by the state during the Crimean War was a way to mobilize and confirm the allegiance of the Kurds both within the empire and outside it, particularly in Iran on the other side of the Ottoman border, and only reaffirmed the increased insecurity and impossibility of equality for all peoples. The allegedly liberalizing regulations, practices, and administrative and structural tools of Tanzimat turned Armenians into the empire's most vulnerable subjects.

It could be speculated that without the military conquests of the first half of the nineteenth century and the alliances established during its middle period, the course of events could have led to a much different situation than what existed at the beginning of the twentieth century. The new order, namely, one of insecurity of life, property, and honor for autochthonous groups, with injustice and impunity for the perpetrators, marked the beginning of the end. Provincial oppressions were a chief feature of the Tanzimat period as well as the entire nineteenth century. The asynchronous relationships between the Armenians of the capital and those in the provinces, along with the violent synchronization policies of the Ottoman center, created a new temporality and territoriality by the turn of the twentieth century. Thus the emergence of a Benjaminian *Jetztzeit*, with all its revolutionary potentialities for a better future, was prevented once and for all.

1

The Armenian Administration and Its Legislative and Executive Entitlements within the Ottoman Empire

In this chapter, I will introduce the mechanisms of the Armenian administration, which underwent considerable changes throughout the Tanzimat period. I will utilize archival documents, official publications of the Armenian administration, including memorandums, orders, and regulations, to show that the Armenian administration and its mechanisms were not static institutions based on a single text of the Nizamname/Constitution, but instead consisted of various components that were adopted according to political and social conjunctures and needs. Primary sources utilized in this chapter include the text of the Nizamname, publications of the patriarchate and the Armenian Hospital, the resignation speech of Patriarch Khrimyan, and accounts from Armenian and Armeno-Turkish newspapers of the period. The available literature on Ottoman Armenian institutions and their functions such as Avedis Bērbēryan's *Badmut'iwn Hayots'*, historian and philologist Hagop Siruni's valuable four-volume work *Bolis ew ir terě*, and historian Arshag Alboyadjian's work published in the Armenian Hospital's 1910 yearbook were utilized to contextualize the archival documents and the official publications of the Armenian administration.[1] The body of sources that I examine shows that there were administrative structures in place before the ratification of the Nizamname. Hence, Armenian ecclesiastical law and legal practices, derived from the traditions of Eastern Christianity, were already in force prior to the nineteenth century. I will focus on Armenian ecclesiastical law at the end of this chapter in an attempt to clarify the principles of this legal tradition and its relevance to this study.

Having a Nizamname was closely linked with having the status of a *millet*. Siruni's books emphasized the impact of the newly emerging *millets* such as the Catholic and Protestant ones as deliberate tools aimed at weakening the Armenian Apostolic Church and the Armenians in general. Supporting evidence for the repercussions of these divisions between Armenians can be found in the books of both Bērbēryan and Vartan Artinian. Artinian explains in detail the eventually failed efforts made toward uniting the Catholic and Apostolic Armenian Churches.[2] This failure might have been regarded as an opportunity from the perspective of Ottoman governance, which then established the Catholic *millet* in 1831. In 1840, Patriarch Hagopos, in alliance with the locum tenens of Jerusalem and the Greek Orthodox Patriarch Antimos, applied to the Kadi of Istanbul against Catholic Armenians, who occupied the Assyrian churches in Damascus and Berea. As a result of the court case, the churches were returned to the Assyrians, and thus to the entitlement of the Armenian Apostolic Patriarchate.[3] An interesting point raised by Siruni notes that Christian missionaries were not allowed by the state to publish the New Testament in Perso-Arabic lettered Turkish, but were permitted to do so in Armeno-Turkish. Doing so allowed their ideas to be circulated first and foremost among Armenians.[4] Thus, from the perspective of the state, the Muslim population was protected from the missionaries' influence, but more important, the local Christian groups were exposed to new confessional rivalries, giving the state more tools of governance over them. Protestant missionaries began their activities in the empire in 1831, which confronted the Armenian Apostolic Patriarchate with not only a number of challenges but also the opportunity for growth through competition. Vartan Artinian refers to this situation as a crisis, mentioning that in 1837 Patriarch Istepan of Brusa had demanded Armenians withdraw their children from Protestant schools and published an order prohibiting their participation in Protestant activities altogether.[5] The Armenian administration responded to its faithful converting to Protestantism by investing in education and founded the Üsküdar Jemaran boarding school in

1838.[6] The first Protestant church was founded in Constantinople in 1846, followed over the next two years by ones in İzmit, Adapazarı, Trabzon, Erzurum, Antep, and Bursa. In 1850 the Protestant *millet* was established by the firman of Sultan Abdülmecit.[7]

During the first half of the nineteenth century, the Armenian Apostolic Church and its administrative units were undergoing changes in response to the demands of Ottoman Armenian society. Reading Siruni, one can take the pulse of the Armenians in the capital through their reactions and vigorous struggle for change. Even before the proclamation of Tanzimat, the Armenian administration was undergoing structural and administrative changes, a transition that reduced the power of the economically influential *Amiras* (high-level economically influential Armenians) through the inclusion and participation of a wider range of the societal strata. Already in 1837, ten out of twenty members of the Supreme Council were artisans, an unprecedented occurrence in the Armenian administration, sidestepping at least for the time being the powerful *Amiras* who had previously dominated the administration.[8] In December 1841, a twenty-four-member administrative council was inaugurated that completely excluded the participation of the *Amiras* in an attempt to create sustainable administration without their input. However, by 1844 during the period of Patriarch Madt'ēōs Chukhajyan *Amiras* reentered the administration, with sixteen of them and fourteen artisans in the administrative committee.[9] Before the ratification of the Nizamname, a firman read on May 7, 1847,[10] allowed for the establishment of the Religious and Supreme Civil Councils, which were to administer Armenians until 1860.[11] Patriarch Madt'ēōs and the *Amiras* were called to Emirgan, the mansion of the minister of foreign affairs, Âli Pasha, for the first reading of the firman.[12] The Religious Council consisted of fourteen members, responsible for both religious and civil affairs, and the Supreme Civil Council consisted of twenty laymen.[13] Varujan Köseyan refers to the period between 1847 and 1860 as one of transition from the system controlled by the most influential Armenians, namely, the *Amiras*,[14] to a constitutional system.[15] This period was marked by a series of administrative crises, such as in 1857 when the Ottoman administration refused to ratify the comprehensive governing regulations that the Armenian administration had accepted. Alboyadjian has a detailed account of the background of this constitutional crisis between the *Amiras* and the charismatic Patriarch Hagopos, who opposed their power. According to Alboyadjian, Hagopos wanted to avoid such a conflict and so resigned as patriarch, but was reinstated by Ottoman decree.[16] This act was followed by the establishment of a Supreme Council constituted completely of laymen, such as artisans and public educators, without even a single *Amira*.[17]

The process by which the empire restructured the Armenian Patriarchate in Constantinople for the ratification of Nizamname was also one by which the patriarchate centralized itself and claimed the authority and entitlement over all Armenians living in the Ottoman Empire. However, the version of the Nizamname that was approved by the Armenian administration in 1857 was rejected by the Sublime Porte.[18] The Armenian administration continued to systematize the process of administration around the constitutional regulations that it had already made. The Nizamname/Constitution went through multiple revisions before its acceptance by the Porte, resulting in at least three versions discussed in the literature dating from 1857, 1860, and the one finally ratified in 1863. The work of Alboyadjian and Ōrmanyan outlines the differences between the version of the Nizamname that was prepared, finalized, and accepted by the Armenian administration and the one ratified by the sultan.[19] While this study will not go into the details of these versions, it will discuss structural changes undertaken after the ratification of Nizamname, showing that it was not a static text but rather one that continued to undergo considerable changes. It is important to mention that the period between the approval of the Armenian Constitution by the Armenian administration in August 1860 and its ratification by the Sublime Porte in 1863 was not an easy one. The public pressure was immense, with Armenians demanding that the Armenian administration guarantee it be ratified by conducting demonstrations and even episodes of violent interference in the meetings of the Armenian Joint Assembly.[20]

While Köseyan did not mention how the entire Armenian administration functioned between the turbulence of 1856 and the Nizamname's ratification in 1863, there are some hints to be found in Ōrmanyan, who mentioned that the period of 1857–60 was characterized by the search for a compromise among all sides. Siruni also gave some details on the proceedings of the first meeting of the administrative bodies in 1860 and their constitution. His remarks on the problems occurring between the Patriarchate of Constantinople and the Patriarchate of Jerusalem upon the election of a new patriarch of Jerusalem in 1861 are also directly related to the issue of the former's administrative centralization process. The Patriarchate of Constantinople asserted that according to the Nizamname, it should now govern the election process by sending a locum tenens, which caused a severe reaction from the Jerusalem-Armenian clerics. As the Nizamname had not yet been ratified by the Ottoman administration, Âli Pasha argued that the patriarch in Jerusalem should be elected according to ancient Armenian tradition, regulations that existed prior to the Constitution. For those Armenians who supported a constitutional system of governance, this meant a second rejection of their Constitution since 1857. They protested by forcing the patriarch to sign a public statement against Âli Pasha's order and against the Armenian congregation in Jerusalem, demanding the application of the Constitution. Hence, the election for the Armenian Patriarch of Jerusalem, which took place in the capital of Constantinople at that time, was not a peaceful one. The Ottoman administration also intervened in the process by sending its full security forces to the proceedings, seizing this golden opportunity to again halt the Nizamname ratification process.[21]

Armenians longed for a constitutional system that would include a better and more just system of representation, yet this process was not only about idealistic principles of good governance. It was first and foremost subjected to the Ottoman administration's own centralization process, for which there was a completely different set of priorities. Inspired by Tanzimat and the Reform Edict of 1856 that followed the Crimean War, Armenians in the capital were ready and willing to utilize the opportunities offered by these processes. However, the nature and core of the centralization underway actually intended something else altogether, a reality the Armenians in the provinces had already realized.

Arshag Alboyadjian, in his five-hundred-page work on the Armenian Constitution and Armenian administration published in the Surp Pırgiç Hospital's 1910 yearbook, sheds light on the historical evolution of the Armenian Patriarchate as a power-centralizing institution. He deemed

1612 as the year this process began, when the patriarchate started creating prelacies under its jurisdiction.[22] However, the process taking place in the nineteenth century was far different from the creation of prelacies; it was the installation of a completely different mode of administration altogether. To what extent was the Nizamname/Constitution, or *Sahmanatrut'iwn* as it is referred to in Armenian, a reflection of an already existing administrative mechanism? In other words, is it possible that the Nizamname came about as a result of the patriarchate's pruning of the powers of local authorities, such as influential monasteries and the catholicosates of Sis and Aghtamar?

The Armenian Nizamname was a legal and administrative structure mainly based in the capital of the empire, and its implementation in the provinces has never been thoroughly researched. Although the patriarchate existed as an institution since just after the takeover of Constantinople by Mehmed II, its role, the area of its authority, and its legislative and executive powers became much more structured and centralized during the eighteenth and nineteenth centuries. According to Alboyadjian, the religious and administrative power attributed to the Armenian Patriarchate was the result of the central Ottoman government's political will, for which he suggested four main reasons. First, the Ottoman government wanted to have one person or institution to deal with rather than various representatives, so this consolidation of power was a pragmatic administrative practice. Second, the realm of authority given to the patriarchate regarding marital issues strengthened the establishment of its central authority among the empire's Armenian institutions. Third, the Armenian Church's most important institution, the Catholicosate of Echmiadzin, was not just outside the borders of Ottoman lands, but in a country with which the Ottoman Empire had rather hostile relations. Fourth, the needs of the provinces were met through the Armenian Patriarchate in Constantinople both intellectually and spiritually.[23]

Based on my own research, I agree with Alboyadjian's first argument that the centralization of the Armenian Patriarchate of Constantinople was a pragmatic tool for the Ottoman government and administration. However, the Armenian Church had other institutions in the provinces, such as the Catholicosates of Sis and Aghtamar, which were also within the borders of the Ottoman Empire. In fact, before Ottoman rule, the Armenians of the provinces were under the jurisdiction of the Cilician Catholiscosate. Alboyadjian wrote that the Patriarchate of Jerusalem had come under the authority of the Constantinople Patriarchate in the seventeenth century, which consolidated the authority of the latter.[24] Yet, as seen in the election process of 1861, the Armenian Patriarchate's authority could be contested at any time by the Ottoman administration. I consider these interventions to be discrepancies created between the Armenian power centers that served as strong signals from the Ottoman administration in order to remind the Armenian administration of its subjection to them. A similar Ottoman method of governance was applied regarding the authorities and entitlements of the Catholicosate of Sis, wherein by not touching upon those in the text of the Constitution, the Ottoman administration secured its arbitrating power over the Armenian one. In other words, the Ottoman government saw the existence of these other power centers to be an ideal tool of governance for fostering power clashes among them.[25] The entitlements given to the Armenian Patriarchate by the ratification of the Nizamname should be understood first and foremost in this context. Furthermore, the archival documents reveal that the legislative power of the patriarchate was not just restricted to marital issues, but on the contrary, the Ottoman administration envisaged a patriarchate that functions as an interface between the provinces and the capital. However, from the patriarchate's point of view, being an interface did not necessarily mean they were given the appropriate tools to operate vis-à-vis the Ottoman administration. The agency of the patriarchate and its limits could arbitrarily be changed by the Ottoman administration according to the interests of the empire. While a *berat*[26] given in 1875 to Patriarch Varjabedyan mentioned specifically—as did *berats* given in 1764 and 1831—that the patriarch should submit *takrirs* to solve the problems of his people,[27] this arbitration of power was only a restating of the obvious. It had long been a common practice by 1875 to submit *takrirs*, even if they were typically ignored. The Armenian National Assembly had already stated in 1871 that the *takrir* process was totally ineffective.[28] As early as 1866, Âli Pasha asked the patriarchate to refrain from submitting any *takrirs* not directly related to religious affairs.[29] Masayuki Ueno reads this restriction or prohibition in terms of stopping the flow of *takrirs* about oppressions carried out by Muslim Kurds.[30] Therefore, the limitations on the submission of *takrirs* already proved to be ineffective by the end of the 1860s. *Takrirs* continued to be submitted, most of the time in service to the bureaucratic mechanism, despite their lack of any factual or legal efficacy. In 1872, after the Armenian administration had already discussed and documented the inability of *takrirs* to solve the problems of the Armenian *millet*, especially in the provinces, the Ottoman government repeated its prohibition on *takrirs* regarding nonreligious issues.[31] This was a clear statement by the Ottoman administration that it had the arbitration power to decide what constituted a religious issue and what did not, creating new hurdles in the bureaucratic mechanism in order to muffle the voices of complaint.

Alboyadjian's fourth point mentioned above, the importance of the capital to the provinces, should be reconsidered through the data provided in this study. The various archival documents, as well as publications from the provinces like *Ardzuig Darōnoy*, show the multilayered and multidimensional nature of power relations in the provinces and their repercussions (or lack thereof) in the capital. The Armenian administrative bodies of the provinces were designed to be similar, if not identical, to those in Constantinople. Although we cannot know to what extent this goal was reached, the petitions and local councils' detailed reports from the provinces allow us to trace the administrative bodies stipulated by the Nizamname. More important, the existence of organic and institutional relations between the central and provincial administrations meant greater empowerment for the patriarchate and less autonomy for the Armenian administrations in the provinces. This argument is based on the fact that there were at least two sets of power relations to be taken into consideration: one between the Armenian and Ottoman administrations in the capital, and the other involving the local administrations, both Armenian and Ottoman, which included various institutionalized and informal power structures in the provinces, such as the begs, aghas, tribal relations, moral codes, and so forth. Although the patriarchate had mechanisms and ways to communicate with the imperial administration or other leading representative institutions in the capital, it had relatively little impact on local power relations. The centralization process of the Armenian Patriarchate of Constantinople required the prelacies in the provinces to interact only with the Ottoman administrative units regarding their unresolved problems through the patriarchate itself. However, the Ottoman administration was generally not interested in resolving their problems, as it was not necessarily in its interest to do so, and even if it was supportive in some cases, the solutions it handed down were not enforced or followed up on. The primary matter for the state was the empire's centralization, with the patriarchate's centralization only a secondary process that needed to be subjected to the will of the former. Hence, the process of centralizing the patriarchate's power vis-à-vis the provinces did not always empower the latter, but often became a tool of governance for the Ottoman administration to facilitate control over the provinces. Through attempting to establish its own centralized power in the provinces, the Armenian Patriarchate enabled the establishment of Ottoman centralization in those provinces.

An example is the patriarchate's involvement in the defeat of Bedir Khan and Nurullah Beg in the eastern provinces that brought them under Ottoman control. Ōrmanyan informs us that the patriarch had applied to the grand vizier time and again to find solutions to the issues of the Armenians in the eastern provinces, as they were suffering at the hands of Bedir Khan and Nurullah Beg. Yet his efforts remained unanswered for a long time, a common Ottoman temporal method of governance, which envisioned reacting and solving problems exclusively according to the Ottoman temporality, meaning when it was in the interests of the Ottoman administration and not necessarily of the Armenian.

Upon the patriarch's final plea for help to the Ottoman administration of the eastern provinces in 1847, stating that otherwise he would not be able to stop his flock from emigrating to the Russian Empire, the administration finally offered military support against the begs led by Osman Pasha. Then-patriarch Madt'ēōs Chukhajyan commanded the participation of Armenian men in the operation by sending an order to the prelates of Van, Erzurum, Bitlis, Palu, and Diyarbekir. As an autochthonous population of that region, the Armenians were one of its most resourceful and knowledgeable groups and played a key role in the Ottoman victory, which facilitated the centralization of the Ottoman administration in this area of reconquest. After Bedir Khan's exile to Crete and Nurullah Beg's to Silistra in northern Bulgaria, Chukhajyan wrote a decree to all Armenians in the provinces celebrating the victory of the Ottoman Army, thanking them for their support, and informing them about the satisfaction the sultan had expressed to him.[32] While the Kurdish emirs were defeated and exiled, the oppressive conditions against Armenians took on another and more complicated form. They were forced to fight on the side of the Ottoman Army, yet still shared the same geography with the other Kurdish and Muslim power holders, groups that were much more alluring allies for the Ottoman state than Armenians, especially after their defeat. Neither these aspects nor the newly established Ottoman institutions of centralization and their impacts are included in Alboyadjian's 1910 analysis. Therefore, while agreeing with him on the political motivations of the Ottoman government behind the centralization of the Armenian Patriarchate's power, I consider this process to actually be the subjugation and forceful integration of Armenians within the Ottoman administration's centralization, both territorially and temporally. Following the military victory, it was easy for the Ottoman administration to gather very detailed data regarding the population, structures of villages, and relations between Muslims and non-Muslims through multiple sources, namely, the newly established local administrative councils, the practices of petitioning through the administrative mechanisms of non-Muslim groups, the reports of religious leaders, and, last but not least, through their newspapers.

As shown above, the Armenian Nizamname/Constitution was not a sudden phenomenon but the result of a process, existing mechanisms, and the strong will of the Ottoman administration to gain power over the provinces and local administrations in Asia Minor as a whole, including the eastern provinces of the country from the Pontus region in the North, along the Mediterranean, and elsewhere. Each of these regions had a considerable Armenian population; therefore, the Armenian administration started to become centralized along with the Ottoman administration both in the capital and in the provinces.

As a result of the centralization of the Armenian Patriarchate in Constantinople, the entitlements and limits of authority of the local Armenian administrations were regularly controlled, contested, and redefined.

The authorities and entitlements of the Armenian administration in the provinces were to be enforced through prelates and *vijags*. *Vijags* were administrative units, which according to Ōrmanyan had been in complete disorder and confusion during the mid-nineteenth century. The Armenian Patriarchate drew up a list of *vijags* that consisted of the names of local religious leaders and institutions such as the monasteries, churches, and local Armenian administrative bodies, but not in a systematic fashion, and submitted it to the Catholicosate of Echmiadzin in 1858. Prelacies were based on the location of the prelate (*arachnort*) of the province, making that central city also the seat of its Armenian administration. According to this list, there were forty-five Armenian prelacies (*arachnortutiwn*) in the Ottoman Empire.[33] Avedis Bērbēryan's book *Hayots' badmut'iwn (1772–1860)*, published in 1871, stated there were actually fifty Armenian *vijags*, one of which was Constantinople. While the Patriarchate of Jerusalem was included in the *vijags*, the churches and monasteries under its authority were not. Similarly, Aghtamar was on the list of *vijags*, but it is unclear whether that refers to the catholicosate or not. The case is the same for Sis, as its catholicosate was not mentioned as such, but the town of Sis was grouped together with Cyprus and Darson (Tarsus) as one *vijag*.[34] As we will see later in this chapter, a memorandum from 1865 mentioned that orders were sent to sixty *vijags* regarding the expansion of the Constitution/Nizamname system into the provinces. Thus, it appears in 1865 there were sixty *vijags*, rather than fifty or fewer.[35] This may indicate there was a constant reorganization of certain *vijags*, if not a series of disagreements regarding their reorganization after the ratification of the Nizamname. The second chapter of this book will discuss the *vijags*' changing borders and areas of authority as detailed in the Armenian patriarchate's correspondences.

For the Armenian administration, centralization required collecting more accurate data on its population, leading to the establishment of the statistics office within the patriarchate's structure. Centralization in the provinces also meant having the same type of administrative bodies there as in the capital. Therefore, the Armenian administration in Constantinople at the center of the system required the provinces to establish administrative units according to the Nizamname. Last but not least, centralization meant that the patriarchate became an interface in almost all issues between the Ottoman administration and the Armenian *millet*, an interface that served as a tool of governance for the Ottoman administration since it had the privilege to make decisions regardless of existing laws and regulations. For instance, in 1866 the Ottoman Empire's foreign minister and one of the most influential Tanzimat bureaucrats, Âli Pasha, suspended the Armenian Constitution and appointed a council that remained in charge of the Armenian *millet* for two years.[36] Therefore, in the long run, the centralizing of the patriarchate's power in Constantinople implied the weakening and extinction of the provincial power centers, while the power, authority, and entitlements of the patriarchate were directly subjected to the sultan, grand vizier, and Ottoman administration in general.

In 1872, Patriarch Khrimyan presented the *First Report on the Provincial Oppressions* after compiling information gathered through decades of reports, petitions, and unresolved issues in the provinces. At this time, the Nizamname had officially been in place for ten years, preceded by an additional thirteen-year institutional structuring process that set its foundations, so almost a quarter of a century in total. The proclamation of the first Ottoman Constitution in 1876 was four years away, yet when it came to the application of the Armenian Nizamname/Constitution, the influence on the system by various power holders and their associates was still there. Artinian draws attention to how young Armenians actively involved in the Ottoman state administration were able to effect institutional change and problem resolution through their friendships and social relations with high-ranking Ottoman officials. Prominent cases include Dr. Servichen, who was a friend and personal doctor of Âli Pasha, and Dr. Rusinyan, who was the family doctor of Fuat Pasha. Artinian stated that these interactions were already accelerating the process of constitutional preparation among Armenians[37] even before the proclamation of the Reform Edict of 1856.[38] Ueno makes a similar remark, pointing to friendships between high-ranking Ottoman officials and Armenians, adding that Patriarch Khrimyan was advised by Midhat Pasha in 1872 to deliver documents, presumably petitions, *takrirs*, or surveys, through Krikor Odyan, one of the most influential Armenian figures of the day.[39]

The Armenian administration was thus forced to perpetuate a pattern of governance based on personal relationships with the Ottoman administration, which ultimately left their political structures, legally binding texts, and norms vulnerable to subversion by the state. This method of governance was an attempt to circumvent the Nizamname, undermining the process leading to its ratification and reminding the Armenian *millet* of the sovereign's arbitrating power regarding its issues by attributing a fragile agency of representation to individuals based on personal affinity. By doing so, the Ottoman government in essence not only committed itself against solving any of the problems of its own Armenian citizens but also pretended that these problems were bureaucratically nonexistent. It can be assumed that any petitions submitted through the "friends of Ottoman administrators" ran a high risk of not being processed at all.

Until its ratification and even after, the Nizamname's text continued to be a contested matter. After the resignation of Patriarch Khrimyan, considerable amendments and changes were made to it under the general title of Reordering/Reform Regulation, as found in the following parts of this study. In the "Order of National Administrative Organization" of 1880, we again find a different set of rules and regulations imposed regarding the Armenian administration.

Main Administrative Units of the Armenian Administration

Surp Pırgiç Armenian Hospital

The Nizamname clearly defined the regulations for the administration of the Armenian Hospital, acknowledging its central place within the entire Armenian administration. The Political Council was responsible for selecting nine people, including two doctors, to administer the hospital.[40] It was established by a firman of the sultan in 1832 and began operating two years later. Hence, the hospital with its numerous functions had already been in operation for thirty years when the Constitution was ratified. The Nizamname stated that the hospital had to be active in four main areas: health services to the poor, shelter for elders and people in need, care for mentally ill people, and orphan education.[41] Indeed, at the beginning of the 1860s, the hospital held only 40 sick patients but 350 unhoused people, for whom a special budget called *Sandık* (Coffer) was established.[42] The coffer was funded by income-generating properties owned by the hospital both inside and outside of Constantinople—for instance, an olive garden in Çanakkale/Dardanelles.[43] Each local Armenian administration similarly made coffers for their own constituencies. In chapter 4, I will demonstrate the central role of the Armenian Hospital as an institution that served the various needs of the Armenian *millet* and was also used as a place of incarceration.

The Record Office

In the Nizamname of 1860, the second one proposed but still not ratified by the state, we read about the establishment of a record office called "Azkayin Tiwanadun." The Record Office consisted of three departments: the Office of Correspondence, which handled letters sent to and from the patriarchate; the Office of Registration, dealing with the issues of the National Assembly and the councils; and the Census Office, established to gather information and provide statistics regarding births, deaths, and marriages, as well as being responsible for travel and trade documents. The Census Office was proposed to have a notary elected by the Political Assembly and confirmed by the patriarch. The Record Office would have an administrator responsible for all three departments and would collect birth, death, and marriage information every five years from all provinces and once every year from the districts of Constantinople. The administrator of the Record Office was fluent in Armenian, Turkish, and French.[44] The articles defining the duties of the Record Office remained more or less the same in the ratified version of the Nizamname, but its title was changed from the "National (*Azkayin*) Record Office" to the "Patriarchal Record Office." Interestingly, the frequency of statistical data collection from the provinces changed from every five years to annually in the ratified Constitution of 1863.[45] More changes to the Armenian administration's internal rules are found in an official publication of the patriarchate from 1876, which are listed under the title "Regulations of the Internal Reforms of the National Patriarchate." In this publication, we also find the functions of the *Tiwanadun* and the *Tiwanabed*, the Record Office and its head, and the office of *kapı kahyası* (written as *kap'uk'ēheasē*, chamberlain) to have been redefined. The head of the Record Office and *kapı kahyası* were mentioned as the two main officers of the patriarchate. The composition of the Record Office has slight differences in this document compared to the Nizamname. There were three departments within the Record Office: the Compiler's Office (*Khmpakrut'ean Kraseneag*), the Registration Office (*Artsanakrut'ean Kraseneag*) and the Office of Statistics (*Vijagakrut'ean Kraseneag*). The Compiler's Office processed all written documents in Armenian, Turkish, and French, as well as documents produced by the Religious and Civil Assemblies. The Registration Office was responsible for all incoming and outgoing documents as well as the registration of all correspondence in a register (*domar*). The Office of Statistics was responsible for collecting statistical data regarding the people and properties of the monasteries and churches in the provinces.[46] The Nizamname of 1860 contained a detailed definition of the Record Office and changed the titles of two of its departments: the Compiler's Office (formerly the Office of Correspondence) and the Office of Statistics (formerly the Census Office). Their duties and responsibilities were redefined by the patriarchate in a very sophisticated manner via a memorandum in 1876. The Office of Statistics became responsible for not only birth, death, and marriage records, but also all movable properties and real estate belonging to Armenian institutions, such as monasteries and churches. It can be argued that the Record Office, with its departments, changing rules, and regulations, must have become a pivotal part of the patriarchate's centralization, as it allowed the patriarchate to strengthen its direct relations with the provinces, registering not only its population but also its properties. This process gave the patriarchate, and through it the Ottoman administration, a much better knowledge of and command over the Armenian *millet*'s territorial entities and their governance.

Khrimyan's Resignation and Changes Undertaken

The resignation speech of Patriarch Khrimyan in the summer of 1873 was an important moment for the evolution of the Armenian Nizamname, as it spurred changes in the Armenian administration via new regulations two years later, which will be detailed here. Patriarch Khrimyan was a leading Armenian figure throughout the nineteenth century in multiple respects. He was first known as a political figure from the provinces who vigorously advocated for its residents' issues, and then for his strong belief in the idea of progress and education, and finally for his clerical leadership roles. He was elected patriarch of Constantinople in 1869 but resigned four years later, only to be elected Catholicos of all Armenians at Echmiadzin in 1893, serving until his death in 1907.

His resignation speech of August 3, 1873, given during the sixty-fifth meeting of the Armenian National Assembly, contains valuable hints about the economic, social, and political life of Ottoman Armenians. That very same day, the Political Assembly had submitted its own resignation in protest of Khrimyan, arguing that as patriarch he was not properly applying the rules of the Nizamname.[47] Khrimyan's speech detailed the intractable problems he saw within the system that, despite his best efforts, were not being resolved, causing him to resign out of frustration. In his resignation speech, Khrimyan mentioned that he had unsuccessfully asked for structural changes to be made to the Nizamname during the four years of his mandate. According to him, there were several issues to be addressed, such as oppression in the provinces and a special administration for the capital. Meeting just once a week, he felt the Armenian National/General Assembly was unable to meet the needs of the "3 million [Armenian] people of Turkey."[48] He also felt that provincial affairs should be dealt with separately so that the Armenian General Assembly could operate effectively, suggesting the creation of a "Local Council" and a "Provincial Council."

On July 11, 1873, he submitted a letter to the committee that had been established to restructure the Nizamname in which he wrote: "I would like to draw your attention to the most important issue of the nation [*azg/millet*].[49] . . . Neither would the Provincial Armenians [*Kawaṛatsin*] find solutions to their most urgent issues nor the Armenians of the capital [*Mayrak'aghak'tsin*] [to theirs]." He finished his letter to the Armenian Administration with an emphasis on the issues of the provinces: "They [Armenians of the provinces] waited for so long that they are tired of waiting [*ach'k'ernin halets'aw*]; hopelessness is not far away, there is a need to draw attention to the issues of the provinces. The only way to do this is the division of the administrative mechanism." In this document, written shortly prior to his resignation, Khrimyan made his main concerns clear, and it might be assumed that he was confronted with strong opposition to his proposals, resulting in his resignation. Indeed, in his resignation speech, he noted that the measures he called for were regarded as anti-constitutional, since it was assumed that the patriarch should respect each and every article of the Constitution, but his requests were not in direct accordance with its principles. Khrimyan criticized those accusing him of being against the Constitution, and after emphasizing its importance he said: "Now and forever, I object to this statement."[50] He also added that he wanted to embrace the Constitution but not smother it with compassion. He regarded the Constitution as a system of administration based on rights and duties that should be adjusted to meet the needs of the people, not just those living in the capital. He mentioned time and again his frustration concerning the Armenian administration in Constantinople's lack of understanding in regard to the problems of the Armenians in the provinces.

I read Khrimyan's argument as an intervention into the Armenian administrative mechanism that drew attention to the temporal and territorial differences between the Armenians living in the capital and the provinces. From this perspective, Khrimyan's aim was a historic one, yet can be regarded as a mission impossible. He was well aware of the situation in the provinces, yet there were various layers to the gap and connections between them and the capital, including the influence of numerous local power networks in both places. Armenian centralization, within this process of subordination to the Ottoman one, was not equipped to solve the problems of the Armenians in the provinces alone. The Ottoman centralization of the 1860s had nothing else to give to Armenians other than a ratified Nizamname, and definitely no solution to their problems in the provinces.

One of the most remarkable comments in Khrimyan's resignation speech was on the involvement of the police, about which he said: "I start shivering whenever the police is involved, I mean, when visionless people ask for the help of police guns in criminal cases."[51] Apparently, in Khrimyan's view, the involvement of the police in Armenian (*azkayin*/*milli*) affairs undermined the Armenian administration's authority. Indeed, the official 1876 report of the patriarchate officially incorporated the police as an institution into the affairs of the Armenian administration through the position of *kapı kahyası*. This publication stated that the *kapı kahyası* was to have two assistants, one at the Sublime Porte and the other with the police.[52] Hence, I take Khrimyan's statement to be a reference to the involvement of the police in the *millet*'s affairs even before the process was codified in 1876, which hints at the impact it likely had on the functioning and entitlements of the Armenian administration. By considering the resignation speech alongside the report of 1876, it can be seen how the new regulations legitimized the already existing institutional involvement of the police. Hence, it can be clearly observed that the Armenian Patriarchate's offices were totally integrated with the Ottoman administration in the capital through the position of *kapı kahyası* and the involvement of police, hinting at the further subordination of Armenian centralization to the Ottoman one.

In Khrimyan's speech, he mentioned the lack of clergy, institutions, and churches, especially in the provinces, as another reason for his resignation. This lack meant not only that the religious needs of Armenians were not being met in various places, but that they were completely left alone, abandoned to their fate. Their voices would not be heard in the capital, their rights would not be defended, and eventually, the flock was in danger of being lost as a result of oppressions and pressures by local Muslim power holders. His remarks regarding the lack of clergy in the provinces may be traced to many of the petitions submitted from the provinces. He gave examples from Kharpert (Harput), Agn (Eğin), Tercan, Erznga (Erzincan), Muş, Van, Amasya, Marzvan (Merzifon), Chamshgadzag (Çemizgezek), Tokat, and other places where there were no Armenian clerics and the local communities' numerous complaints and requests remained unresolved. Khrimyan also mentioned in his speech that the issue of the Catholicosate of Sis, its status and entitlements, vis-à-vis the Patriarchate in Constantinople remained unclarified.[53] While Khrimyan drew attention to the unresolved problems of the Armenian administration, especially in the provinces, Siruni pointed to the fact that the provinces' issues not only were lived in the provinces but also extended to the capital. In the city's Galata district, there were large numbers of provincial Armenian migrant workers (*bantukhd*) from Van and Muş who were sharply divided over the issue of Khrimanyan's leadership.[54]

In the period that followed Khrimyan's resignation, we see various reports published on the situation of monasteries, on issues related to the Sis Catholicosate in Cilicia, on orders for educational reform, and about the relations of the provincial and local administrations. Thus, Khrimyan's resignation must have had at least some effect in bringing attention to the issues for which he had advocated, and two years later led to structural changes that sought to address them.

Kapı kahyası *(the Chamberlain)*

One of the interesting changes to the Nizamname was the creation and/or definition of the position of *kapı kahyası (kapukehyası/kap'uk'ēheasě)*, an office whose duties were defined by the patriarchate in an official 1871 memorandum. I could not find a similar position to the *kapı kahyası* in the Nizamname of 1863.[55] *The Memorandum of the Political Assembly (1870–71)* suggested replacing an old, inefficient office called *kapu oğlanı* with the new offices of *kapı kahyası* and his deputy *kapukehyası muavini.*[56] Based on more information about the *kapı kahyası* in the report published in 1876, we find it had become one of the two most important officers of the patriarchate. He was elected by the Political Assembly, based on the recommendation of the patriarch along with that of the head of the Record Office and the locum tenens (deputy patriarch). He was responsible for the communications between the Sublime Porte and the patriarchate and was accountable to the patriarch and his deputy. He was tasked with participating in the sessions of the Political and Mixed Assemblies. As mentioned above, the *kapı kahyası* had assistants at the Sublime Porte and the police.[57] *Kapı kahyası* was also a position in the Ottoman bureaucracy that played a similar role for the governor (*vali*) at the capital in order to communicate with the Sublime Porte.[58] According to the Nizamname, it was the patriarch who had been the only mediator between the Ottoman and Armenian administrations ("*Badrikin Devleti Âliye ile Millet beyninde vasıta olmak hasiyeti sabıkı vechle ikba olınub*").[59] Yet the report of the patriarchate from 1876 seems to indicate that the *kapı kahyası* had a similar mediation entitlement.

In an order (*hrahank*) published in 1873 by the Armenian administration to codify the relations of the prelacies and provincial administrations with the local Ottoman government,[60] it was stated that the *kapı kahyası* in each prelacy was charged with submitting *takrirs* to the local Ottoman administration. The *kapı kahyası* was responsible for the communication between the prelacy and the Ottoman administration in the provinces. He had to be present whenever the *arachnort* (the leading archbishop of a provincial administration) visited Ottoman officials. Hence, the duty of mediation did not remain in the capital but extended itself into the provinces. The following arguments can be made regarding this territorial extension of the role. First, as part of centralization, the provinces needed to have the same structure and institutions as the capital, which resulted in the creation of *kapı kahyası* there too. Second, the *kapı kahyası* mediated between the patriarchate and the Ottoman administration in the capital, and so it would also mediate between the prelates and local administrations, weakening their position and the authority of representatives of the Armenian administration vis-à-vis the Ottoman administration. In other words, the position gave the Ottoman bureaucracy and administration the opportunity to arbitrate power between patriarch/prelate and the *kapı kahyası*, both in Constantinople and in the provinces.

Provincial Committee or Provincial Assembly?

The Nizamname of 1863 had set forth a Provincial Assembly and its functions. The religious leader of each prelacy (*marhasalık*) was the head of the local provincial council with the duty of implementing the Armenian Constitution in his province. It was decreed that just like in the capital, prelacies in the provinces should have district councils, a district coffer, and a district registration office and that a religious assembly, political assembly, and a provincial coffer should each be established.[61] The same structures were anticipated to exist for both the capital and the provinces, which sounds ideal in theory but is actually impossible in practice. The General Provincial Assembly and the Provincial Administration (*Kawaṛagan Varch'ut'iwn*) were established by an order of the patriarchate published in 1861, as was stipulated by the 1860 version of the Nizamname that still lacked ratification by the Sublime Porte. According to this document, the provincial administration should follow the model of the central administration and have its own parliamentarians. It elaborates on the electoral mechanisms and the election procedure of the General Provincial Assembly.[62]

The Memorandum of the Political Assembly to the Armenian National Administration (1865) contains the first instance I encountered of a section titled "*Kawaṛagan*," meaning "Belonging to Provinces," or "Issues of the Provinces." It begins with a clear statement that relations between the patriarchate and the provinces had always been complicated and difficult. The memorandum's tone is one bordering on a complaint in regard to the numerous issues that needed to be dealt with, such as how the number of administrative units in the provinces was too high, the extreme difficulty of implementing the Nizamname/Constitution, the insufficiency of the budget, and the high number of grievances from the provinces. Furthermore, the memorandum states that "the most important and the most insignificant issues of the provinces were at the center of the patriarchate's agenda as a result of the Constitution." The Political Assembly expressed the need for controllers and inspectors in order to secure the application of the Constitution, which would mean the synchronization of the provinces to the administration in the capital. However, it also stated that the Armenian administration did not have the financial means to do so and that there were other unspecified reasons standing in the way. Consequently, according to the document, there were a number of unresolved national problems, disturbances, and difficulties in applying the Constitution.[63]

The memorandum from 1865 stated that the provinces' main problems derived from oppression and heavy taxes and included various complaints from the provinces and descriptions of how they were handled by the patriarchate. It is the first time we are given such a detailed account of the provincial problems, which should be contextualized within the framework of the ongoing centralization of the Armenian Patriarchate. It contains two chapters, one of which is called "Provincial" (*Kawaṛagan*), which includes all the issues related to and happening in the provinces, starting from the regulations of the prelacies, including the unresolved problems of Çarsancak, Aghtamar, Muş, Van, and others. The other chapter is titled "Program: The Situation of Provincial Administrations," which states that out of the "approximately sixty *vijags*" that had been requested to provide their programs for implementing the Constitution and organizing district administration elections, only twenty-five had responded with their plans.[64] Out of those, fifteen had already established their district administrations and were functioning accordingly. It specifically noted that the status of the district administrations of Amasya, Erznga (Erzincan), Muş, Etesia (Urfa), Antep, and others remained unknown. Considering that these areas were heavily populated by Armenians, the lack of a plan on the district level must have been greatly frustrating for the Armenian administration in the capital.

We learn in the 1871 memorandum that after the election of Khrimyan as patriarch, a Provincial Subcommission was tasked with handling the issues of the provinces over the past years but had little success. The memorandum states that the Provincial Committee wanted to be renamed the Provincial Assembly, but its request was rejected by the Political Assembly as being contrary to the Constitution, which established that there could be only two assemblies, with the Provincial Committee as an administrative unit under the Political Assembly.[65] This must have been what Khrimyan referred to in his resignation speech when he mentioned that the issues of the provinces should be separated from the ones of the capital and delegated to another assembly dealing exclusively with the provinces. However, it seems despite his influence, the establishment of another assembly with the same rights and entitlement could not be achieved.

During the first half of the 1870s, the Armenian Patriarchate strove for more control over the institutions of the Armenian administration in the provinces by issuing orders to regulate their relations with the local Ottoman administration. This proves that Armenian administrative bodies in the provinces integrated themselves not just to the Armenian Patriarchate in Constantinople but also to the Ottoman centralization process. The Armenian administration's order from 1873 codified the relations of the prelacies and provincial administrations with the local Ottoman government. It established de jure the limits of the authorities of the local Armenian administration and their relations vis-à-vis the local Ottoman administration and the Armenian one in the capital. Its first part states that the prelates (*arachnorts*) and the provincial administration with its religious and civil members were entitled to administer relations with the local Ottoman administration. While the patriarch represented "all Armenians living in Turkey" at the Sublime Porte, the prelate (*arachnort*) and members of the local Armenian administrations represented the Armenians in the provincial administrations of the Ottoman Empire. This paragraph was followed by strict rules, which limited the authority of provincial administrations exclusively to their provinces. First, the prelates and Armenian provincial administrations were prohibited from contacting the Sublime Porte directly. If there was a need to apply to the Sublime Porte, they had to do it through the patriarchate.[66]

Second, they were also not allowed to contact any Ottoman administrative body outside of their own vilayet, and the members of the Armenian local administrations could contact only the governor of the vilayet through their prelate. Hence, this order strictly hierarchized the relations between the provinces and the capital, as well as the administrative relationships within the provinces. Although they may have previously been hierarchical, this order emphasized the limitations of the authorities, subjugating the provinces to the capital and forcefully synchronizing them to the temporality of the patriarchate. It also stated that all communications with the provincial Ottoman administrative bodies had to be done with extreme politeness and sweetness (*k'aghts'r linelu ē*), and that the prelates and local Armenian administrations should be well informed on the troubles and issues they present to the local Ottoman administration because if their information was found to be inaccurate, they would be withdrawn from their positions immediately. It once again urged that prelates and local Armenian administrations should be very cautious in their language and behavior toward the Ottoman administration. *Takrirs* that were to be presented to the Ottoman administration should be composed very carefully and edited by people who mastered the Turkish language and thus would know the best ways to express the subject matter.[67] This is one of those sentences that makes the severity and fragility of the situation more tangible. The prohibitive and authoritarian language of the document must be regarded as the result of the reaction to the compendium of complaints from the provinces compiled by Patriarch Khrimyan and submitted to the Ottoman administration in April 1872, after which official petition submissions were not welcomed anymore.[68]

The order refers to the Ottoman administrative units that came into being with the Provincial Regulation (*Vilayet Nizamnamesi*, 1864–71) and underlines that the religious leaders of a province (*reis-i ruhani*) were to be present in those units.[69] Moreover, the same document called for the members of the local Armenian administration to take a more active role in the administration of their respective provinces: "It is not the duty/right of only the Prelate (*Aṛach'nort*) to sit on the Administrative Council; the civil members should also participate in the councils in the offices of *Kaymakam, Mütessarrıf, Vilayet, İdare, Deavi* and *Temyiz-i Hukuk ve Cinayeti* Councils."[70] Although the participation of Armenians in local administration was required by the Provincial Regulations, as noted by the patriarchate's order, such participation was not easy. In practice, it meant placing Armenians into a constant state of struggle at every level of local governance.

The Provincial Regulations established Nizamiye courts that were to serve both Muslims and non-Muslims.[71] These courts were formed with the election of three Muslim and three non-Muslim members. The Administrative Assembly of the Province (*Vilayet İdare Meclisi*) was an administrative unit established through the Provincial Regulations with minor changes made to it between 1864 to 1871.[72] It had a wide range of faculties, including tax issues, supervising the decisions of municipal councils, road construction, establishment of hospitals, and administration of zaptiah soldiers.[73] In this assembly too, non-Muslim representatives and their religious leaders sat alongside Muslim participants. However, according to Çadırcı, this participation did not always run smoothly, which is evidenced by cases presented from Erzurum (1871) and Bursa (1872) where non-Muslim representation was either nonexistent or faced troubles.[74] The Imperial Edict of 1839 and the Reform Edict of 1856, as well as the Provincial Regulations (1864–71), anticipated the participation of non-Muslims on various levels of the administration. While Armenians in the provinces were trying to become part of local administrations and faced numerous bureaucratic obstacles in the process, they publicly expressed and reported the problems and oppressions they faced to the patriarchate, which increasingly made their situation at home even more fragile. For instance, the newly established Assembly of Kastamonu was completely under the control of the local governor. Despite the fact that the Sublime Porte sent a *takrir* to the governor requesting the inclusion of the Armenian representative in the Assembly (*Meclis*), the governor argued that there were not enough Armenians living in Kastamonu to justify that and rejected it. As a result, the Armenians had to prove the density of their population in the area and asked for reconsideration of the issue.[75] As is seen, the Ottoman administration actually continued to benefit from the existing conflict as they obtained vital demographic and administrative information in the process.

An 1873 order of the Armenian administration reveals the Armenian administration's hopelessness, yet it still had to put on a brave face for its audience of government officials, making two hopeful references to Tanzimat and the government's goodwill of promoting "the security of life, property, and honor." In the next paragraph, it mentions *arachnorts* were entitled to submit *takrirs* to their local governments on issues in cases where the principles of Tanzimat and laws in general were being disregarded or violated.[76] While the 1872 *First Report on Provincial Oppressions* was filed and submitted to the Ottoman administration without the government offering any solutions in return, local Armenian administrations were strictly hierarchized and urged to be cautious in what they did, although they were the ones who were in urgent need of solutions to their problems. Despite the optimistic references to Tanzimat, the bans and strict administrative rules as well as the need to word the language in communications to the government very sweetly indicate that as of 1873, the ways of finding solutions for the Armenian *millet* in the provinces were already at a deadlock.

The Monasterial Council

The Monasterial Council was an institution stipulated by the Nizamname to be established, and its bylaws were prepared by the Joint Assembly. This work required the collection of statistical data from the monasteries; two years later, the memorandum from 1865 stated that the council's duties and entitlements had still not been clearly defined, as the monasteries were not responding. It notes the only monastery that had responded with a governance program synchronizing it with the capital as requested was one prepared by Archbishop Khrimyan for the monastery of Klag in Muş, but it had not yet been ratified by the Armenian administration in the capital. The same memorandum mentions that the implementation of the Nizamname/Constitution had been successful in only some cities, while attempts in the provinces generally remained administratively "barren [*amul*] and formless [*angerbaran*]." Monasteries and other national institutions were either not functional or desolate, while most Armenians in the provinces faced incessant oppressions and lived under conditions of insecurity of life, property, and honor.[77]

As the bureaucratic mechanism developed over the 1870s, the Armenian administration's policy of collecting data became more systematic, especially regarding the institutional presence of Armenians in the provinces, where the monasteries were mainly located. A memorandum released by the patriarchate in 1874 informed the Armenian administration about the properties and number of clergymen employed in the monasteries. It states that the first meeting of the Monasterial Council had taken place in the capital in 1872. This forty-four-page memorandum includes a "List of All of Turkey's Monasteries" (*Ts'ang Turk'ioy ĕnthanur vanōrēits'*), a total of 160 monasteries, including 2 ruined ones in Nakhchivan and Kars, but the list did not include the monasteries in Cilicia. The memorandum informs its readers in a footnote that there were many monasteries in ruins that were not listed and a few monasteries under the authority of the Catholicosate of Sis about which the Monasterial Council did not receive any information.[78] We can assume that the Monasterial Council asked the catholicosate to send information about the monasteries under its authority but received no response, which again proves that the issues of authority and entitlement between the patriarchate in Constantinople and the catholicosate in Sis remained unclear. The memorandum states that the monasteries were asked for statistics, and provides us with a detailed account of 43 monasteries, including their properties, how many people they employed, what their means of income were, the amount of revenue they collected from properties, where their properties were located, whether agricultural or breeding activities were regularly held, and how many villages belonged to a given monastery's area of entitlement.

Furthermore, we find information on the confiscation of lands and enslavement of Armenians in certain regions—for instance, in regard to the Monastery of Gets'an Smpadashen Holy Mother Mary, which was located in the southwestern part of Lake Van in the vicinity of Garjgan and at that time under the authority of the Bitlis Armenian administration. Gets'an Monastery had four villages within its area of authority whose inhabitants were "slaves" of Khalid and Mahmud Begs.[79] Its lands were occupied in exchange for the monasteries' debts. According to the information in the memorandum, the local Armenian villagers were neither able to stay, as they could not endure the oppressions, nor allowed to go, since as peasants they could not leave the land. A very similar situation will be described in depth in chapter 2.

The monasteries played a pivotal role in the local administrations, since they were the ones whose area of entitlement and authority were directly subject to subordination, while at the same time they had their own methods of administration for being the center of local economies, responsible for financing their personnel and other national (*azkayin*) institutions such as schools. Thus, gathering data on monasteries and knowing their entitlements, capacities, and constituencies were integral to the centralization of the Armenian Patriarchate in order to integrate them within its administrative system.

The Juridical Council

Arshag Alboyadjian wrote in his lengthy article on the Armenian Nizamname/Constitution that the Juridical Council within the Armenian administration was established in 1840. He contextualized this within the framework of the juridical reorganization of the Tanzimat period. The Juridical Council had both ecclesiastical and lay members and was headed by the deputy patriarch.[80] In the original Armeno-Turkish text of the Nizamname, this body was named the Judgment Commission (*Muhakeme Komisyonu*) and had four lay and four ecclesiastical members, all jurists, married, and over age forty. The Nizamname also indicated that this judicial body heard family law cases as well as those referred to the patriarchate by the Sublime Porte. According to the Nizamname, legal affairs in the provinces had to be handled by the regional assemblies of the churches and monasteries governing the local Armenian communities.[81]

A section of an official report prepared for the years 1874 to 1876 and submitted to the Armenian central administration explained the constitution of the Juridical Council. According to it, members of the Juridical Council were required to have staff knowledgeable of the law and well versed in the bureaucratic language (*dajgakēd*). Another person was to be put in charge of registering juridical and marital affairs. Thus, apart from the members of the Juridical Council, there were two additional personnel, editors for Armenian, Turkish (*Dajgerēn*), and French materials within the administration of the patriarchate.[82] The memorandum from 1865 also contains a short paragraph on the duties of the Juridical Council, mentioning that the council meetings took place every Wednesday and heard cases related to marital, monetary, and other family matters. Reports of the Juridical Council's proceedings were submitted to the Political Assembly. More detailed information can be found in *The Memorandum of the Political Assembly (1870–71)*, which shows that the cases handled were not restricted to the realm of family law, listing 93 marital cases, 46 about trade, 43 related to issues of immoral behavior, 21 related to honor, 15 property issues, 11 about inheritance, and 6 miscellaneous. The Juridical Council had handled a total of 233 cases in fifty meetings over fourteen months.[83]

In another official publication of the patriarchate, which can be translated as *The Rule of the National Administrative Organization* from 1880, we find the most detailed definitions regarding the juridical function of the Armenian administration. *The Rule* has a total of forty-five articles, and, interestingly, its longest section (Articles 26–40) is about the Judicial Councillor (*Tadagan Khorhurtagan*). It is important to note that this title is a change from the Nizamname in which it was the Juridical Council (*Tadasdanagan Khorkhurt*).[84] *The Rule* has a whole section on "Courts," of which there were three types: local (district level), central, and the Supreme Court. Any case unrelated to national officers or the protection of the church would first be handled in district courts. In case of disagreement, the Central Court would review the case and make a decision that could also be brought before the Supreme Court for review. All judges were elected to two-year terms.[85] The Central Court had three subdivisions: marital, individual, and administrative. These were not called courts, but *seneags*, meaning "rooms." While the Marital Room (*Seneag*) handled only cases related to marriage, the Individual Room took care of inheritance and family issues, compensations, crimes against honor, reparations, and other individual matters. The Administrative Room entailed all regulatory matters, including local issues, administration of monasteries and educational institutions, teachers, issues of the Armenian *millet*, and electoral rights.

The Supreme Court consisted of two branches, one for religious and the other for political issues. Their members were all trained in law, with the religious branch consisting of five clerics and the political branch of five lay members.[86] This order is the most detailed publication of the Armenian administration that I have encountered for the period between 1860 and 1880, meaning by that point the juridical function of the Armenian administration had increased by a considerable extent, as is evidenced by the large amount of ongoing and unresolved cases from the provinces as well as the capital. Having said this, I have to note that the language of the document, even its status as a rule rather than even a regulation (*ganonatrut'iwun*) or anything more authoritative, undermines the institutions of the Armenian administration in various ways. For example, what had been called councils were renamed councillors, and *juridical* was replaced with the term *judicial*. Even the juridical subdivisions had their terminology downgraded from courts to rooms (*seneag*), which obscured whatever specific legal function they were supposed to have. After the strict, hierarchical tone of the order from 1873, here we have a complete undermining of Armenian administration, its institutions, authorities, and entitlements. It can be argued reasons for this subversion could include the fact that the reign of Abdulhamid II had already started, the short-lived Ottoman Constitution had been suspended after the defeat in the Russo-Ottoman War, and the Congress of Berlin in 1878 aggravated the already decades-long oppressions in the provinces for Armenians. However, as demonstrated in this chapter, the Armenian administration was already losing its entitlements and authorities gained from the Nizamname by the time of the 1872 *First Report on Provincial Oppressions*. In other words, the style and language of the order were not the direct results of political conjunctures but a forshadowing of the events to come.

Armenian Ecclesiastical Law

This book makes extensive use of numerous secondary sources on the Armenian administration in the nineteenth century that detail the Nizamname and its significance. However, not even a single analysis based on archival sources has ever been published, at least to my knowledge, in regard to the juridical functions of the patriarchate during the nineteenth century. Under these circumstances, my only alternative has been to follow Melik'-T'ankyan's early-twentieth-century analysis of the evolution of Armenian ecclesiastical law starting from the fourth century. He brings together all available primary sources of ecclesiastical law, many of them in classical Armenian (*Krapar*), and puts them alongside their modern Armenian versions and explanations in order for the reader to understand the evolution of a certain juridical principle or law in a systematic way over the centuries.[87] The Armenian Church had numerous councils of its own in various places—for instance, the five councils at Dvin between 507 and 719, and the council of Shahabivan in 447 that is mentioned in Melik'-T'ankyan's book as one of the most influential.[88] The rules established by Basil the Great between 370 and 378 are especially relevant to understanding family law for the purposes of my study, as, for example, Melik'-T'ankyan noted that villagers still applied Basil's rules in his time for cases of adultery. Hence, I will refer to these as a set of rules that may have been the principles followed by the Armenian churches under Ottoman rule, as there are not currently any other sources available to suggest otherwise. It may well be the case that the patriarchate followed similar legislation to the canonical laws described by Melik'-T'ankyan while also taking into consideration their hierarchically superiors' existing legal, social, and traditional practices in place.

Conclusion

In this chapter, I showed the dynamics of the Armenian administration's centralization process starting from the 1830s. This chapter demonstrates through reports, memorandums, and orders published by the Armenian administration that while this development gained a more structural form after the proclamation of the Tanzimat in 1839 and the Reform Edict in 1856, it had actually begun prior to them. However, this does not necessarily mean that the establishment of the Armenian Nizamname/Constitution and the process of Tanzimat were not interrelated. On the contrary, the centralization policy of the Armenian Patriarchate at the capital was an integral part of Ottoman centralization, a process to which it was subordinated. Especially in cases such as the military support provided by the Ottoman Army to Armenians against the Kurdish emirates in those regions where Ottoman territorial and temporal policies were yet to be implemented, Armenians were forcefully integrated and synchronized to the Ottoman centralization process, for the sake of which Armenians were deprived of their own territorial and temporal entities.

Gathering information was an integral part of the centralization processes of both the Ottoman and the Armenian administrations. As is shown in this chapter, ordering the establishment of local administrations in the provinces according to the Armenian Nizamname/Constitution in itself required engaging in a number of data-gathering mechanisms. I explained the evolution of certain institutions within the Armenian administration—for instance, the position of *kapı kahyası*, the Juridical Council, the Monasterial Council, the Record Office, and the Armenian hospital Surp Pırgiç. I chose these institutions and demonstrated their evolution through the Tanzimat period because they were the ones most closely related to the archival documents that will be analyzed in the other chapters of this study. Furthermore, I showed the evolution of the Armenian administration based on the Nizamname and its official publications up until the 1880s. Tracing the administrative and institutional changes throughout the Tanzimat era, I compared the text of the Nizamname and the content of various memorandums, orders, and regulations that were passed and published by the Armenian administration as a result of shortcomings that had been exposed or policies that had been newly introduced through the Ottoman centralization. Thus, this chapter shows that the Armenian administration was not a static structure but one that underwent several changes not just before but also after the ratification of the Nizamname.

It is important to outline the temporal and territorial regimes and their differences in the provinces and the capital. The period studied here is one in which for the first time emphasis was placed on the issues of the provinces through the advocacy of Patriarch Khrimyan, who highlighted the need to consider them separately, or at least not lumped together with all the problems of the capital. It is clear that Khrimyan left his seat without being able to bridge the gap between the administrators in the capital and the Armenians in the provinces. The challenge Khrimyan realized, probably even before becoming patriarch, was that the Armenian administration in Constantinople would never fully understand the depth of the structural and institutional problems of the provinces and that even if it did, it would not have the capacity to intervene unless the Ottoman administration was willing to allow it. Thus, I suggest reading Khrimyan's resignation not merely as a response to internal turmoil within the Armenian administration, but as an objection and therefore intervention into the entire process of undermining the Armenian administration's authorities and entitlements.

Last but not least, I outlined the legal framework of Armenian ecclesiastical law to which this study will refer when analyzing the juridical processes and cases of family law. Melik'-T'ankyan's two-volume work of more than one thousand pages helped me to understand the origins of Armenian canon law and make sense of the archival material at hand. However, Armenian administration with all its juridical entitlements on the issues of family law was not an independent agent that could simply apply its own customary law, as it was always subject to a hierarchically superior juridical authority, and more important a social order that could always contest its decisions. Throughout this book, I will trace the (im)possibilities for Armenians to make their own juridical decisions and the limitations they faced.

2

"Either Save Us from This Misery or Order Our Murder" (*Ya Derdimize Derman, Ya Katlimize Ferman*)

Tanzimat of the Provinces

> Before we presented our problem, we had faced fewer oppressions. Now it is much more and of greater severity. Our lives are not anymore ours. We pay the tax of property [*emlâk*], but the property belongs to the agha, we pay the tax for the land, and the land belongs to the agha, the oxen and the sweat are ours, but the product belongs to the agha. On this earth, even birds and ants have a nest, but the people of Çarsancak do not. What does it bring us to have a Patriarch, a prelate [*arachnort*], and why did you actually come here?
>
> —Kēōrk Erewanyan, *Badmut'iwn Charsanjaki Hayots'*

These striking words, depicting the condition of the Armenian peasants of Çarsancak, illustrate the magnitude of the extraction they were subjected to by 1879. They were recorded by Karekin Srvantsdyants', who had been sent to the eastern provinces to gather statistical data regarding the provincial institutions, monastic properties, schools, and churches, and reflected the wall of despondency he found there. Particularly remarkable is the confession from the peasants of Çarsancak that they suffered even more troubles and oppressions after presenting their problems to the administrative bodies, as it shows how the mechanisms of representation established throughout Tanzimat actually functioned against the interests of Armenian peasants. Furthermore, it clearly shows that as peasants, they owned nothing, not even their lives.

Ottoman historian Nadir Özbek states that at the center of the rebellions in the eastern provinces, known as the Kurdish or Armenian question, lay the issue of peasantry (*köylü*), and thus the issue of class.[1] This chapter will demonstrate the new methods of governance that the Armenians in the provinces were subjected to throughout Tanzimat that turned them into completely unprotected outcasts. Military operations, wars, and massacres were central components, along with the administrative and structural changes that followed them, in reorganizing the Ottoman Empire around new temporalities and territorialities. Tanzimat, with its many new regulations, codes, and institutions, was first and foremost the result of these reconquests by the state. The reconquests of the eastern provinces not only imposed new temporal and territorial regimes throughout the empire but also introduced an oppressive and abusive taxation, leading to the deprivation of Armenian peasants' rights to the lands they cultivated. Tanzimat's promise of security of life, property, and honor was in actuality a guarantee of their unprotectedness.

As will be described in this chapter, a series of massacres against the region's autochthonous populations blighted the first half of the nineteenth century.[2] The role of these massacres was to end the existing rules, temporality, and regimes of territoriality in a given area, which would subjugate the surviving population to the victorious perpetrators. Furthermore, policies of massacre and annihilation were methods of creating emptiable places that in turn opened new paths to "affect, control, and influence" the populations in a given territory.[3]

Military conquest is primarily about territorial control, but any such control requires information gathering both prior to and after it, which is then utilized in the postconquest period for integration of the conquered territories. For example, Dina Rizk Khoury draws attention to the connection between military conquest and administrative reforms in the seventeenth-century Ottoman Empire,[4] one that this study will show is also relevant to the period of Tanzimat. While there is near consensus that Tanzimat and the Reform Edict were predominantly the results of territorial loss, economic weakening, and the industrial backwardness of the empire,[5] this book will instead suggest that Tanzimat was a process of applying new methods of territoriality, especially in those areas that were not yet fully under the empire's control. Doing so offers a new perspective to center-periphery relations in the field of Ottoman studies, incorporating into the debate the use of unabashed violence and the administrative changes that followed to integrate the peripheries to the center both temporally and territorially.

Inner Conquest and Reorganization

The significance of the reconquest of the Ottoman Empire's eastern provinces typically goes unnoticed, especially against the European territorial losses that are prioritized in the historiography. However, far from deserving to be an overlooked footnote, the establishment and consolidation of Ottoman territoriality in the eastern provinces during the first half of the nineteenth century set long-lasting practices not only within the Ottoman Empire but also later in Turkey and the region as a whole.

From the perspective of the Ottoman administration, the stalemate of the Ottoman-Iranian War of 1821–22[6] made for a good opportunity to restructure its eastern borders, a process that involved two critical issues. One was the need for military conscription after the disbanding of the Janissaries in 1826, and the other was the changing of power relations in the eastern provinces. Notably, Kurdish emir Muhammad Pasha of Rawanduz massacred Yazidis and Christians there in 1831, proclaiming his cruelty to be an act of religious necessity aimed at consolidating his power in the region. He killed the majority of the Yazidi population east of Mosul, from the Greater Zab to the Habur River, as well as Assyrians in the area, attacking one of their most important monasteries, Robban Hormizd. However, rather than consolidating his power, the pasha of Rawanduz's act of emptying actually prepared the ground for his own end[7] and that of the rest of the Kurdish emirates by the Ottoman Army. In 1837, the Ottoman Army attacked the Kurdish emirs in Cizre, Sincar, and Telafer, defeating them and capturing three thousand Yazidi children for the army.[8]

After Ibrahim Pasha of Egypt defeated the Ottoman Army at Nizip in 1839,[9] one of the most influential Kurdish rulers, Bedir Khan Beg[10] of the principality of Bohtan, took the opportunity to join forces with his distant relative and ally Nurullah Beg and enlarge his area of authority from Diyarbekir to Mosul. However, like Muhammed Pasha of Rawanduz, in seeking to expand their power by first killing the autochthonous populations, Bedir Khan and Nurullah Beg ended up completely losing their territorialities and temporalities, because these massacres against the local Nestorian population (1843–46) paved the way for the Ottoman inner conquest.[11] As Hans-Lukas Kieser points out, from the perspective of the Ottoman administration, neither a large Nestorian presence nor a powerful Kurdish emirate was desirable in the region, so there was no reason for the Ottoman administration to intervene in the massacres.[12] By using their military power to annihilate the local autochthonous populations, the Kurdish rulers of the region emptied the land, which in turn resulted in their quick defeat and subjugation by the Ottoman Empire.[13] Thus, in a relatively short period of time between 1830 and 1847, said to be one of the weakest periods in Ottoman history, the empire succeeded in subjugating the most influential Kurdish power holders under its central control. Furthermore, by allowing the autochthonous populations of the region to be massacred, the sovereign gained a long-lasting tool of governance to use whenever necessary, fixing the set of new rules of survival from then on for those who remained.

The establishment of the Vilayet of Kurdistan in 1847 marked a historical turning point for the empire, with its subjugation of the majority of the powerful Kurds in the eastern provinces, integration of the empire's eastern peripheries into the temporality of the center, and most important the territorializing of their administration. Robert David Sack draws our attention to the fact that the upper echelons of a hierarchy, in this case the state, tend to use territory to define, enforce, and mold groups, thus creating a territoriality that delineates their social relationships.[14] The constant redefinition of Kurdistan's borders is a good example of this case, a process that was alluded to by Tuncay Baykara. He made references to Van, Muş, and Diyarbekir each having been the center of the Vilayet of Kurdistan, but from his description, it is hard to understand when those cities served as administrative centers. We know that the new vilayet's borders already changed in 1849. While Muş, Van, Hakkari, Diyarbekir, and Cizre were still part of it, Baykara wrote that "*some years later*," Van, Mardin, and Cizre were reorganized into the Vilayet of Hakkari, which in turn was again "*some years later*" renamed the Vilayet of Van. I emphasize Baykara's terminology of "*some years later*" as it refers to the Ottoman temporal regime, even if covertly. The temporality of the changes undertaken remains unclear to the reader, which gives an arbitrary feel to the Ottoman government's systematic reorganization of temporality and territoriality in that region. Baykara wrote that in 1856 the Vilayet of Kurdistan had forty-nine *sanjaks* and encompassed Diyarbekir, Mardin, and Siirt, so we can assume that all the aforementioned territorial changes took place within the relatively short period of time between 1849 and 1856. Baykara also added that the Vilayet of Kurdistan was dissolved by the Provincial Regulations of 1864–71, but without giving an exact date or details.[15] Following Sack, we can assume that the demographic profile of the Vilayet of Kurdistan and the people being governed there changed constantly over the twenty-year-period before its dissolution. Sack further argues that territoriality can help engender more territoriality and more relations to be molded,[16] leading us to read the vilayet's constantly changing borders as territorialities engendering more territorialities. In that sense, the constant changes were not a weakness in governing, but on the contrary demonstrate the Ottoman administration's strength in keeping the situation on the ground subject to change, a constant instability that served to discipline its new and "untrustworthy" allies.

The establishment of and constant change to the Vilayet of Kurdistan was one of the most important forceful integrations made in the region but by no means the only one. Sabri Ateş underscores that it is impossible to understand Kurdish history without studying the demarcation of the Ottoman-Iranian border that began in 1848. With the collaboration of Russian and British experts as well as Iranian and Ottoman plenipotentiaries, the Ottoman administration succeeded in dividing the Kurdish tribes and regions along the Iranian-Ottoman border from Mount Ararat to the Gulf of Basra. For years "diplomats, engineers, botanists, geologists, archeologists, meteorologists, cartographers and military personnel of the Tsar and her majesty, in the company of the servants of the shah and sultan, located, classified . . . and mapped the physical and human geography of the region. . . . In addition to their geodetic and topographical work, they collected and cataloged geological, botanical, and zoological specimens. They . . . interacted with different ethnic, linguistic, and religious groups. . . . They also collected ethnographic and socioeconomic data about them."[17] The demarcation of the Ottoman-Iranian border and the survey that accompanied the entire process provided information on demography, linguistics, geography, and ethnicity in the militarily subjugated regions.

War is one of the most efficient tools of governance and the ideal opportunity to apply newly developed mechanisms derived from the data gathered, such as that accumulated by the Ottoman-Iranian demarcation process. For the Ottomans, it came in the form of the Crimean War of 1853–56, which served as the testing ground for many of the policies of Tanzimat, providing them with a reservoir of knowledge and experience that was to be utilized for at least the next half century. The Ottomans' proclamation of jihad was one of the most important instruments applied during the war, as it allowed them to secure Kurdish military support on both sides of the Ottoman-Iranian border and create a powerful alliance in this formerly rebellious area.[18] The division of emirates and large tribes by the border is an excellent example of Ottoman territoriality, as it hindered those groups from potentially collaborating against it. Accordingly, during the four years of survey prior to the war, the Ottoman administration followed a formula of keeping Sunni Kurds on both sides of the border.

Ateş argues that the Crimean War also enabled the Ottoman administration to introduce Tanzimat's new taxes, namely, the contributions to war (*iane-i cihadiye* or *iane-i harbiye*).[19] Combined with administrative and structural changes that consolidated the new territorial and temporal regimes in the region, the empire for the first time gained control over its eastern provinces.[20] Ottoman military operations continued in parallel through the *Fırka-ı Islahiye* regiment founded in 1863. While its name, which translates to the Division of Renovation/Reform,[21] hardly implies an army, it was indeed a military regiment established after the Crimean War, with very comprehensive aims.[22] These goals included taking control of multiple regions such as Cilicia, the Sanjak of Iskenderun, and Dersim and exiling the autochthonous Armenian villages found there. These operations changed the demographic situation in those areas and created new alliances for the empire with the local Muslims. The reservoir of knowledge created during this period was later effectively utilized by the empire during World War I. In other words, Tanzimat was the period during which the peripheries were forcibly integrated territorially and temporally to the center, but not all groups were entitled to full integration. Indeed, Armenians were much more peripheralized as a *millet*, but at the same time, their administration was completely subjugated to Ottoman centralization.

Administrative and Structural Changes: Land Code and Provincial Regulations

Up to this point, I have underlined the importance of the reconquest and the informational basis of the reorganization. During Tanzimat, the Ottoman state introduced two new important administrative and institutional tools of governance, the Land Code[23] and Provincial Regulations. The former defined the administration and division of land, while the latter did the same for administrative units. The Land Code of 1858 was the first attempt at creating a unified property regulation across the empire.[24] Both the Land Code and the Provincial Regulations were of crucial importance, especially in reshaping the villages where the Ottoman state settled Circassian migrants coming from Russia in the mid-1860s. One of the Land Code's main principles was that if land remained uncultivated for more than three years, the government had the right to redistribute it, in this case to the migrants. The Land Code prohibited the collection of all village lands under one person, but at the same time it actually gave no limit to the amount of property one person could acquire.[25] Through this loophole, there was actually nothing stopping a local power holder from appropriating just about all the land in a village. The Land Code did not intervene into the local power structures, but on the contrary supported their reproduction on the basis of new regulations. As will be shown in this book, provincial oppressions resulted in the de facto pushing out of Armenian villagers, depriving them of their right to use the land in order to open it to others. Therefore, we have to consider the nexus between provincial oppressions and the Land Code that remained in force after the establishment of Turkey.

On the other hand, the Provincial Regulations of 1864–71 were a set of techniques and applications at the disposal of the empire consisting of a means for data collection, mapping, administration, and control. The final version of the Provincial Regulations was accepted in 1871, at which time the new regulations were already being harshly criticized,[26] as Roderic Davison points out, citing the newspaper *La Turquie*'s claim that the regulations were "setting up 'little absolute states' in which governors (*valis*) had the powers of proconsuls, quasi-independent vassal princes [and] *derebeyi*s revived."[27] Many of the cases in this study indicate governors were in fact only briefly effective in the provinces until they too were overtaken by the control of tribal chiefs and overarching Ottoman political interests.

While the Land Code restructured the proportion of Muslim and non-Muslim landownership, the Provincial Regulations took the further step of reterritorializing administrative units. In other words, the latter changed the administration of the lands territorialized by the former, demonstrating how territoriality engenders territoriality.[28] If the distribution of land and its ownership was the first step of applying new territorial regimes on the smallest unit, the village, the second step was the Provincial Regulations that reterritorialized those new territorial units on the level of the empire's administrative practices. Both the Land Code and the Provincial Regulations were devised as methods to secure the sustainability of the empire's military success in those regions and were the most important policy tools for Tanzimat's restructuring of the empire both territorially and temporally.[29] Land should be considered first and foremost an economic parameter, especially in the Ottoman Empire, as the primary activity for creating surplus was the peasantry's working of it, which places the Land Code, peasantry, and taxation policies all within the same context. Thus, the territorialization enacted through the Land Code was primarily a political one, aimed at changing economic and political structures in the long run. Consolidation of power for local aghas, begs, and sheiks was enabled by the possibility to register the land in their own names.[30]

The government's need to develop new administrative methods, along with laws about land and provincial administration, should not exclusively be regarded as a result of territorial loss in the west and the weakening of the empire in general. Rather, considering the importance of the

Ottoman Empire's military successes in the east and the administrative effectiveness in controlling, encapsulating, and consolidating those provinces, both the Land Code and the Provincial Regulations should be seen as efficient tools of governance.

One of the most important tools of Ottoman territoriality, mapping, was largely carried out by Prussian cartographers who were commissioned for the work. For example, Prussian engineer Wilhelm Fischbach was commissioned to prepare a map of Prizren in the Vilayet of Danube. His detailed professional map drawn with both administrative and natural characteristics of the region was completed as early as January 1870.[31] Later, he was sent to the eastern provinces where he created an administrative map of the *sanjaks* of Harput and Maden, dated 1879,[32] denoting the borders of the governorates (*mutasarrıflık*), district governorates (*kaimakamlık*), and head of subdistricts (*müdirlik*). The types of maps created, when they were mapped, and even the reasons those areas were selected were not coincidental. These maps were used as administrative tools wherever necessary for introducing new regulations, making them visual and mathematical tools of territorialization. Fischbach must have spent a considerable portion of his life in the Ottoman Empire, as the earliest document I could access with his name was from 1870 and the latest from 1909.[33] Besides mapping the empire, his career included a search for mines around Gallipoli,[34] time spent living in Adana,[35] and finally working as a public servant to the empire in Kastamonu.[36] It is striking that I could find no information about him except in the Ottoman Archives. While Fischbach may be one of the least notable figures who took part in mapping the Ottoman Empire, he is representative of the long tradition of Prussian cartographers working there, a member of the second generation of Prussians who followed in the footsteps of Helmuth von Molkte and his colleagues.

Von Moltke was the most prominent Prussian officer in the Ottoman Army during the second half of the 1830s and served on the battlefields of the eastern regions.[37] Dr. Johann Samuel Heinrich Kiepert was another well-known cartographer and geographer with numerous publications to his name. Together with officers Karl Freiherr von Vincke[38] and Friedrich Fischer, they published the book *Memoir über die Construction der*

Karte von Kleinasien und Türkisch Armenien in 1854.[39] Their works were extensively used throughout the nineteenth century and even in the twentieth. A file in the Ottoman Archives shows that the demographic maps of the empire in 1914 were based on the work of Kiepert and von Moltke.[40] I consider their cartographic, demographic, and philological work and know-how to have been essential to the creation of the Ottoman administration's new territorialities and the implementation of its temporalities through their maps. As early as the 1830s, the activities of these Prussian Army officers prepared the necessary foundation for the structural and administrative changes to come, and their followers continued to be an important point of reference for the Ottoman administration and even the Republic of Turkey. Sabri Ateş makes a similar remark in the context of the Iranian-Ottoman border survey, noting that "mapmaking, a modern technical feat, was seen as a task that could only be undertaken by the European powers."[41] I often came across the names and maps of Prussian cartographers while trying to locate a certain village whose administrative unit had been altered. Very interestingly, in 1900, one of Kiepert's maps, "Anadolu-yı Şahane," was prohibited in the Ottoman Empire.[42] I could not find any copy of that map, but it may well be the case that having been drawn in the mid-nineteenth century, it was no longer territorially and temporally acceptable by the start of the twentieth century. This could be because the state did not want reminders of defunct territorialities and temporalities that were no longer in its interests.[43]

Applying Robert David Sack's theory of territoriality to this situation, we can that state that both the Land Code and the Provincial Regulations were instituted to affect, influence, and control people living in a certain village or province, and their relations were to be restructured through these administrative and structural changes. Thus, all the changes that occurred as a result of these processes, whether it be to the borders of districts and vilayets or through the constant rotation of governors, should be regarded as a part of the new Ottoman territorial regime. Seen from this perspective, the eastern provinces were almost completely redefined, recategorized, and restructured according to the Ottoman administration's interests between the 1830s and 1870s, the very period of the administrative and structural changes of the Tanzimat era.

The inner conquest of the eastern provinces and military mobilization during the Crimean War must have had some benefits for the Kurdish population (both Sunni and Alevi). In other words, their service to the empire must have been rewarded, a result that can be traced in the correspondences of the Armenian Patriarchate throughout the 1850s, 1860s, 1870s, and beyond in the form of provincial oppressions by the Muslim populations in the regions where Armenians and Kurds made up the majority of the combined population. Instead of keeping with the principle of equality enshrined in the Reform Edict, the Ottomans administered the Land Code in such a way that they guaranteed the superiority of the Kurds over non-Muslims, confirming and reiterating a power hierarchy. This enabled Kurdish begs to appropriate and register lands that Armenians formerly had the right to use. Kemal Karpat argues that while the Land Code of 1858 originally intended to provide better control over state land, it ended up privatizing them.[44] However, he fails to mention which groups benefited from this privatization and who previously had the right to use the land. Taking a look at the bigger picture, the increase in petitions about land issues sent by Armenians both to the patriarchate and the Sublime Porte after the Crimean War should be considered structural and not coincidental. Accordingly, the Land Code should be reread in light of the surge of complaints made by Armenian villagers that followed its introduction.

One of the most important components of Tanzimat, therefore, is its denial of the coevalness of Armenians living in the provinces vis-à-vis the Ottoman and Armenian administrations in the capital.[45] Allowing the provincial oppressions to take root and leaving them unresolved for decades, forcing Armenians to petition every authority in vain, were methods of governance throughout Tanzimat. Armenians living in their autochthonous lands were not coevals of the Ottoman administration or even of Armenians living in the capital, and thus the provincial oppressions in their entirety should be regarded as policies aimed at fostering a temporal and territorial separation of Armenians from one another and their lands. Provincial oppressions included onerous taxation, lack of timely response to petitions, corvée labor (*angarya*), and many others that will be analyzed in light of territorial and temporal methods of governance. Hence, I argue that although the Ottoman administration introduced the principle of equality for all its subjects on paper through the Reform Edict, in practice it did not just fail to enforce those laws but tacitly supported all manner of oppression in the provinces. These oppressions increasingly grew in severity after the Crimean War, as the Ottoman state solidified its previously established alliances with local power holders. The practices of the Ottoman administration at the provincial and village levels made it clear that the empire intended to only cooperate with Muslims thereafter. For Armenians, there were few options left: either die in their villages or die on migration routes.

In the meantime, the Armenian administration went through a process of centralization with the ratification of the Armenian Nizamname/Constitution. The requirements of the central Armenian administration and the reactions to it by local ones provide insights into the ongoing centralization processes. In this sense, as Armenian centralization was subordinated to Ottoman centralization, they cannot be considered as two separate developments. At the same time that provincial borders were being changed, immigrant populations were being settled in the Armenian villages and the status of those Armenians was becoming increasingly fragile. The policies of Tanzimat, rather than granting promised legal protections and rights, in actuality disenfranchised Armenians from their lands and turned them into wageworkers. This change and other economic policies also forced Armenian peasants in the provinces to become migrant workers in Constantinople or other cities, separating them from their families and leaving that already vulnerable population in an even more imperiled situation.

Ottoman centralization meant the creation of new territorialities extending Ottoman temporality to new lands. The time for potential alliances between the local Christians and Muslims, as well as the temporalities of the Nestorians, was over. A new order with new temporal and territorial regimes was established based on the know-how and mapping work of Prussian cartographers. The constant changes of the provincial borders proved Ottoman sovereignty in the region rather than its weakness. The Ottoman administration had a very dynamic nature when it came to its own interests. As will be shown next, however, the same dynamism was not deployed for Armenians; they had to wait.

An Integrated and Subordinated Process: The Reorganization of the Armenian Administration

The centralization of the Armenian administration had no choice but to be subordinated to the process of Ottoman centralization. The Archive of the Armenian Patriarchate contains abundant material on the changing borders of Armenian administrative units (*vijags*) throughout the 1860s, which grew out of this centralization of administrations.

Both the APC and official publications of the patriarchate show that the central Armenian administration in the capital sent out orders to establish local administrative units according to the Nizamname in March 1864. A month later, the implementation of those orders is shown in two documents signed by the administration of Archbishop Kevork of Amasya, who was the prelate of a *vijag* that also included Marzvan (Merzifon) under its authority.[46] The prelate asserted that the local assembly (*taghagan khorkhurt*) of Amasya had been established and that he would be doing the same in the rest of the towns and districts under his jurisdiction as soon as he could visit them.[47] In the second document, which carries the same date as the first, he specifies that he has received the orders for the establishment of the constitutional order according to the Nizamname in Amasya, Sinop, and Bolu. While he had carried it out in Amasya and Sinop, which were under his authority, he had not done so in Bolu, as it was under the jurisdiction of Kaghadia (Galatia).[48] As is seen in this case, the units of the Armenian administration in the provinces were being reorganized by order of the Armenian and Ottoman administrations in the capital, becoming centralized to their overall authority.

The biweekly magazine *Zhamanag* published a lengthy article in September 1865 on the changing status of Garin (Erzurum) Province. It is noteworthy to point out that the author referred to the Vilayet of Danube's recent establishment, saying that Garin was similarly being organized into a regional center for the densely Armenian-populated provinces, including Van, Bayazıd, and Erzincan, and that its Armenian administration would be second only to the one in Constantinople.[49]

In the book *Badmut'iwn Darōni ashkharhi* by Garō Sasuni, we find a description of the creation of Provincial and Political Assemblies for Muş in June 1864, which shows the repercussions of the ongoing administrative changes.[50] Provincial Assemblies were elected in five districts, or better put in five churches. Sasuni also mentioned that Khrimyan, then the head of Muş's Surp Garabet Monastery, was always busy either in Constantinople or in Erzurum dealing with the oppressions against Armenians or with internal unrest at the monastery. Two collective petitions (*arz-ı mahzars*), one with sixty and the other with seventy-seven seals/signatures against Khrimyan, were sent to the capital with the aim of evicting him from Muş and sent elsewhere, an example of the discontent the process was causing.[51] The establishment of the Armenian Nizamname in the provinces along with all the other regulations and changing power relations on the ground was not a smoothly operating process because, as will be shown, it was not in the Ottoman administration's interests for this process to run smoothly.

Ottoman Centralization and Provincial Oppressions: Territorial and Temporal (Dis)integration of the Armenians of the Provinces

Settling Migrants, Changing Borders, Exiling Armenian Villages: Pingean, Niokisaria (Niksar), Beylan and/or Belen, Payas, and Ocaklı

In the 1860s, the policy of settling Circassians in Armenian villages was reported in the Armenian newspapers, which emphasized the undue hardship it brought on those existing communities. Based on Ottoman statistics, Davison wrote that thousands of Tatars and Circassians entered the Ottoman Empire between 1855 and 1864. Although he only wrote "thousands," he explained in the footnote that the number was much higher, perhaps six hundred thousand people from 1855 to 1864 and four hundred thousand more in the next two years.[52]

Pingean, 1864

One of the cases related to Circassian immigrants was from Pingean in Agn (Eğin). The news item celebrated Pingean for establishing its constitutional order with local assemblies according to the Nizamname thanks to the new bishop on duty, Nigoghayos. At the same time, the article informed readers that ten households of Circassian migrants had been settled in Pingean, approximately eighty to one hundred people. The Armenians of Pingean were asked to feed, shelter, and find jobs for the immigrants for one year until they found places to live and work, after which time lands would be given to those immigrants to earn a living. However, the majority of the Armenian men of Pingean had left to become migrant workers (*bantukhd*) in the capital and elsewhere, while the Circassians arrived as intact families. This worried the Armenians as 180 Armenian houses consisting mainly of women, children, and the elderly were left unprotected. Consequently, the Armenians of Pingean submitted a complaint to the Armenian administration about the high number of Circassians being settled in their village and asked for them to be settled in Muslim areas instead, as such a large presence could pose a danger to their region.[53] The news item stated that this kind of settlement had become a common practice that Armenian villagers faced in the provinces. This case brings up a number of questions that should be addressed. First and foremost, how would an Armenian village whose residents were already unable to sustain themselves economically, as evidenced by its men becoming *bantukhds*, be able to feed and finance the presence of so many immigrants? In addition, which and whose lands were to be given to the immigrants? The fact that the Circassian immigrants were armed and in such great numbers was one of the biggest issues of concern for provincial Armenians, and would soon become a life-threatening crisis in Pingean. Hence, it should be considered that settling armed Muslim immigrants in the vicinity of Armenian villagers at the height of the *bantukhd* waves had both territorial and temporal motives. Not only was asking them to feed the immigrants under such conditions a heavy economic burden on the Armenian villagers, but given their poor living conditions, not being able to do so would in turn also pave the way to violence. While Armenians had nothing to gain, both the migrant groups and the Ottoman administration obtained clear benefits from the process.

Niokisaria/Niksar, 1868

In petitions written in 1868 from Niokisaria (Niksar), we see two different problems. The first is the conflict with the Circassians, and the second entails repercussions of the Provincial Regulations. The first petition we have, with twenty-nine signatures, was written in May stating it was actually the third collective petition of complaints they had sent. It describes in detail how it was impossible for Armenians to leave Niksar to trade or buy provisions, as they were constantly being attacked and robbed on their way, with many already killed by Circassians and other Muslim groups. The petition blames these troubles on the fact that Niksar had recently been removed from its traditional position within the Vilayet of Sivas and placed under the administration of Ünye, and asked for this change to be reverted.[54] Although Niksar has historically been part of the Vilayet of Sivas, apparently after 1864 for at least some time it was administered by the *kaimakamlık* (a smaller unit of administration) of Ünye. The petition also stated that while Ünye and Sivas were equidistant from Niksar, a twenty-two-hour journey, the road to Sivas was far safer and of better quality. The Ottoman Archives contain documents on the administrative change of Niksar from Sivas to Ünye and the maltreatment of locals as early as 1865.[55] During this time, the area also received a considerable amount of Circassian immigrants. On August 26, the Armenians of Niksar wrote another petition with the same request, this time with twenty-eight signatories. They repeated their plea for Niksar to be taken back under the authority of the Vilayet of Sivas rather than that of the "lawless" Ünye outside the vilayet. The Armenians of Niksar emphasized that they wrote numerous petitions about this issue to both the patriarchate and the Sublime Porte and that their lives and properties were under constant threat. The governor-general (*vali*) of Pontos had been informed about Niksar's situation and promised to create a new *kaimakam* administered within Samsun, but his plan met resistance and he returned to Constantinople before it could be carried out. The Armenians expressed their fear of remaining under the authority of Ünye that would result in even worse treatment and inevitably they would have to leave Niksar as a community.[56]

In these petitions, we see administrative decisions being part and parcel of the provincial oppressions against Armenians. Those in Pingean complained about the inappropriate and disproportionate settlement of Circassian immigrants in their village, as it placed undue financial and security burdens upon them, which was undoubtedly part of engineered demographic changes. The petition from Niksar made repeated pleas about the dangers they were enduring from attacks by Circassians and other Muslims to the point they were unable to earn a living or even buy provisions, blaming the local administration of Ünye because it was incapable of handling the situation. Hence, administrative transfer from Sivas to Ünye was not a merely bureaucratic decision, but one that engendered perils for the Armenian inhabitants of Niksar. The consequences Armenians reported in these petitions should be contextualized within the Provincial Regulations. In just a four-year period between the first and second cases, we can draw a line from the initial warnings about the mass settlement of Circassians in Armenian regions to a situation in which life for Armenians had become practically unsustainable as a result.

A number of methods of governance can be traced in this situation. First, the demographic makeup of the region was changed along with its administrative unit. Controlling the relations of the people living in a certain territory by changing its demographic profile as well as administrative structure is part of the territorial method of governance. Allowing criminality to take root in the region as a result of one of these policies is yet another tool of governance. The temporality of these methods is also of utmost importance because the Armenians of Niksar, as is seen here, wrote multiple complaints both to the patriarchate and to the Ottoman administration that were ignored. This common practice left the provincial Armenians without proper solutions to their problems. In fact, as will be shown throughout this chapter, the cultivation of prolonged problems was a component of Ottoman temporal and territorial governance. In this case, the Armenians were implying that the Ottoman administration would refrain from acting *for so long* that the situation in Niksar would reach a point of no return.

Çork Marzvan (Dörtyol), 1868: "Either save us from this misery or order our murder" (Ya derdimize derman, ya katlimize ferman)

In the correspondence files of the Armenian Patriarchate, I came across several complaints from the villages of the Sanjak of Iskenderun about the miserable situation of the villagers who were suffering from exiles and oppressions by the Ottoman authorities throughout the region. Documents from Belen and/or Beylan in the Sanjak of Iskenderun, Payas, and Çork Marzvan asking for help were all written in the summer of 1868. (Belen and Beylan are two separate files in the APC, but I believe that they both refer to the same place.)

The first document I will introduce and discuss is from the APC file of Beylan of the Sanjak of Iskenderun. It is marked with only one seal, that of the Armenian district council of Beylan. This document, written in Armeno-Turkish on August 11, 1868,[57] mentioned that the populace of three villages, Çork Marzvan, Ocaklı, and Özerli, were forced to move to Payas, causing the villagers many hardships. The document notes the presence of officers in the village for the past thirty days, meaning the government had sent its representatives there in July 1868. It was stated that the villagers were not allowed to harvest their fields, and subsequently, the villages' crops and gardens were all destroyed (*telef oldu*). According to the document, the local Armenian cleric Bishop Artin contacted the *Mutessarrıf* in order to stop the village removal process but to no avail. We see a note by the patriarchate at the rear that it reacted to the petition by sending a *takrir* about the matter on August 24, 1868.[58]

The second document is from the APC file of Belen, written by Archbishop Harut'iwn of Antioch on August 9, 1868.[59] Per his account of the issue, the Armenian notables (*ishkhans*) of Payas had brought him there to ask its pasha to give the villagers time to finish their harvest, cure their sick, and pass the scorching summer days before having to move. It does not state which of the villages this request was about, but it contained thirty-seven houses (*hane*), two of them Muslim and the rest Armenian:[60]

> Lawlessly forced, without the security of honor, the ones who seem to be semisick were tied to the animals while the others who were in severe conditions were rafted and brought to Payas. They sit under the walls, miserably, having nothing to eat and drink. One cannot stand seeing them like this; they are poor and dying of starvation. (*Cebri ganondan usuldan dışarı ırz ve ayal ölümcül khasda olarak eyicelerini khasdaların hayvanlara sararak ve koetülerini salıla payasa getirdiler her biri bir duvar dibinde kaldılar perüşan aç susuz telef olmaladadalar efendim buna can dayanmaz fakhir ve fukharalar açlarından ölüyorlar.*)[61]

The third document is a single-sheet mailer written on the same day as the previous one from Belen. The same situation was depicted, this time by another cleric, Istepan Vartabed, who stated that the Belen Armenians' miserable situation was the result of extreme oppression by the *Mutasarrıf* ("*aşırı derecede zulüm ediyor*"),[62] with the word *zulm* meaning an abuse of power, particularly concerning property. Historian Safa Saraçoğlu draws attention to the word's context, pointing out that the ruler was not supposed to take from certain groups to give to others, as doing so would constitute an attack on property rights.[63] However, in this case, not only were the property rights of Armenians in the region attacked, but they were exiled altogether, losing their properties, fields, houses, stores, and in some cases most likely their lives. Istepan Vartabed unsuccessfully tried to convince the *Mutasarrıf* to give the villagers some time to prepare for their exile.

The most detailed account of this same issue was a collective petition (*arz-ı mahzar*) in the file of Çork Marzvan written on September 1, 1868, with nineteen signatures, three of whom were clerics.[64] The petition was sent because it appeared that none of their previous attempts at correspondence with the patriarchate had received a response. As a result, they sent their religious leader to the patriarchate to directly inform it about what was happening. We learn from the petition that just a week prior, on August 24, cavalry regiments came to their village and asked them to leave Payas that very day:

> Saying that the houses that ought to leave Payas will leave today, by beating up, by cursing us, they are forcefully migrating us, from evening to the morning without our consent the zaptiahs are beating us up, they feed their horses with bulgur instead of barley, they take our food as if it was theirs. The slander and the torture we have been going through has never taken place before. They would eat one chicken, but they would kill three of them. (*Payasa göçecek khaneler bugün kalkacak deyerek dög(v)erek söy(v)erek zor ile göçürüyorlar bizlerimizin akşamden sabaha irademiz yok iken zaptiyalar dögerek atlarına arpa yerine bulgur asıyorlar kendilerine yiyecek bulduruyorlar bizlere olan. Hakaret ve aziyet zannımıza göre daha e(i)şitilmemiştir. Şoeyle ki bir tavuk yiyecekler ise üçünü birden kesiyorlar.*)[65]

After describing the physical tortures that the villagers were subjected to, the petition asserted that the integrity of the entire village was being targeted through a number of strategies. The officers forced a percentage of the villagers to move to Payas, while not allowing the artisans who remained behind to practice their crafts. This method of territorial governance denied the ability to earn an income to both those who were forced out of the village and those who remained. Thus, the plan was not to merely transfer the Armenians to Payas, but to divide and resettle a part of each village there, undermining the existence of the Armenian villages as a whole.

The forceful exile of these Armenian villagers in the mountains of Iskenderun Sanjak, without any explanation or plausible reasoning, began in July 1868 and lasted until mid-September. The practices described in these documents attest to the temporal and territorial policies of Tanzimat that clearly targeted the Armenian villages, even though from what is visible in the documents they contained no conflict, no unrest, or any objection to authority. In other words, the Ottoman administration intervened and disrupted the provincial administration and life of Armenian villages that had not been the cause of any trouble. In addition, the Ottoman administration chose not to react dynamically in its temporal governance but instead waited until issues grew severe. Armenians reported the situation repeatedly to the patriarchate as well, apparently with no result. The exile took place through bullying and terrorizing the inhabitants, banning the harvest of their products, confiscating and abusing the villagers' provisions, threatening their lives and livelihoods, and finally dispersing the village.

What was happening in Cilicia and the Sanjak of Iskenderun in the summer of 1868? Ahmet Cevdet sheds light on these disturbances in great detail in his *Tezâkir-i Cevdet.* He states the *Fırka-ı Islahiye*, which consisted of "distinguished [*güzide*] Georgians, Circassians, and Kurds," had already been operating in the region, assigned the duty to control and reform ("*zabt-u ıslah*") the village of Kozan, reform the rebellious Zeytun region ("*hali isyanda bulunan Zeytun nahiyesini ıslah*") and bring the Kürd-dağı region up to Cebel-i Bereket (Gavur Dağı) under full obedience. The wording of "reform" (*ıslah, ıslahiye*) applied to military operations in both the *Tezâkirs* of Ahmet Cevdet and in the title of the army is noteworthy. In this way, the Ottoman administration continued its military conquest of the past decades, this time focused on the regions of Cilicia and Iskenderun up to Aleppo. The documents sent from the regions' villages show that these operations continued into the summer of 1868, the time of the Çork Marzvan petition. The long passages found in Ahmet Cevdet's *Tezâkir* on the Armenian administration, the Armenian Catholicosate in Sis, and demographic, denominational, and ethnic differences of the region, as well as its geographic characteristics, resemble the work of the Prussian cartographers published in 1854. *Tezkire* no. 36 is about the administrative structures of Cilicia and Iskenderun Sanjak, including demographic, ethnic, and denominational data for Aleppo, Payas, Adana, Kozan, Maraş, and Urfa. *Tezkire* no. 38 is exclusively on Armenian ecclesiastic institutions as well as their entitlements, historical developments, and the regions of the sovereignty of the Catholicosate of Sis and other power centers.[66]

There were economic factors intertwined with the issues of the military conquest of Cilicia and the Sanjak of Iskenderun. The agricultural products and high capacity for exports made the region economically very attractive. Cilicia, with all its economic assets, had a high Armenian population and was ruled by Muhammad Ali's son Ibrahim Pasha between 1832 and 1840, who rediscovered the region's economic importance.[67] Later, Cilician cities and towns came under the control of Kurdish and Turkoman *derebeys*.[68] In 1864, the US Foreign Office launched a large-scale survey in the region, which determined that over the previous year the land cultivated with cotton had doubled.[69] The region already had the attention of foreign investors, and the complaints sent from these regions to the patriarchate in the summer of 1868 must be read within this context. The Ottoman administration aimed to gain full control of the region, in line with Ibrahim Pasha's strategy to gain the best economic assets possible and to control the Kurdish and Turcoman local power holders while getting the Armenians out of the way. This strategy was especially important in those areas where Armenians were historically autochthonous. By exiling and dispossessing the Armenian villagers and hindering their alliances with other Armenians in the region, the Ottoman administration was sending a strong message to the "rebellious" Zeytun as well. The Armeno-Turkish newspaper *Manzume-i Efkar* reported in August 1868[70] that armed confrontations had been taking place in Zeytun since 1862 and that the Ottoman forces were not always successful in controlling the area.[71]

The Armenian villages of Çork Marzvan, Özerli, Ocaklı, and Belen were under the authority of Adana, but in the structural reorganization, they were to be taken under the authority of Aleppo.[72] Ahmet Cevdet confirms in his *Tezâkir* that Adana, Kozan, and Payas were put under the jurisdiction of the Vilayet of Aleppo.[73] More important, his work depicts military operations and administrative and structural changes as integral parts of the "reform." In his *Tezkire* no. 38, Ahmet Cevdet describes the process for the ratification of the Armenian Nizamname and the omission of the Sis Catholicosate's entitlements from it, as Kozan (Sis)[74] was not under the complete control of the Ottoman administration.[75] Hence, from Ahmet Cevdet's account, it can be assumed that the Ottoman administration was *waiting* to see the developments in Sis and therefore kept silent on the entitlements of its catholicosate within the Nizamname of the Armenian *millet*. Here again, waiting and keeping silent were tools for creating temporal and territorial methods of governance. By remaining silent on the entitlements of the Catholicosate of Sis while it was not yet fully under its control, the Ottoman administration reserved its priority and privilege to arbitrate power by creating power clashes between the Armenian power centers of the Patriarchate in Constantinople and the Catholicosate of Sis.

The correspondence of the Armenian Patriarchate chronicles the repercussions of military conquest against the Armenian villages of the region, who had lived there for the past five hundred years. The petitioners from Çork Marzvan stated that the problem was their very existence, as there were hundreds of Christian houses in these villages, a situation the authorities did not want. Moreover, they pointed out that their drive to establish a school was also opposed. The teacher Garabet was severely beaten up and his head cracked open by someone named Beyazit and his brother Molla Mehmet from Kara Kise (Karakise) village. Armenian villagers went to court and sued the perpetrators, but the court requested they bring four witnesses. Once four witnesses were found, it was argued that infidels (*gâvur*) could not witness anything ("*gâvurun isbatı tutulmaz*").[76] Almost three decades after the proclamation of Tanzimat, the state was neither willing to secure the life, honor, and property of Armenian villagers, nor interested in applying the principles of equality before the law.

The signatories of this petition complained that their voices were not heard and people were living helplessly on the streets in misery. Their desperate cry was articulated as follows: "If we are considered a *millet*, either you save us from this misery or order our murder. (*Eger biz de millet isek, aman el aman, yakın günde ya derdimize derman, ya katlimize ferman.*)"[77] This powerful statement by Armenian villagers about the state violence that they were subjected to at the height of Tanzimat should be considered a response of Armenian villagers to Tanzimat in an area where there had been no conflict. Despite any prior cases of unrest in Çork Marzvan, it still received an unprecedented military intervention, which divided and exiled inhabitants of the Armenian villages.

By dispersing the inhabitants of this old Armenian village in the mountains of Iskenderun Sanjak, the government might have contemplated settling these areas with immigrants or other Muslim populations in order to "control" and "secure" the way from Cilicia to Aleppo. These administrative and demographic measures did not cease in the region after this period of reorganization either. In a document from 1897–98 (1315) in the Ottoman Archives, the population of Payas was to be moved to Ocaklı.[78] In 1906, yet another document ordered Payas to be moved to the north to Dörtyol, and for Ocaklı to become part of the administrative unit of Payas.[79] This shows that Ottoman territoriality during Tanzimat deployed disruptive methods of exiling autochthonous populations, and uprooting them from their ancestral lands proved to be so effective that the practice continued well into the twentieth century. The experience and knowledge gathered during Tanzimat were utilized on a larger scale, during both the Hamidian massacres of the 1890s and the massacre of 1909. Thus the roots of these cases of mass violence should be looked for in the period of Tanzimat.

Famine, Starvation and Migration: Çarşamba, Galatia, Yozgat, Kayseri, and Çarsancak

It was mentioned in a report of the Armenian Patriarchate from 1876 that the Armenian inhabitants of the Pontic region of Çarşamba had to leave their houses and lands as a result of the ongoing oppressions. They tried to flee to Russia but were stopped on the way and returned to Samsun. They asked for assistance from the patriarchate both politically and financially to resolve their issue. A *takrir* was written to the Sublime Porte by the patriarchate asking for a stop to the oppressions in the villages of Çarşamba. However, the oppression and attempted migration had already resulted in the villagers facing starvation. The Armenian administration decided to immediately send money to Samsun to rescue the population.[80] In many cases like this one, oppressions in the provinces resulted in the forced migration of entire villages collectively. In this example it also resulted in famine, further endangering the villagers' lives.

Famine was not a rare phenomenon. An official publication of the patriarchate documents one faced by 150 Armenian households in the region of Galatia because of the high price of agricultural products.[81] The report explained the Galatia Armenians' difficulty in paying the taxes and how the Armenian administration in the capital wrote to the governorate asking for its support in order to relieve the oppressions against the famine-hit population. This same report also states the Ottoman administration had already established a commission to help Armenians facing famine and starvation.[82] A news item in the *Manzume-i Efkar* about the growing cases of famine throughout the provinces drew attention to the ban on leaving one's own village. Like in the Armenian administration's report, the news item connected the famine with the burdensome taxes provincial Armenians had to pay to the Sublime Porte. It was stated that the villagers were not permitted to find refuge in other places or leave the empire unless they could appoint a guarantor to pay their taxes. The only other option was to take the risk of escaping without permission, as a request to the Sublime Porte for special permission to leave would be denied. While the peasants' main obligation was to cultivate the land and they were not allowed to leave the land uncultivated,[83] those hit by famine could neither leave nor sustain their livelihood in their villages. The article suggested that the patriarch should ask for a firman in order to get special permission for the Armenians facing famine to migrate.[84]

The starvation, famine, and migration in these documents were clearly interrelated, as was the taxation policy. Özbek describes the taxation policies of Tanzimat as unjust and says that collection methods were oppressive and corrupt.[85] He also refers to the common practice of levying the taxes collectively, especially in the case of the special tax (*vergi-i mahsusa*), one of the most burdensome taxes of the Tanzimat.[86] Armenian sources referred to the oppressive taxes and abusive methods of tax collection as provincial oppressions. Hence, with economic oppression at its core, taxation and tax collection were the most prominent of the provincial oppressions. In addition, they were coupled with a number of other methods such as bans on harvesting as in the case of Beylan, and on leaving the village even to buy provisions. Such oppressions helped lead to the famines in Çarşamba, Galatia, Kayseri, and Yozgat.

Çarsancak: A Struggle for Land and Survival

Forced migration, famine, starvation, unemployment, and loss of wealth and property were consequences of oppression in the provinces. One of the longest-lasting examples is the case of Çarsancak village.[87] In a memorandum of the Political Assembly of 1865, we read an account of the Çarsancak Armenians' struggle as they had been constantly submitting complaints about the injustices of twenty-four Kurdish *derebeys* and the unfair distribution of imperial taxes. The issue was landownership because while the Çarsancak Armenians had assumed that the fields they harvested, the houses they resided in, and the shops they ran belonged to them, the *derebeys* claimed ownership over it all. The Armenians asked for trials to be held in the capital against the *derebeys*. In a memorandum of the patriarchate's Political Assembly of 1870–71, the issue of Çarsancak was categorized under the title "Negotiation of the Patriarch with the Grand Vizier regarding the Armenian millet's five most important issues." Although no details were given regarding the content of the negotiations, it was stated that the grand vizier lent his approval to a report on the provincial oppressions being compiled by the patriarchate.[88]

Çarsancak was addressed in this report under the heading of "Provincial [Issues]," which stated the Armenians of Çarsancak were not content with the long-lasting local juridical processes as they consistently had no result. They went to the patriarchate to inform the Political Assembly about the situation in Çarsancak and made severe complaints about the local judge. It was decided that the patriarch should write a request to the grand vizier to resolve the issue and another request through the judge to the Sheikh-ül Islam. It was included in the report that the begs were opposed to all decisions taken in favor of the Armenians of Çarsancak and continued their oppression. In the meantime, the Çarsancak Armenians decided to emigrate, as too much time had elapsed with their problems still unresolved. Forbidden to work in their fields and unable to sustain a living, they could not hold out forever. While the report was being written, the conflict between Kurdish power holders of the region and the Armenians worsened, and a number of murders took place. The Çarsancak Armenians decided to resubmit a *takrir* to the Sublime Porte including the latest oppressions. The Council of State (*Şura-yı Devlet*) decided in their favor, but the decision was not enforced, and Çarsancak Armenians in Istanbul reported that oppressions continued and a case of murder was added to the existing complaints. It was decided to submit a new *takrir* to the Sublime Porte, in light of all the oppressions, asking the Ottoman administration to either enforce the decision of the Council of State (*Şura-yı Devlet*) or at least permit the Armenians of Çarsancak to emigrate elsewhere.[89] The situation depicted in the memorandum of 1870–71 clearly testifies that the state was not ready to enforce its own legal decisions made at the highest level in order to appease the local power-holding *derebeys*.

One of the new institutions of Tanzimat was the Nizamiye courts, which aimed at making justice more accessible for both Muslims and non-Muslims. An example from Perri, also in Dersim in the vicinity of Çarsancak, gives an indication of to what extent these courts met the needs of the people:

> Perri had a *bidayet* court; however, its functions were quite limited because of the following reasons: The court was under the control of aghas and begs, and it was not in a position to make free and fair decisions. The people of Çarsancak were deprived of using these mechanisms to claim their rights. For instance, a simple villager could never think of claiming his rights, . . . as he would know that, not only would

> he not get his right, but also this could lead to a worse catastrophe for him in the end. . . . On the other hand, aghas and begs had no reason to go to court to settle their issues with Armenian villagers and merchants. . . . Regarding the cases of murder, the court remained almost ignorant. . . . Against the thieves and bandits, there were no investigations either. Hence, the *bidayet* court often had nothing to do, and the prison in Perri was empty most of the time. . . . The turbaned judge of Perri usually was sitting next to the *musalla* stone in the center of town resting under the white poplar trees. The same was with Pertag and Mezgerd, where tens of zaptiahs and governmental institutions just watched and kept the situation going as it was.[90]

This account demonstrates the judicial dead-end for the Armenian population of the region. As will be shown later in this chapter, the patriarchate's report of 1872 expressed hope in the Nizamiye courts,[91] but this was more wishful thinking than anything else. The bidayet court, as was mentioned in this account, was part of the system introduced with the Nizamiye courts. Like any other juridical and/or administrative body, the bidayet court also remained only a superficial mechanism totally within the status quo.

The cases introduced in this part of the study from around Payas, Çork Marzvan, Beylan and/or Belen, Ocaklı, and other Armenian villages in the region, along with those from Çarşamba, Galatia, Yozgat, and Kayseri, prove that the provincial oppressions were not solely found in the eastern provinces. They occurred almost everywhere in the empire and were part and parcel of the new administrative tools of Tanzimat like the newly introduced taxes and administrative structures, military operations of *Fırka-i Islahiye*, the Provincial Regulations, and the Land Code. Almost all the cases presented occurred at the height of Tanzimat after the Reform Edict of 1856. I demonstrated at the beginning of this chapter that the partitioning of Kurdistan, the defeat of the region's Kurdish begs, and their mobilization by the empire against Russia consolidated the empire around the idea of Muslim unity as early as the mid-1850s. On one hand, the central Ottoman administration was promoting the idea of equal citizenship, but on the other hand, it was further dividing provinces on the basis of religion and confessionalism. For this reason, the strengthening of Muslim and Sunni allegiances throughout Abdulhamid II's reign[92] was not a coincidence, but the result of policies consistently pursued throughout the nineteenth century. The Kurdish, Circassian, Turcoman, and Turkish Muslim alliances became central to the structural changes undertaken after the Crimean War and the Reform Edict that followed. The same thread can also be seen in the activities of the *Fırka-i Islahiye.* While Ahmet Cevdet's *Tezâkir* gives detailed accounts of the military operations and administrative changes undertaken, the archival documents of the Armenian Patriarchate show the severity of the situation on the ground. The land issues of Çarsancak, Zeytun, and the Sanjak of Iskenderun did not end in the nineteenth century. Çarsancak and Zeytun were severely affected during the genocide period, whereas the Sanjak of Iskenderun continued to be a region of perpetual exiles for Armenians even post-1923.[93]

Ardzuig Darōnoy: *"Khachadur is . . . the Tanzimat of the Provinces"*

By the mid-nineteenth century, the Armenian Apostolic Church had two Catholicoi within the Ottoman Empire: one in Cilicia and one at Aghtamar in Van, and two patriarchates, Jerusalem and Constantinople. With the ratification of the Armenian Constitution, the Armenian Patriarchate of Constantinople systematically strove to centralize its power to govern over all the empire's Armenians. The Catholicosate of Aghtamar in Van, with its geographic proximity to Echmiadzin, had its biggest rivalry with the Mother See.

The murder of Catholicos Bedros of Aghtamar in 1864 occurred during what Garo Sasuni defined as a period of constant insecurity between 1850 and 1880.[94] *Ardzuig Darōnoy,* a biweekly published by Karekin Srvantsdyants' in Muş, released details of this murder and the subsequent proclamation by Archbishop Khachadur of himself as the new Catholicos of Aghmatar.[95] According to news received from the region, Catholicos Bedros had been thrown into Lake Van and remained on the shore of the lake overnight. The next day he was taken to his brother's house in the nearby village of Pshavank, and that same night a single gunshot was heard in the village. A follow-up article added that Bedros had been killed by two Kurdish gunmen,[96] specified by Bishop Eremia Degvants to be a son of Derviş Bey and a grandson of Mahmud Khan, who in his time had been an ally of Bedir Khan Beg of Bohtan.[97] The murder of Catholicos Bedros is perhaps the most striking example of the magnitude of violence that prevailed in the provinces, but it was far from a unique case. Indeed, Yaşar Tolga Cora draws our attention to the fact that starting in the mid-1850s, there were several cases of attacks and murders of prominent non-Muslim people. The British Consul at Erzurum called the murder of prominent Armenian citizen Khachadur Efendi Pastırmacıyan[98] a common case that he attributed to "the fixed fanatical jealous rancour all Moslems bear Christians here, and the easy impunity with which they can act."[99]

Ardzuig Darōnoy published a detailed analysis of the situation at the Catholicosate of Aghtamar, saying it had become a "feudal chiefdom" (*derebeylik*), a violent and oppressive power that in his words was "cooperating with Kurdish tribal leaders." Referring to the self-declared Catholicos Khachadur, the newspaper wrote: "This Khachadur . . . is the Tanzimat of the provinces."[100] This phrase likens Khachadur's ordering of Catholicos Bedros's murder to the author's understanding of Tanzimat's reform in the provinces, a replacement of the old order through oppression and murder. The article in *Ardzuig Darōnoy* was anonymous, as was an earlier similar article published in the Constantinople-based *Giligia.* The latter informed its readers about the incident via a letter received from Van that "illuminated the sad incidents which took place."[101] Based on the details provided in the article and its stylistic resemblance to those published in *Ardzuig Darōnoy,* it appears to have been written by the same anonymous person.

While these incidents occurred in October 1864, Srvantsdyants' had already been lamenting the situation in the provinces that January when he wrote a lengthy piece in the Constantinople-based *Zhamanag.*[102] This periodical almost exclusively published articles and news items on two major themes: the Armenian administration in the new constitutional era and the situation in the provinces. Considering the political and social atmosphere of those days, publishing anything from the provinces would be held by the state as quite troublesome, and as will be shown in this chapter newspapers were sometimes temporarily closed for publishing critical news items or articles related to the provinces. *Zhamanag*'s relative freedom, however, might be attributed to two possible reasons, the first being that it was published biweekly and thus not considered as influential as newspapers and magazines published daily or thrice a week, and second because it was published in Armenian and so its readership was more restricted than the Armeno-Turkish newspapers.

Darōn/Muş, 1864: A Station of Disaster

The January 1864 article by Srvantsdyants' about provincial oppression described the situation of Darōn in the region of Muş, saying there were already more than six hundred households (*hane*) that had abandoned their belongings, fields, animals, and homes as a result of the oppression and constant injustices. An average household might have consisted of ten people, which means that even in 1864 at the height of the Constitutional fervor and Tanzimat, more than six thousand Armenians left just this region because of ongoing oppressions. In his words, Darōn was a station of disaster. Animals were dying from hunger, houses were being raided, and people were forced to leave. Srvantsdyants' pleaded with the Armenian administration to take care of the situation, or else soon it might not have a population in the region to administer.[103] Time once again was working against the Armenians and in favor of the local power holders and the state, for whom it became a primary tool of governance in keeping the provincial oppressions going.

At this time Bishop Hovhannes Muradyan of Muş was visiting its villages in order to introduce the Armenian Constitution and guide local communities in establishing local administrative bodies. He wrote a report about his findings, and while his notes were partly published in the newspapers, his full report can be found in the published volume *Tiwan Hayots' Badmut'ean*, which was compiled by Father Kiwd Aghanyants' and eventually published in Tbilisi in 1915. Bishop Muradyan's report included sixty cases pertaining to the villages of the Muş Plain that occurred just between mid-May and mid-July 1864. While many of the cases are criminal in nature, they include hints at the destruction of core family structures among Armenians, especially in the numerous cases related to women. I chose some of these cases and kept their original numbers as given in the source.

> 1—In the village of Motkan, an Armenian man, Tukhman, was killed with an axe by a Kurd from the village of Asdre . . . while weeding. Eight years previously, the same person also killed Yakup Aga and Ghugas, the brother of milletbaşı Krikor from Diyarbekir, in their houses.
> 4—In the village of Ardvots, an Armenian man, after letting his wife go, took another woman together with his uncle as a common wife of both. They adopted the Kurdish tradition.
> 6—We gathered the villagers [of Vartenis] in one of the houses to inform them about the Constitution. At 7 o'clock in the evening, bandits knocked on our door. Since there were three brave fighters, they had to run away.
> 25—In the village of Trmed, there were 50 houses of Armenians. From April until June, 25 families left the village. The remaining families had to face the Kurdish and military oppression, which resulted in the evacuation of the village, the villagers left all their belongings behind.
> 37—In the village of Havadorig, the Kurds collect one sheep from each Armenian family. The reason is that when Kurds kill each other, they collect blood money from Armenians.
> 41—Kurds from Motkan kidnapped the bride of Kre from the village of Musheghen. They offered her to the Sheikh and Kurdified her.
> 55—An Armenian woman from the village of Hunan was kidnapped by the Kurds with her valuables. Father Mkhitar found her. However, Kurds stole her heart and had her say that she was a Muslim (dajik). Father Mkhitar took the case to court and rescued her.[104]

There were many regulations that structured the institution of marriage and family life within the Armenian *millet.* As I will demonstrate in the last chapter of this book, Armenian ecclesiastical law strictly forbids having a second wife. However, the gendered nature of the violence seen in this report hints at a larger and much more comprehensive strategy, namely, targeting the nucleus of Armenian society, the family, and outlawing Armenians in the eyes of their administration. If the Armenian administration attempted to intervene, the accused could easily evade it through conversion to Islam. In 1871, Archbishop Grigoris, the prelate of Muş, also reported that some Armenian men were taking two wives and that conversion had become a method of escaping penalization.[105] These practices were undermining both the familial institution of the Armenian *millet* and the authority of its administration.

As is seen in the articles of Bishop Muradyan's report, violence was omnipresent. It not only had an economic component through double taxation and the confiscation of animals, agricultural products, and land, but also systematically criminalized the Armenians within their legal structures through the adoption of "Kurdish tradition."[106] This culminated in the outlawing of "Kurdified" Armenians and their full subordination to the aghas and begs. By taking a second wife and converting to Islam when questioned by their local administration, Armenian men would leave their first wives and family destitute, further deepening the desperate situation in the provinces. More important, not all of them officially converted to Islam, but instead existed in a de facto reality estranged from the Armenian administration yet not officially part of the Muslim one, leaving them completely at the mercy of the local Kurdish beg without legal protection. Regarded as criminals within their own system and pushed into poverty by heavy and unjust taxes, they had no other choice than to become an outcast with practically no legal framework of rights. In other words, criminalization as a method of governance subjugated and gave the local power holders full control over the autochthonous people.

Similar news items and letters from the provinces were published in *Zhamanag*, sometimes with a signature and sometimes anonymously. For instance, in August 1864 there was a three-and-a-half-page report on the Surp Garabet Monastery of Muş and Armeno-Kurdish cooperation resisting the patriarchate's attempts to implement the constitutional order. Considering the heavy censorship of the Armenian press by the Ottoman as well as Armenian administrations, it is noteworthy to see such lengthy articles in *Zhamanag*. The newspaper also published Bishop Mgrdich Pakraduni's report on the region of Sasun and Motkan. Bishop Mgrdich reported that there were many villages of Armenians in the provinces where Kurds spoke Armenian and Armenians worked for Kurds. The same kind of *derebey* system prevailed there as in Çarsancak. Bishop Mgrdich reported the following:

> The Kurds of these regions were speaking in the language of Armenians. But their religion is not known. There is no circumcision, no mosques, no marriage ceremonies [*nikâh* written in Armeno-Turkish]. Their entire income is based on Armenian labor. . . . They [Kurds] collect yearly taxes from them [Armenians]. They [Kurds] control the monasteries; they choose the head of a monastery, or fire him as they wish. Only with their written orders are these changes allowed to take place. The bishop representing each monastery is called to account from the Kurds. There is a famous monastery in the region by the name of St. Aghperits; it has a large constituency. It is in the hands of Kurds. They hold the seal of the cemetery too. A Kurd is doing the duties of the abbot [*vanahayr*]. . . . Most of the time, they force poor Armenians to have a second wife, especially when they see that the first woman did not have a child. The reason for this is that they do not want the Armenian population to decrease as this would spoil their comfortable life.[107]

The bishop, being a local cleric, would know all the groups living in the area. His statement of "their religion is unknown" may mean two things. Either he meant that they were Alevi Kurds, a group that does not attend mosques, and thus their villages did not have a mosque, or he meant that they were not classified under any ruling or religious authority. In this case, what mattered to them was to maintain their lifestyle by exploiting Armenian labor, as seen in Bishop Muradyan's report. The provincial oppressions were pushing the limits of the *millets*, forcing Armenians to become criminals in the eyes of their administration, and creating outcasts who were under the complete control of their begs.

The situation of the Armenian administration in Muş was not any better than that of Sasun and Motkan, at least when it came to the administrators of Surp Garabet Monastery, the region's central monastery where Srvantsdyants' and Khrimyan served at the time. Also in the *Zhamanag* newspaper, we find an anonymous letter lamenting the collaboration of local Armenian notables with Kurdish tribal forces against clerics sent from Constantinople to centralize the monastery. It explains how the monastery's administration commissioned Kurds to kill Archbishop Hagop from Constantinople, who was shot dead in front of the monastery. Archbishop Bedros was exiled, and Archbishop Grigoris fled to Erzurum during the night. Bishop Madteos from Yozgat was threatened with guns and kicked out of the monastery. Guns were fired upon Khrimyan from five in the afternoon until sunrise the following day. Kurds would also independently dismiss the head of the monastery and appoint whomever they desired.[108] In those days, the Monastery of Surp Garabet fed 186 people daily and owned more than one thousand animals.[109] Consequently, it was a large abbey with agricultural, educational, and publishing facilities. In the autumn of 1864, Armenian clerics in the provinces were trying to introduce and establish the constitutional order of the Nizamname by visiting all the remote villages, where they were often confronted with situations similar to those described in these reports.[110]

As shown here, the centralization of the Armenian Patriarchate had many layers, including but not limited to the implementation of the Nizamname. As for the Ottoman administration, reform and centralization meant strengthening the alliances with Kurdish tribal chiefs by territorially and temporally subjugating them to the structures and institutions of the center. Keeping criminality and impunity high was a method of governance that was very effective in hindering any alliance between the Armenians and Kurds in regions where they lived together. An alliance between the Kurds and Armenians could be allowed only if they were in line with the state's interests, such as the murder of Aghtamar Catholicos Bedros.

Erzurum, 1857, and Van, 1866–1871: Water Theft

As early as 1857, right after the Crimean War, Bishop Hovhannes from Surp Giragos Monastery in Garin/Erzurum wrote to the Patriarchate in Constantinople complaining of two locals, namely, Molla Yusuf and his uncle's son Faruk, who were oppressing Tsermak, an Armenian village with one hundred households.[111] Access to water was being hindered. As explained by Bishop Hovhannes, Molla Yusuf and Faruk changed the waterway, and water was accessible only at their mansion, preventing the villagers from getting water to irrigate their fields. Unable to work in the fields, the villagers were unsure how to sustain their livelihoods. Molla Yusuf and Faruk occupied the village, burned down the threshing floors, and sent animals into them. They also intentionally damaged the villagers' crops by releasing animals into their gardens. They kept the *aşar* (*öşür*) tax for themselves that was supposed to be sent to the government. Conditions had become unbearable for the villagers, and they were ready to leave their homes and descend on the capital to complain at the Sublime Porte. Bishop Hovhannes wrote that they wanted to send a testimonial (*mazbata*), but their previous negotiations (*müzakere*)[112] had been heard by the Muslims (*aylazki*) who slandered them as a result, leaving them no other way to complain. The document requested that the patriarch write a *takrir* on the issue to the Sublime Porte, send an order (*emirname*) to the governor of the sanjak, and follow up on the results, as "patience was running out."[113] Monopolizing natural resources such as water creates momentum intrinsic to the logic of territoriality, which in turn creates inequalities.[114] The hijacking of the water supply against Armenians happened quite often in many other places as well, which I read as intensifying existing inequalities leading to the enforcement of differential access, in which one group is prioritized over others. Irrigation and access to water were the most critical issues for peasants, as not having water meant the end of life in the village.

The same document from Erzurum also reveals another aspect of oppression, the hindering of religious practices. The Reform Edict ratified religious freedoms, but the idea of equality between Muslims and non-Muslims could not be accepted, as inequality had been intrinsic to power hierarchies for centuries. The idea of being equal to a non-Muslim could be regarded as a disgrace for a Muslim. One of the common practices for Christians was to call the community to prayer by knocking on a piece of wood, called *tahta çalmak*, signaling the beginning of the church service. This practice had been established as an alternative to ringing a metal bell, which was often forbidden. The document explains how Molla Yusuf and Faruk would stand in front of the church on Sundays complaining about the loud prayers coming from inside. Bishop Hovhannes lamented that the villagers would avoid coming to church because of them. Hindering the call for religious services or encumbering the gathering of the community was part of the provincial oppressions in many places. In fact, there are complaints in the Ottoman Archives about hindering Armenians' *tahta çalmak* as early as 1846.[115] The practice of knocking on a piece of wood in the absence of bells is a matter of temporality. In other words, the practice was part and parcel of the Christian temporalities of calling people to church, and thus hindering it should be seen as a forceful synchronization of Armenians to the temporality of the sovereign.

Another case of water theft was reported in December 1866 by four bishops and one layman from the monastery of Varak, again near Van. They explained the troublesome situation and possible solutions in detail. One of the most striking parts of this report was the exact description of the problem, namely, how their water was being stolen: "Every day they come, 2–3–5, sometimes ten bandits, with guns and daggers under their belts, without even asking first for the permission of the monastery; they carry the water, and then they eat, drink and sleep, not allowing anyone to approach the water, even those coming from the monastery." The matter was not a new one. It was stated that this same policy had been deployed at Lake Keşiş, which dried up as a result of overconsumption. Another critical point from the text gives striking insight into the authors' feelings about their lives in the time of Tanzimat: "We do not believe that even in this period of liberating illumination, the oppression experienced in the monastery will vary from those barbarisms [of the past]."[116]

The Armenian Central Administration and the Provincial Oppressions

The term of Patriarch Mgrdich Khrimyan (1869–73), a native of Van born in 1820, is uniquely defined in Armenian historiography by his attachment to the provinces. During his reign, a section appeared in the memorandum of 1871 called "The Issue of Provincial Oppressions." Prior to this change, provincial oppressions were merely reported under the subtitle "Provincial [Issues]" (*Kawaṛagan*). This adjustment of wording signals that by this time it had already been determined it was futile to attempt to solve the provincial oppressions by writing *takrirs* to the Sublime Porte and that something more needed to be done. Thus, the patriarch took it upon himself to discuss the issues directly with the grand vizier and submit a brief memorandum to him called a negotiation (*müzakere*). He also issued an order for the prelacies in the provinces to similarly conduct their relations with the Sublime Porte by this principle, essentially requesting them to stop contacting it about their issues altogether.[117]

I will introduce and analyze one of these detailed reports sent to the central Armenian administration from a provincial prelacy that year, found in the Correspondence File of the Armenian Patriarchate's Archive. The report from the *Vijag* of Erznga/Erzincan is exemplary of many others that were utilized to prepare the final report of April 1872, as a result of the meticulous research conducted by the Armenian administration in the capital. The provincial oppressions it detailed are emblematic of those endured during Tanzimat and would only intensify after the Congress of Berlin.

A Report from the Vijag *of Erznga/Erzincan, 1871*

This report, prepared by the Armenian administration of Erznga and Paperd (Bayburt) at the request of the patriarch, includes almost all types of oppressions, and so is worth discussing in detail because it gives hints as to how the final report came into being. The document has a registration number in its marginalia along with a note restating that the report was sent in accordance with the Armenian Patriarchate's memorandum on provincial oppressions. It was signed by the prelate (*arachnort*) of Erznga, Krikoris Alatjyan, on March 10, 1871, and was processed in the capital on April 5, 1871.

Erznga was one of the principal cities on the way to Erzurum and was under its jurisdiction at the beginning of the twentieth century. According to data from 1914, Erznga had some 37,612 Armenians (5,207 households [*hane*]), 103 churches, 35 monasteries, and 63 schools across 66 villages. As Erznga lost a considerable portion of its population during the massacres of 1895, we can assume that in 1871 the area's Armenian presence was much better structured and the number of Armenian households much higher.[118]

The report titled "Report on the Oppressions of the Province of Erznga" consists of thirteen pages with thirty-four articles. The twentieth article has ten subarticles all related to the oppressions done by Kasaboğlu

Haji (Hacı) Selim. A second section of the report contains thirty-four solutions, one for each oppression mentioned in its first part.

The first nine articles are on tax issues, demonstrating the centrality of Tanzimat's tax regimes in the provincial oppressions. The first one is about the unjust collection of the military exemption tax (*Bedel-i Askeri* or *Bedelat-ı Askeriye*). This tax replaced the poll tax (*cizye*) for non-Muslims after the proclamation of the Reform Edict.[119] It was owed for the exemption of non-Muslims from military obligations, and the amount to be paid would be determined by registering the population at the age of military service. Musa Çadırcı mentions that there were troubles in the distribution and collection of this tax but does not elaborate on them.[120] The report provides some valuable information regarding what those troubles were, indicating that this tax was due not only for people whose whereabouts were known but also for those who had been away from the region for the last ten to fifteen years. Hence, the Armenians of Erzincan were expected to also pay taxes for their Armenian neighbors who used to live in the same district or village but left years ago.[121] There is a similar case from Tercan in a memorandum of the Armenian administration for 1870–71 in which the military exemption tax (*bedel-i askeri*) for Armenians who had emigrated from Tercan to Erzurum (Garin) was charged to the Armenians remaining in Tercan.[122] Consequently, in order to avoid paying extra taxes, each household was responsible for making sure its neighbors stayed in the village. While Özbek refers to the practice of collective payment of the *vergi-i mahsusa*, the special tax introduced by Tanzimat,[123] cases included in this report prove that the military exemption tax was applied similarly. To resolve this problem, a new registration (*tahrirat*) was suggested to adjust for and register those who had moved away or died or whose whereabouts were unknown, thus freeing their neighbors of the tax burden of continuing to pay for them.[124] The solution offered by the local Armenian administration was nothing more than to carry out the law as it existed on paper. This request asked for the population to be properly registered and taxed accordingly, something decreed but not enforced. While the lack of enforcement of laws was a common complaint, this study considers it to have been owing to a choice rather than an inability. In this case, too, it is an issue not only of unjust taxation but also of creating a mechanism of social control, one in which neighbors had to keep an eye on each other in order to avoid the burden of unfair taxes. More important, it has to be assumed that state officials were well aware of this problem and how it could be rectified, but instead found this temporal and territorial method of governance to be more advantageous left in place.

The second article is about the unjust distribution of the Registration of Property (*Tahrir-i Emlâk*) and Taxes on Profits (*Temettüat*). The Department of Registration of Property (*Tahrir-i Emlâk Nezareti*) was an institution of Tanzimat founded in 1858 to establish revenue sources for the empire. Introduced in 1860, the Regulations for Registration of Population and Property (*Tahrir-i Nüfus ve Emlâka Dair Nizamname*) clearly defined how the registration of valuable property and the population was to be conducted.[125] Yet as the report stated, there was an imbalance between the registration of properties belonging to Armenians and those of Muslims. The houses or shops of Armenians were registered with double or even greater value, whereas the houses or shops of Muslims (*Dajig*) were undervalued.[126] The other tax referenced, *Temettü*, was collected based on the estimated yearly income of tradesmen and artisans. It started at 3 percent and was increased in 1878 after the end of the Russo-Ottoman War to 4 percent.[127] It can be inferred from the solution offered that neither the yearly income estimates nor the registration of valuables was done fairly. In the second part of the report, it was requested that the Ottoman administration establish a special commission jointly with Christians to verify the registered values and correct them when necessary.[128]

The third article is about the Property Registration (*Tahrir-i Emlâk*) and Tax on Profits (*Temettü*) for the year 1856–66 (1282). The *tahrir* registers that year were exaggerated causing an overly high assessment of the taxes, which led to many objections and people being unable to pay them. Furthermore, relatives of people who had died after that year's registration of the tax on profits were held responsible for paying the deceased's full exaggerated amount.[129] The solution offered was to ask for the mercy of the government, to correct the exaggerations, and then to ask the families to pay the taxes of their dead relatives.[130]

According to the report, the order instituting the registration of properties through *Tahrir-i Emlâk* arrived in Erznga only in 1870 but was never applied,[131] and it requested that be done immediately and adequately.[132] Çadırcı stated that the regulation had been put into effect in 1860 and was first instituted in Bursa followed by the Province of Yanya (Ioanina).[133] Apparently, when the order did finally reach Erznga ten years later, its application did not go as smoothly as it had in Bursa and Yanya. This was likely the case in many other areas as well, where the registration of land was a highly charged political issue in terms of maintaining the existing power relations of certain begs and aghas.

An Armenian from each district of the city and for each village was required to work with the government's tax collector to collect the tax on profits (*temettü*) and property taxes (*emlak*). This meant that the Armenians of Erznga/Erzincan had to pay the heavy burden of monthly salaries for almost thirty tax advisers.[134] The second part of the report suggested that tax collection should be the duty of the government alone and that Armenians should not surrender to these unlawful demands.[135]

Grapes, gardens (*bostan*), cotton, and other crops that were not weighed were subjected to unjust tax estimations by tax collectors (*mültezims*). They would look at each field to estimate how much it would produce and take one-tenth as tax. However, the estimations of tax collectors were so high that often nothing would remain for the farmer. As a result, the farmer could not cultivate the land the following year, preventing him from earning a living or paying taxes.[136] Çadırcı wrote that in Bursa, where these registrations were first undertaken, the best practice was to appraise the gardens and vineyards according to their size and productivity.[137] However, the report contends that in Erzincan/Erznga they were not measured, nor were their sizes estimated fairly. To stop unjust taxation on these products, it was urged the fields and *bostans* be taxed according to their exact measurement in order to allow the farmers to continue their occupation.[138]

There was also a tax on the farmer's unsold products and those he used personally such as mulberries and grapes. For this reason, houses were often unexpectedly raided in search of mulberries and grapes to tax,[139] a practice regarded as improper by the report. It was suggested to tax just what is sold and stop raiding homes.[140] House raids should also be seen as a method of temporal as well as territorial governance, meaning not even the gardens and houses belonged to the owners but to the sovereign, and his representatives were entitled to enter those spaces *whenever* they wanted to. It was yet another practice that had a criminalizing effect on the inhabitants.

According to the Provincial Regulations, it was stipulated that a tax of one bushel of wheat should be created to support poor farmers in order to provide them with seeds and food when necessary. Though this support tax had been collected for two years at the time of the report, no Armenian had ever been permitted to benefit from it, and it remained unknown where the collected wheat was actually going.[141] The suggested solution was to cancel the extra wheat collection altogether, as the economic situation of every farmer was practically uniform.[142]

The cleanliness of the city and the construction of buildings were under the authority of the municipal council, which was funded by fines. The Armenians were assessed far more fines while receiving the least amount of municipal services in their districts, with the money collected exclusively used in Muslim districts.[143] The report objected to this discriminatory funding and requested the proceeds be applied equally for all *millets* as well as to distribute the budget fairly among every district.[144]

According to the report, Erzincan/Erznga's water sources were mostly found in the Muslim districts, even inside their houses. Armenians generally did not have access to water and so were forced to pay extra money to the water sellers, but even then still did not have enough water for their households. There was a campaign to collect money to construct more fountains, but despite raising 10,000–12,000 *gurush*, no new fountains were built, and the money disappeared.[145] The second part of the report suggested finding that money, which had been collected during the governorship of Derviş Pasha, and use it to build waterways.[146] Derviş Pasha was the commander of the Fourth Army in Erzincan in 1864, prior to which he served in the Ottoman Army as the commander of the division in Herzegovina. He was in charge of the war against Montenegro and in 1863 was appointed governor of Yanya (Ioanina). After his military services subduing the westernmost parts of the empire, Derviş Pasha was suddenly sent to the easternmost part of the empire, Erzincan. He was made the head of the Fırka-ı Islahiye Army in 1865, which brought the regions of Cilicia and the Sanjak of Iskenderun under Ottoman control.[147] His career seems to be a materialization of Ottoman temporalities and territorialities. The experience and know-how he accumulated through military operations and restructuring in the west must have been regarded as useful to control and establish the empire's sovereignty in the east, a choice that should be considered among its methods of temporality and territorial governance.

Another issue in the report is in regard to zaptiah officers. When they would visit villages, the expenses they incurred in the course of their work would be paid from their budget. However, the zaptiahs would demand everything from the Armenian villagers for free. They would finish their duty in Muslim villages and go to the next Armenian village to stay overnight. It was noted that these practices were done only in Armenian villages and never in Muslim ones.[148] This abuse of power was not only practiced in the eastern provinces. Çadırcı gives examples from Hüdavendigar (Bursa) Province where zaptiahs demanded free food and fodder from the villagers.[149] The report's solution affirmed that the existing regulations regarding the zaptiahs paying for their own expenses were suitable but lacked enforcement, so methods should be applied in order to enforce the existing rules against unlawful practices.[150] Here as well, not enforcing the law should be read as a method of governance rather than a lack of authority. Forcing Armenians to pay the zaptiahs' expenses, serve them food, and provide them a place to stay overnight were policies with both temporal and territorial aspects that encouraged them to abuse their authority and entitlements.

A major obstacle for Armenians is that their testimony was not held as sufficient proof in court, leaving them unable to prove crimes committed against them. Whenever an Armenian attempted to protect their rights, the other side would bring Muslim witnesses, meaning that not only were Armenians unable to defend themselves, but in the end they would be the ones found guilty and imprisoned.[151] The report stated that by law, the testimony of Armenians is acceptable in court, but the law was not applied. One of the most commonly repeated sentiments in the report is that the existing laws should be enforced.[152] When this report was written in 1871, the principle of equality was being reiterated time and again, based on not only the 1839 proclamation of Tanzimat but also the Reform Edict of 1856. Yet the rhythm and direction of the time were that of Ottoman arbitrating power, so by not enforcing the existing laws and regulations as time passed, it actually created a de facto reality that reproduced more inequality and oppression.

Indeed, one of the most important criteria for becoming equal was equality before the law, that is, the right to testify. Although the Reform Edict accepted the equality of all citizens of the empire in theory, as shown in this report from Erzincan and the cases from Çork Marzvan and Çarsancak, this equality was not applied and had no societal or institutional support. Therefore, the assumption of equality on paper actually triggered further inequality, in that it provoked a reaction of Muslim superiority which reinforced the impossibility for them to accept the equality of Muslims and non-Muslims.

The report had an article on the use of the term *infidel* (*gâvur*). The Muslims of Erzincan would call Armenians infidels (*gâvur*), "thinking that they still lived in the old times."[153] With this quote, the Armenian administration in Erznga was making a reference to the quality of time in accordance with the Ottoman administration's temporality, which regarded the Tanzimat as a new period of progressive change. However, some things apparently had not changed, as there was no punishment for this slur either.[154] The solution offered was to punish those using the word. It mentioned that "years ago" when such defamations were subject to fines, everybody was very careful with their words. However, seeing that enforcement was not taking place, the use of such defamations actually increased despite technically being illegal.[155] Not enforcing the law in this case can be read as encouraging the crime and granting impunity to the perpetrator.

The report stated that the lieutenant of the zaptiah in the region, Feyzullah Beg, was using harsh and military methods exclusively upon the Armenians, interfering in all their matters, provoking the Muslim population against them, and even imprisoning them arbitrarily.[156] It was suggested that Feyzullah Beg should be suspended from his position and that this would be good practice for the future.[157]

There are more than ten complaints in the report regarding the misdeeds of Kasaboğlu Hacı Selim from the village of Hayrabed (Üçkonak).

According to the report, his oppression of the peasants had earned him the nickname "the Tamerlane of Erznga." For example, he hindered the construction of a church despite the existence of a firman permitting it. In order to bring water to his garden, he opened numerous wells that were left unmaintained and became a burden for farmers, whose animals fell in them and died. He used the villagers of Hayrabed as forced labor to bring the well water to him, and his claiming of the wells caused the Armenian farmers' fields to dry out.[158] He left his animals to a female shepherd who let them graze in the Armenians' fields, as they could not do anything about it since the consequences would be grave, and most of their agricultural products were subsequently eaten by his animals.[159] In addition, properties belonging to the daughter-in-law of a stonemason (*taşçı*) Mangasar from the same village were apparently forcefully registered[160] in Hacı Selim's name. Kelleryan Avedis was beaten severely because of the water problem, causing him to barter away whatever he had and leave the village. The local Armenian cleric of Hayrabed village was harshly beaten up while he was overseeing the preparations for the construction of the local church. Whenever Hacı Selim entered a place, all those present had to stand up or else be beaten.[161] Once again, here we see that territoriality occurs in the form of a number of oppressions, such as violence against the Armenian inhabitants and their clerics, confiscation of their property, and the monopolization of natural resources in favor of the local Muslim power holders.

In the second part of the report, it was suggested to take all measures possible to rescue the Armenians from Kasaboğlu's hands, even calling him to Constantinople if necessary, as his absence would make it much easier to issue an official request (*istilam*) that would probably be used to bring him before a judge.[162]

Another case in the report was from the Armenian villages of Erznga/Erzincan to the south of the Euphrates, which were complaining about a Kurd from Srpehan Village named Süleyman, son of Seydi Khan. He and his brother were oppressing the villagers with their many demands and were known to be murderers who were not afraid to kill again.[163] The solution to their oppression offered by the report was to exile them elsewhere.[164]

The village of Ghuzulchan,[165] described as being "behind the mountains" far away from the center of Erznga/Erzincan, was once a densely Armenian-populated area, but they had been forced out as a result of oppression by the region's Kurdish inhabitants. The remaining fifty Armenian families, scattered around a few local settlements, had been protesting their treatment by *kaimakam* Shah Hüseyinzade Hüseyin Beg. He was one of the long-rebellious regional Kurdish leaders, the head of the Alevi Kurdish Çarekanlı tribe, who was finally brought into line by the state, pardoned, and called for military duty.[166] The local Kurds could only approach Armenians if he permitted them to, meaning he had the ability to protect the Armenians if he wanted. However, there were several complaints from the villages about homicides, theft of animals, and other offenses against them. Armenians living in these villages were far from the administrative center in Erzincan/Erznga and therefore had weak relations with the local Armenian administration.[167] As a solution, like in the case of Hacı Selim, the report suggested removing Hüseyinzade as *kaimakam*.[168]

Debit-credit issues between Kurds and Armenians were another type of problem that would result in Armenians being forced to leave. It was stated that in the village of Dandzig, the Kurd Mahmud grandson of Bozo borrowed money from Pilibos Ghugasyan of the same village. Not only did Mahmud not repay his debt, but he oppressed Pilibos to the extent that he had to flee to the city. Mahmud confiscated Pilibos's fields, houses, and wheat.[169] The solution requested was to give the properties back to their rightful owner and punish Mahmud.[170]

In the vicinity of Dandzig, four fields of the monastery of St. Tateos the Apostle were confiscated by a Kurdish inhabitant of Dandzig, Zemzi, the son of Mehmed.[171] The report determined that the confiscated fields should be returned to the monastery.[172]

In the same village, Kurd Mahmud occupied the fields of Sarkis, son of Faroghgents Mardig. In the same village, the Kurd Veli, son of Mehmed, occupied the Armenian Trakoshents Krikor's fields. The two Armenians fled to the city in order to save their lives.[173] The same solution was offered as above: the confiscated properties should be returned to their owners.[174] The fields of Babig and Markar and those of Harut'iwn, son of Stepan, were confiscated by the Kurd Ghulabi, son of Mehmed. He oppressed them so much that they left everything and moved near Apshda village, where they lived in extreme poverty.[175] Here it was suggested the oppressors should be punished severely to set an example against such behavior in the future, taking into account the fact it would be impossible to exile the perpetrator to other regions in every case of oppression.[176] The Kurd Ghulabi, known as Ghulabi-Zade Halil, and his son Gül Agha were from the Balaban tribe. This same tribe would later be actively involved in the massacres of 1895, and in 1915–16 was complicit in the crimes of the Committee of Union and Progress at Erzincan/Erznga.[177] Hence, Ghulabi's oppression of the Armenians was already notorious by 1871, and through the principle of impunity, it continued well into the twentieth century.

The report said there were a considerable number of Armenian carpenters in Erzincan who were often taken from their construction sites and forced to work elsewhere. If they resisted, the zaptiahs were called to take them forcefully, intimidating and insulting them, sometimes even beating them. At times they faced imprisonment and usually were subjected to *angarya*.[178] *Angarya* was a common practice of corvée labor, which forced peasants into doing unseemly and demeaning work without payment, tearing them away from their own daily routines that they had to maintain in order to sustain a living. *Angarya* can only happen in a hierarchical system. Indeed, in the Ottoman Archives, there are various cases of *angarya* complaints, in which one side is held as superior to the other.[179] Superiority owing to religion or confession is usually the case in the complaints. The solution insisted that all forms of *angarya*, including defamation, beating, and imprisonment, should be strictly punished as they were against the laws and regulations of the empire. The workers should be free to choose where to work and earn their living, as they had to pay taxes on the money they earned during this time.[180] Hijacking the people's time and energy and tearing them away from their own temporality and necessary work, corvée labor was yet another method of impoverishing the Armenians in provinces.

The report pointed out that about five years prior, it had been decided to build a police station (*karakolhane*) in Erzincan for which a large sum of money was collected. However, the police station was never built, and the money vanished.[181] The report suggested that impoverished people should not be manipulated and forced to pay money for nothing and requested an order to prohibit these kinds of practices.[182]

The last article of the report is about the irrelevance of the local Armenian administration in the eyes of the local Ottoman administration, as it would ignore the Armenians' entitlements established by the Nizamname. *Takrirs* submitted by the local Armenian administrations to their Ottoman counterparts were disregarded with the argument that "the essence of this issue is not a religious one, the government should decide" (*O ruhani mevadden deyil, hökümetin bilecigi iş*).[183] Written in Armeno-Turkish, it was a sentence that must have confronted the Armenian administration quite often. Whether an issue was regarded to be a religious or nonreligious one was decisive as to which jurisdiction would resolve it. However, more often than not, there was no clear separation between religious and nonreligious issues. Further, not only did Nizamnames recognize the religious entitlements of a *millet*, but the Armenian Nizamname was a comprehensive administrative text that detailed rights and responsibilities beyond just religious issues.[184] The sentence quoted in the report was an alibi to restrict and undermine the Armenian administration's authority as well as to keep issues unresolved. An issue of *Masis* newspaper from 1872 discussed this problem of the intertwined nature of religious and nonreligious issues, as well as the arbitrary nature of decision making.[185]

As depicted in this report, provincial oppressions had a wide range of practices encompassing every part of daily life, including unjust and disproportionate taxation, confiscation of property, stealing water, and hijacking irrigation routes that in turn made village agricultural activities impossible. These practices all created conditions that led to the impoverishment of Armenians who then were forced to emigrate to survive. However, every Armenian peasant in his or her helplessness had to police their neighbors in order to avoid the added burden of paying the taxes on those who left. Chaining Armenian peasants to one another by this taxation policy should be regarded as an important part of the provincial oppressions because it resulted in keeping the peasants in their villages and locked into the despair of *waiting* to die from hunger or subject to attack on the road trying to emigrate.

The report defined not just Alevi and Sunni Kurdish tribes as the oppressors but the zaptiahs as well for their abuse of the villagers and for forcing them into *angarya*. Although new regulations on the zaptiah were adopted as part of the Provincial Regulations in 1869,[186] we understand from this report that no de facto changes had taken place. The report also pointed to discrimination by municipal organizations in the amount of services they provided to Muslim and non-Muslim districts. The government is often depicted as failing to enforce the laws and regulations, which in turn allowed the oppressions to occur. This method of governance also meant it was in the position to stop them, and indeed some cases of good governmental policies were identified, such as the outlawing of the use of the word *infidel* (*gâvur*). Yet while there were rules against such defamation, when it became clear there was no enforcement of the law, the slur became even more prevalent. Therefore, in this report, the government was not directly the oppressor, but an institution that did not react appropriately to enforce the laws and regulations it adopted. Thereby, the state was still an institution that Armenians in the provinces looked to with hope, *waiting* for its justice.

The Report of the Armenian Assembly, 1872

The First Report on Provincial Oppressions Submitted to the Sublime Porte in the Name of the Armenian National Assembly was submitted on April 11, 1872, based on the reports sent from the provinces such as those I introduced above. A special committee had been appointed by the Armenian administration in November 1870 to prepare this report on the provincial oppressions. The committee contacted the prelacies asking for reports on their condition and grievances without exaggeration. The past twenty years of documents from the patriarchate's archives were also scrutinized.[187] The October 9, 1871, edition of *Manzume-i Efkâr* contains a lengthy news item about the ongoing preparation of the report, stating that the text had been presented to the Armenian National Assembly. The news item stated that more than five hundred *takrirs* had been written over the past twenty years. The head of the committee that prepared the report was Archbishop Nerses Varjabedyan, who went on to become patriarch after Khrimyan.[188] Among the complaints, Patriarch Khrimyan had collected were issues of *angarya*, money exaction, forced Islamization of women and children, and abuses in the distribution and collection of imperial taxes. The tax issues included assessing the military exemption tax (*bedel-i askeri*) for deceased people, those who had emigrated, or those individuals whose whereabouts were unknown to their relatives. The *ölçek hakkı* (also called the *Şahnalık* tax) in particular had already been abolished yet was still being levied on Armenians at a rate of one-sixth of the total produce and sometimes more. Also mentioned in the document were the unjust distribution of property (*emlak*) and taxes on profits (*temettü*)[189] and the abuses of tax collectors (*mültezims*) and their agents in the villages. The tax collectors' abuses included not coming in time so that the product would be spoiled or staying as long as they wished, especially when winter was approaching, in the houses of the villagers, who were obligated to satisfy their every whim and desire. Tax collectors also used physical violence and dishonored the women in the villages.[190] The report notes these complaints were more severe in districts where the Kurdish begs held power.[191]

The original version of the report also has complaints regarding inheritance (*tereke*). According to the report, when an Armenian passed away, the judges of the Islamic court (*kadı*) would immediately go to the deceased's home, and whatever they found there was counted as their property and put toward the tax calculation. In such cases, even if the deceased had already left a testimony with the official approval of the court, it would not count.[192]

One of the most critical issues was undoubtedly of landownership in the provinces. There is a special section dedicated to it in an official publication of the patriarchate from 1876, which explained that the government launched a campaign to encourage farmers to register the lands on which they worked in their own names. In practice, however, Armenian peasants of the provinces ended up being disadvantaged by this new regulation, as the local Kurdish begs used their power to register the land in their names instead. This practice turned the Armenians into wageworkers (*maraba*) on the lands that they used to have the right to cultivate. The document considers land registration "the most important issue of the Armenians of the provinces."[193]

Tanzimat envisioned the participation of non-Muslims at various levels of administration, at least on paper. The Provincial Regulations also affirmed the mission of Tanzimat, enabling the establishment of new commissions (known as *Meclis-i Tefrik* or *Tefrik Meclisi*) at all administrative levels—*vilayet, liva, kaza*—in which non-Muslims and Muslims were to be equally represented. The representatives were to be determined by elections,[194] but the Armenian Patriarchate's *First Report* contended that these new commissions (*Meclis-i Tefrik*) were exclusively composed of the subgovernor (*mütessarrıf*), the judge (*hâkim*), the mufti (*müftü*), the registration/correspondence officer (*tahrirat müdürü*), and the leaders of the non-Muslim inhabitants. Though each non-Muslim group was to put forward the names of those they desired for the electoral list, the report claimed it was controlled by government officials. It also emphasized that the wealthy men of the provinces should be prevented from taking undue advantage of their positions and that "the composition of *Tefrik Meclis* should be rendered more *profitable to the people at large and the poorer classes.*" The report suggests local clerical heads, prelates (*arachnorts*), which were apparently excluded from the process, should be allowed to participate in the choosing of members.[195] As is shown in the first chapter, a similar situation of hindering the representation of Armenian *millet* in the local Meclis, was also the case in Kastamonu. Therefore, the problem described in the Erznga Report was not specific to the eastern provinces but was a general problem where Armenians lived.[196]

The report refers to the insecurity of life, property, and honor, the three ideals that made up the motto of the period: "It is superfluous to add here how many rapes, depredations and thefts, and above all murders remain without punishment or have remained undiscovered despite the efforts of the Government itself."[197] It expresses hope in the Reform Edict, a belief that justice would be achieved through the Nizamiye tribunals and that the principle of equality would eventually prevail.[198] This part of the report recalls that the testimony of non-Muslims was not admissible in court, meaning the security of life, honor, and property was not applied and the criminals were not punished.

The First Report underlines the oppressions by armed Kurds, especially in Erzurum, Diyarbekir, Muş, Van, Kığı, Tercan, Bitlis, Çarsancak, and Siirt, among other places.[199] This eight-page report by the patriarchate devoted its last two pages almost entirely to the eastern provinces and Kurdish oppressions, concluding as follows:

> Let either the Kurds who continually oppress our nation be disarmed, or let the Armenians be put in a position to protect their life and property against the oppressors. It is to be hoped that your benevolent Government will adopt some such final measures as by immediately employing the bravery of the Imperial army against the Kurds, by introducing a powerful police force into the oppressed districts, of which we have an example in Roumelia, and by admitting Armenians into all the ranks of such police, then the vital question of equality may be solved to the satisfaction of the people.[200]

As I searched for the repercussions of this report in the newspapers, I ascertained that the newspaper *Manzume-i Efkâr* was banned for almost two months starting in April 1872. Searching for the reason behind this ban, I came across a letter sent to the newspaper by the Armenians of Sivas, published under the title of "Internal News" (*Dahiliye*) with the subtitle "A Request from the Grand Vizier" (*Sadrazam Hazretlerine bir niyaz*). The letter said the Armenians of Zara located near Sivas were oppressed by Bahar Murtaza Kehya and Kındz İçeroğlu, who was described as a "gangster" (*eşkıya*). The former was alleged to have burned down the villagers' stable, killing their oxen and cattle. While a personal petition (*arz-ı hal*) had been submitted to the administration of Zara about their maltreatment, the criminals enjoyed the administration's protection. Therefore, the Armenians of Zara complained to the pasha of Sivas and waited for it to be addressed. In order to travel to Sivas, they borrowed money with interest from a certain Khacher Panigyan. An editorial was included following the letter: "In an era of justice and civilization, during the reign of a Sultan such as Abdulaziz and in a period when Mahmud Pasha is a Grand

Vizier, in some places some people continue their cruelty, barbarity, and commit murders. Not only do they continue to do all these, but they also remain exempt from any punishment."[201]

The May 20, 1872, issue of *Manzume-i Efkâr* explains the reason it had been banned, pointing to two articles[202] it published that were considered to contain "aggressive/abusive language [*mütecavizane lisan*] against the government."[203] Although the offending articles were not named, one can assume "A Request from the Grand Vizier"[204] to be a strong candidate, with its critique of the "reforms" mentioned in the open letter sent from Zara in Sivas. Thus, by 1872, Armenians had spent years bringing public attention to the ongoing problems they faced in the provinces through numerous methods, including petitions, newspapers, going to the capital to ask the patriarchate's help, and through the decisions of the Armenian administration and the *takrirs* submitted to the Sublime Porte. The ban indicates that such methods of protest were no longer tolerated by government circles. A prime candidate for the other article is found in an issue that devoted a complete page to a discussion that was ongoing in the *La Turquie* and *Levant Herald* newspapers criticizing the high salaries of ministers and the miserable situation in the provinces.[205] It is quite reasonable to think that a newspaper like *Manzume-i Efkâr*, published in Armeno-Turkish with a large readership, would be banned for this very reason.

Neither the Armenians' complaints nor their reports brought about any significant changes in the years after the Ottoman-Russian War of 1877–78. As was the case during the military conquests of the provinces and the Crimean War, this war was another convenient excuse to *delay* addressing the Armenians' complaints. The missionary reports from Kiğı in the Vilayet of Erzurum during this time depict a very similar picture to the one I have drawn throughout this chapter. They describe how a Turkish inspector, Osman Efendi, had worked efficiently during the first days of his appointment, but soon he too was taken under the influence of local power holders, and the Christians' situation subsequently became worse.[206]

Conclusion

Tanzimat of the provinces refers to the Ottoman state's temporal and territorial methods of governance put in place after military conquest in the provinces to establish and strengthen its sovereignty there. It involved not only the subjugation of the Kurdish begs, but also the creation of new alliances with them and other Muslim groups such as the Turcomans and Circassians. The cases discussed in this chapter show the wide-ranging variety and everyday nature of the provincial oppressions. Methods utilized by the local power holders, and more importantly by the Ottoman administration against Armenians, included unjust taxation policies, a lack of responsiveness to their problems, the introduction of new structures that reorganized the land and administration of the provinces, the aggravation of famine by forbidding villagers from buying provisions, and demographic engineering through the settlement of approximately a million Circassians in the Armenian provinces, which in turn threatened, exploited, and marginalized the Armenian population.

Criminalizing the Armenians was one of the most effective tools of Ottoman governance. By targeting Armenian family structures, Kurdish power holders aimed to create a society of Armenians who were criminals and outcasts in the eyes of their own administration, leaving them without legal protection. These actions set the necessary ground for the outcasting of those Armenians, rendering them slaves of their begs or aghas. Meanwhile, Armenians also had to deal with day-to-day indignities such as the destruction of their fields and the theft and killing of their animals. The kidnapping and Islamizing of Armenian women was almost a routine practice. The previously mentioned report of the Armenian Patriarchate from 1876 contains an account of the Islamization of six to seven hundred Armenians in Muş alone who converted in hopes it would bring an end to the provincial oppressions they suffered.[207]

Coming back to the discussion of center and periphery, it is crucial to understand that a province was not only a spatial and administrative concept but more important one referring to a certain set of methods of governance, infused by the politics of temporality and territoriality. As has been shown, such methods deployed throughout Tanzimat include changing the borders of administrative units, purposefully interfering in well-administered villages and towns like in Niksar, dispersing the Armenian populations of long-established villages as in the mountains of the Iskanderun Sanjak, exposing villagers to starvation and famine, and leaving their complaints unaddressed for months, years, or even decades. By utilizing Armenian sources, we find that provincial oppressions were not merely a problem of the eastern provinces but found in almost every province. As they were occurring, the Land Code "reform" enabled the Kurdish begs and aghas to register the land of Armenians in their names, turning Armenians into wageworkers. Losing their right to land meant losing their temporality and territoriality in the long run, as they were pushed slowly but consistently out of their ancestral homelands. The case of Çarsancak is one of the most striking examples of these processes. In 1880, Patriarch Varjabedyan expressed his hope for an eastern province modeled after that of the Vilayet of Crete (1867), Vilayet of Archipelago (1867), or even Lebanon, all of which being "privileged provinces" had Christian governors.[208] This call never resonated with the empire's administrative enterprise because Armenians could never be considered privileged in the first place, and second, the developments of the Crimean War period had already shown that Armenians would be left to the mercy of their local power holders. Unlike the treatment of the privileged vilayets, Tanzimat in the provinces determined which groups were to be prioritized and which were to be excluded, or even to be completely disintegrated in a given region by those very policies of forceful integration.

The diametrical opposition between the scholarship on Ottoman and Turkey's historiography on Tanzimat and how it is reflected in the Armenian primary sources is very telling. The second half of the 1850s through the 1860s shows a trend of ever-increasing cases of oppression, demonstrating that life for Armenians had become unsustainable in the villages, with provincial oppressions becoming a part of daily life throughout the Tanzimat period and even more so afterward. This situation is what led Patriarch Khrimyan to collect petitions from the provinces and is the reason the Armenian administration in Constantinople prepared the report submitted to the Ottoman administration in April 1872.

Caught between local power holders and the state, Armenians did not have many choices except to carry on with the legal mechanisms they had been utilizing in vain like complaints, petitions, and submitting *takrirs*. Yet these efforts did nothing to prevent their exile, Islamization, and abandonment to starvation. This everydayness was the Tanzimat experienced by Armenians in the provinces. At its height in 1872, a local cleric from Erzurum, M. Kh. Ballaryan, had the following to say: "There is no security for life, property or honor, there is not even a single quiet night. Nonetheless, the Turkish [*dajgagan*] government assumes that there is nothing [wrong], however, whatever there is, there is."[209]

3

Armenian-Rum Relations

Legal Issues between the Armenian and Rum *Millets*

The first chapter of this book draws attention to the creation of different *millets* as a strategy for dividing groups into smaller administrative entities in order to limit their authority and entitlements while creating as much rivalry among them as possible. Intrinsic to the Ottoman state's strategy was to keep constant conflict between *millets*, making them simultaneously more vulnerable and better manageable. Hence, the main characteristic of the Ottoman administration was to prioritize the rights of the groups according to the circumstances of the day and wielding the arbitrating power to govern them from a superior position according to the empire's best interests.

This chapter will discuss the issues between the Rum and Armenian *millets*, contextualizing them within their regional and local social networks and power relations. These two groups constituted the most significant segments of the Christian population in the Ottoman Empire, but it must be taken into account that Christianity was not regarded as common ground for them since confessional differences could quickly turn into big disputes.[1] Consequently, the Armenian and Rum *millets* did not always regard religion as a unifying institution and were treated differently by the Ottoman government. I decided to write this chapter after reading cases in the Armenian Patriarchal Archive involving intercommunal and confessional matters between these two groups in order to provide deeper insight into the government's method of maintaining constant tensions between the *millets*. As is shown in chapter 2, the protraction of conflicts over decades, the reinforcement of discrepancies between the groups, the dividing of their territorial units, and the interventions made into their temporalities were central tools of governance for the Ottoman administration. The cases analyzed in this chapter demonstrate that all these methods of governance were by no means specific to the eastern provinces, but were the sine qua non of Ottoman administrative policies.

Although their mutual Christianity did not serve as a unifying ground, the archival material shows that the Rum and Armenian *millets* were in close contact at the administrative level. Their patriarchs worked with each other in order to solve their *millets*' problems, and in some cases where there was a large discrepancy in the representation and population between the two *millets* such as in Erzurum and Heraklion, the representatives of the stronger administration would help the weaker one. The support provided by the metropolitan of Heraklion to Armenians in Crete and by the Armenian prelate to the local Greeks in Erzurum was not coincidental. As the Ottoman administration, keen on keeping conflicts between the groups, was not prepared to meet the needs of the people in these regions, the Armenian and Rum administrations were supportive of each other. Unlike as may have been imagined, Armenians and Rum did not typically enjoy harmonious relations throughout the Ottoman territories. The archival materials reveal that this discord was a component of the Ottoman methods of governance, which avoided the consolidation of groups acting in solidarity against oppression, inequality, and injustice.

In this chapter, I will evaluate materials directly linked to Rum and Armenian *millets*. The documents to be analyzed here are from the four corners of what is today's Turkey and the surrounding region, covering issues from westernmost Heraklion to Antalya in the south, Bandırma in the southern part of the Marmara Sea to Giresun, Samsun, and Çarşamba in the Pontus region, Erzurum to the far east, and Konya in central Anatolia. The topics I will examine through these documents are apostasy, mediation, petitions for justice or release from prison, and requests for social help due to disability.

The Archive of the Patriarchate includes unique cases such as the collective petition from Heraklion, the personal petitions sent from the Giresun prison, and those from Samsun and Çarşamba that each shed light on multiple relevant issues beyond routine personal or communal issues.

It also contains various cases related to conversion from different parts of the empire, including two from Bandırma and Antalya. In both cases, the petitions not only shed light on the various layers of conversion practices but offer very insightful details about the functioning of Ottoman social life in the smallest provincial dwelling units. The cases of conversion from Bandırma and Antalya provide detailed accounts of how the local *millets* were administered and the dynamics of social life in these provincial villages.

Most of the petitions in the archive were sent to Istanbul, written as either a personal petition (*arz-ı hal*) or a collective petition (*arz-ı mahzar*), meaning that the local administrations had not been able to solve an issue for one reason or another and thus were compelled to write a petition for help from the patriarchate explaining every twist and turn of the case up until that point. These documents are thus extraordinarily detailed historical sources that provide glimpses into the functioning of the Ottoman social fabric that otherwise would not have been accessible to us.

In addition to the situation in the provinces, the last part of this chapter examines the relations between the Rum and Armenian *millets* in the capital. In cases such as that of a shared cemetery in the capital, we can trace the main form of Ottoman conflict resolution between *millets*, which was based on gaining the sympathy of one group at the expense of the other and thus exacerbating the perpetual conflicts between them.

Heraklion, 1862: The Metropolitan Mediates between Armenians in Crete and Constantinople

In 1862 Dionesios, the metropolitan bishop of Crete, sent a complaint from Heraklion written in Greek and addressed to the locum tenens of the Armenian patriarch. The complaint was originally written in Greek by local Armenians, and the archive file contains a complete translation into Armenian. The original cover letter and the complaint itself were both written in Greek, and the translation was done in the capital. The marginalia written in Armenian on the sealed envelope summarized the content and noted that "an answer was written."[2] The first question to be asked here is why were the Armenians in Heraklion sending a complaint to the patriarchate through the metropolitan bishop of Crete.

The signatories complained about their priest, Garabet, who was in charge of the Armenian community of Crete. The complaint had two central components: the first accused the priest of being irresponsible, having left the island without informing the community, thus depriving it of religious services, and second that he had mistreated his elderly mother and the community.[3] Regarding the first point, leaving one's constituency behind and going somewhere else without prior permission had been banned by ecclesiastical law since the earliest centuries.[4] According to the document, the priest Garabet and his brother Simeon had taken the "*hüccet*" (written as *hoe(ö)ccet*) of their mother's house and left her without care. In this case, *hüccet* meant her right to the property, which means that by leaving he probably left her homeless. According to the document, Garabet's wife mistreated his mother just like he had done, leaving her helpless and forced to beg for money from "Muslim" (*aylazk*) people. As Crete was under the jurisdiction of the Patriarchate in Constantinople, it was asked to examine the case and send a reliable and trustworthy priest. The signatories stated that they were fed up with paying the priest's debts and his improper attitude toward his mother. As a public persona, Father Garabet's behavior was particularly inappropriate, and the signatories emphasized his bad behavior toward his mother, as if to say as he did not even care for his own mother, imagine his attitude toward his community. Thus, the document implied that Garabet's private and public personae made him unsuitable as the local Armenian community's political and ecclesiastical representative. Five men signed this complaint: Hagop the customs worker, Hovhannes the churchwarden, Simeon the quilt maker (*yorğanci*), Serovpe (an illegible abbreviation of the surname), and Harut'iwn the tailor.

An interesting sentence in the petition answers the question of why the signatories had conveyed it through the metropolitan bishop of Crete: "Despite the fact that we have previously sent some letters to our father Patriarch, unfortunately, the son of the above-mentioned priest Garabet, who works at the Patriarchate, was stealing our letters, preventing our Patriarch from receiving and reading them."[5] Therefore, Metropolitan Dionesios's letter mentioned that he mediated between the community in Heraklion and the patriarchate since a letter sent by him would not have been stolen so easily.

This is one of the rare cases in which a Greek metropolitan mediated between the *millets* for the sake of a case. One reason he may have taken this step could be that he was also aware of the situation described in the petition. For the local Armenians, having a cleric who could not meet their needs meant political as well as social fragility vis-à-vis the other confessions. Their rights could not be advocated, and the unfulfilled needs of the *millet* would cause power clashes within the community, which would have repercussions on local power relations. Numerous petitions written by Armenians from various regions of the empire show that they were primarily requesting to be assigned leaders. It was of the utmost importance for the community to have a leader who would not cause hardships, would defend their rights, and had a good command of local power dynamics. The main issue in this petition was that the Armenians in Heraklion were left adrift, and their relations with the other faiths and confessions had become politically and socially as well as religiously fragile. Therefore, this petition should be read in the context of an unprotected Armenian community looking for someone who would represent them adequately, with their struggle supported by the leader of another local *millet*.

Three Personal Petitions: Samsun (1859), Çarşamba (1867), and Giresun (1868)

Samsun, 1859: Istepan Altunoghli Asks for Social Help

The case that I will present here took place in Samsun and is found in its archival file, though the document itself was written in the capital. The addressee is the patriarch, who at that time was Kevork Kerestejyan of Constantinople.[6] This *arz-ı hal*, written in Armenian, is an important one because it was sent by a disabled person and refers to the social assistance mechanism of the Armenian *millet*.

This personal petition was sent by Istepan Altunoghli from Diyarbekir, who went to Samsun as a migrant worker (*bantukhd*) to work in a stonemasonry.[7] By the mid-nineteenth century, *bantukhd* life had become a reality for large numbers of Armenian peasants, which caused the rupture of their temporality in their own villages or towns. Their positions in the cities they moved to were socially vulnerable and fragile, as their daily practices and the socioeconomic, cultural, and political settings were quite different compared to at home. As is discussed in the second chapter of this book, becoming a *bantukhd* was one of the results of the provincial oppressions such as heavy taxation and the engineered inability to earn enough money to pay those taxes and sustain a living in the provinces. Hence, many Armenian peasants were forced to become migrant workers, carrying the yet unseen heavy burden of the transformation of economic relations into a capitalist system.

The migrant worker Istepan from Diyarbekir sent this petition for help because he had become disabled in Samsun as a result of a physical attack. He stated that he had been the only Armenian among the entirely Rum stonemasons, describing the Rum as "religiously radical" (*gronamol*) and noting that their hatred against Armenians was already known.[8] He stated that they hated him for being Armenian and a year and a half prior had beat him up to the point he fainted into a coma for more than six hours, rendering him an invalid and unable to work ever since. Having consumed all his savings in order to live, he borrowed money with interest and accumulated a debt of 12,000 *ghurush*. He had two requests from the patriarchate: to organize a hearing in order to be judged together with the Rum stonemasons and to receive compensation that would ensure his family would be entitled to receive regular income after his death.

The Armenian administration had a coffer for people in need. Most probably, Altunoghli wanted an entitlement to receive money that was set aside for the poor or disabled. His case would be helped by an official document testifying to his disability as a result of the physical attack. Once the disability was verified, it might have opened the door to compensation from the *millet*'s social help mechanism. However, bringing his enemies before the Armenian *millet*'s court would not have been an easy task. As will also be seen in the next case to be examined, a trial against members of another *millet* was very difficult to obtain, but both these applicants regarded it as the only way to achieve some justice.

The document was written professionally from both a calligraphic and a stylistic point of view. The choice of words, use of abbreviations, and utilization of classical Armenian (*krapar*) show the literacy level of the author, a professional scribe. The document also contained Turkish words written in Armenian such as "*hazıren gudem*" (*hazırdan yiyorum*), meaning that he had spent his savings to survive.

This is one of those rare documents found in the Archives of the Patriarchate sent by a disabled person representing himself and asking for the patriarch's help. This might mean that similar cases of requesting social assistance had also been reported to the patriarchate in the past. It may also be assumed that Istepan had tried in vain to find other solutions to his situation during his one and a half years of disability before writing to the patriarchate, but as he had consumed his savings without proving his case, he was forced to apply to the Armenian administration in Constantinople as a last resort.

Çarşamba, 1867: Debt Collection—
Efdim Anasdasialis Wants His Money Back

This is an *arz-ı hal* in Armeno-Turkish sent by Efdim Anasdasialis from Çarşamba to Archbishop Mesrob Sukiasyan in order to collect a debt owed to him from a certain Ananiaoghlu of Gorum (Kurum/Grom) who lived in Ispir.[9] Here we can assume that the indebted person is an Armenian from the region of Kurum, because otherwise it would not have made any sense for him to apply to its local Armenian administration. Indeed, in his ethnographic study on Pontus and Hamshen, P. K. Torlakyan indicates there was a sizable Armenian population living with the Islamized Rum population in Kurum/Grom.[10]

Efdim Anasdasialis had previously contacted the archbishop about the issue, asking him to determine the whereabouts of Ananiaoghlu. Upon investigation, the archbishop told Anasdasialis that Ananiaoghlu was not in Ispir but had traveled to Tbilisi. Therefore, the archbishop advised Anasdasialis not to go to Ispir without making sure that Ananiaoghlu had returned. As we understand from the document, Archbishop Mesrob had offered to collect the debt from Ananiaoghlu himself in the case he returned to Trabzon or Gorum. Efdim's petition was a request for a follow-up meeting with the archbishop to collect his money.

Hence, it could be assumed that the local Armenian administration had to act as an interface between the *millets* and that their duties and responsibilities were manifold. As the various cases related to family law that I discuss in the subsequent chapter will show, the need to locate someone's whereabouts was a common issue, and local Armenian administrations would ask other provinces for information about people who may be there. In addition, in this case, we see a person from the Rum *millet* able to request the help of the local Armenian archbishop in order to collect his debt from an Armenian. This document in the file of Çarşamba suggests that one of the regular duties of the local Armenian administration was mediating in debit-credit issues like this one. Furthermore, it could be assumed that Efdim Anasdasialis was known by the archbishop personally and must have had a large debt to collect on, or else it wouldn't have been necessary to write this petition. The way it is written, mostly in the familiar singular "you" form, makes me think that Efdim Anasdasialis was a notable person in the region, probably a businessman or a tradesman and that Archbishop Mesrob was mediating between him and the Armenian Ananiaoghlu from Ispir in order to avoid any controversy or larger-scale complications that might result for both sides.

The petition is written in Armeno-Turkish, but we can assume that a professional scribe wrote it for Efdim Anasdasialis, as the petition has a good command of Armeno-Turkish orthographical rules. It was signed by Anasdasialis in both Armeno-Turkish and Greek, mentioning that his city of origin was "Tokatlü" (Tokat). His name was written in the Armeno-Turkish and Greek alphabets as Efdim. Although one might think that he would have signed with his original Greek name of "Efdimios," he chose the locally used form "Efdim."

The document shows not only the flexibility of local administrations and their multilayered duties but also that a person from the Rum *millet* could contact the local Armenian administration by writing a personal petition to solve an issue. The next case, a personal petition written in Turkish with Greek script, is also addressed to Archbishop Mesrob Sukiasyan but comes from a much more marginalized person.

The Giresun Prison, 1868: Nikolaus Polikhron Kabakaroghlu's arz-ı hal

This quite interesting document is unique in that it comes from the prison of Giresun. Nikolaos Polikhron Kabakaroghlu from the "*Urum* [Rum] *Milleti*" wrote an *arz-ı hal* to the Armenian prelacy in Giresun asking for its help to rescue him from prison by organizing a hearing for his case.[11] Nikolaos Polikhron sent a one-sheet mailer "to the Armenian School" (*Ermeni Mektebine*), but the letter was addressed to the Armenian Prelate of Trabzon in Giresun (*Kiresonte Trabezonlu Despot Efendi Metropolituna Ermeniyan*).[12] Perhaps he was primarily familiar with the school as an institution, and so hoped it would forward the letter as needed. Kabakaroghlu was in jail owing to a financial issue between him and an Armenian, Haji Asadur Agha Veledoghlu. Kabakaroghlu states in the petition that he has been imprisoned for the past four years and claims his innocence. The nature of this petition suggests that a member of the Rum *millet* could request to be tried by the Armenian prelacy when the case involved a member of it. Considering that Nikolaos Polikhron Kabakaroghlu had been in prison for four years, he may have tried other ways to obtain release through the authorities of his own *millet* such as the Greek metropolitan of Giresun, though no reference is made to any previous efforts. Although we do not know the process that landed him in prison, it is clear that Nikolaos Polikhron Kabakaroghlu placed at least some hope in the Armenian prelacy, even though it may sound unconventional to ask for a trial under its jurisdiction.

His hopes were not baseless, in any case. Thirteen years earlier, in 1855, a news item from the region of Muş had informed readers of the *Masis* newspaper about the problematic situation of the local religious leader Archbishop Krikoris. Although details were not given, we may assume that the political situation in the area was extremely fragile as a result of the Crimean War. Archbishop Krikoris asked to be relocated to Erzurum, from where he would continue to administer the political issues of Muş. The news item praises Archbishop Krikoris and his achievements in the region, and, as proof of his excellent work, it includes the translation of a letter attested by Governor Ismail Pasha[13] and sent to the Sublime Porte to be conveyed to the Orthodox patriarch. The letter was addressed to the Orthodox patriarch and written by thirty Rum families from Erzurum (Garin) stating that the Rum population of Theodopolis (Erzurum) was grateful for the services of Archbishop Krikoris, who defended their rights as a coreligionist, as their own Archbishop Dimoteos mainly resided in the area of Trabzon and thus was unable to care for his flock in Theodopolis.

The letter also stated that the Rum representative in Theodopolis asked their patriarch to convey their gratitude to the prelate. Upon receiving this letter, the Orthodox patriarch sent letters of thanks to the Armenian patriarch and Archbishop Krikoris.[14] Generally speaking, this news item shows that there was a practice of collaboration on administrative matters in the region that the locals would have been aware of. Nikolaos Polikhron Kabakaroghlu's petition to Archbishop Mesrob may well be the result of such relations. At the very least, there was a valid reason justifying his logic of seeking justice through the Armenian administration, and his hopes were not baseless.

Of particular interest in this document is its linguistic particularities, along with the fact it was sent to the prelacy from a prison. The use of local dialect and the writing in Turkish with Greek script reveal the local format of pronunciation. It gives us the opportunity to study a historic local dialect that may have undergone enormous change by our present day or even disappeared entirely. This letter is one of those unique documents that reveal the multigraphization of Ottoman society as well as the ways people regularly expressed themselves in their local dialects and the alphabet of their mother tongue. Hence, this *arz-ı hal* demonstrates that even in places where there were no regular publications in a certain language form—Greko-Turkish, in this case—people still utilized it for practical reasons even in formal applications, knowing that the addressee could read it. In addition, reading and writing about Kabakaroghlu's personal petition help us to reflect on the sources we utilize in our research and reveal the necessity of bottom-up historiography. The fact that his petition reached its intended destination and could be read today demonstrates how he strove to achieve justice for his case.

Bandırma, 1848, and Antalya, 1871: Two Cases of Apostasy

During the nineteenth century, conversion and apostasy across various confessions of Christianity in the Ottoman Empire were not just matters of individual religious belief, but structural issues defining the *millet* administrations' territorial and temporal entitlements, and therefore they were handled at the highest levels of their respective administrations. The Ottoman administration's use of brutal penalties for apostasy came under fire because of the prominent case of Hovagim Tavukjyan (T'avuk'jean) of Samatya in 1843. Hovagim, who first converted to Islam in 1839 and then converted back to Christianity during a business trip to Syria,[15] was identified and arrested for it upon his return to Constantinople. He was executed by decapitation, and his head was put on public display in the capital. The most detailed information on his case is provided by an eyewitness and chronicler of this time, Avedis Bērbēryan, in his *Badmut'iwn Hayots'*, and another account appears in Ōrmanyan's *Azkabadum*.[16] British ambassador Stratford Canning played an important role in the case, unsuccessfully intervening in an attempt to stop Hovagim's execution. According to Bērbēryan, Hovagim returned to the capital and repented for his decision to become a Muslim, only disclosing his secret reconversion to a priest. He wore European clothes to avoid being recognized, but he was reported to the Ottoman administration, arrested, and tortured to convert back to Islam. Yet he did not relent, and neither the patriarch nor the *Amiras* had the courage to intervene, since converting to Christianity was undoubtedly one of the gravest crimes in Islamic law. Instead, his family contacted the Russian ambassador, who advised them to go to British ambassador Canning. Through his dragoman, Pisani, Canning diplomatically asked Grand Vizier Rauf Pasha and the director of foreign affairs for Hovagim's release. He was told that the issue would be handled in a juridical and ministerial meeting scheduled two days later and that Hovagim might be released afterward. Hearing this news, Canning reassured Hovagim's family that their son would be released soon. However, the sheikh-ul Islam, Rıza Ali Pasha, and two more ministers disagreed and decided to proceed with Hovagim's decapitation. He was beheaded at Balıkpazar, one of the gates of Constantinople. Bērbēryan wrote that he was there prior to the decapitation and heard Hovagim be asked for a final time to convert to Islam. Hovagim refused by praising Jesus and bowing his head. His corpse was handed over to the Armenian administration and buried in Zeytinburnu at the cemetery of Surp Hagop.[17]

After the execution, Canning organized other representatives of foreign missions to the Ottoman Empire to write furious reports to their governments about the incident, describing this situation as being in complete contrast to the zeitgeist of the Tanzimat era, as well as against existing political expectations. At the beginning of 1844, the ambassadors demanded an end to executions for apostasy. The Ottoman administration agreed in principle but argued it would be met with strong opposition from the conservative population and asked for seven years to enact the change.[18] Bērbēryan wrote that the "death and martyrdom of Hovagim became the principal reason for granting religious freedoms."[19] He added that, despite the protests of the Ottoman administration, freedom of belief and conversion was eventually permitted, as well as the construction and renovation of churches.[20] Despite all this, the name of Hovagim Tavukjyan, the symbol of religious freedoms in the Ottoman Empire, hardly finds its way into the mainstream historiography, nor is he given credit for the groundbreaking changes his case represented to the Ottoman societal fabric and state policies.[21]

Conversion was a major sin, but at the same time, it was an absolute break from the past, a rejection of one's history, and a new beginning. Therefore, conversion meant a temporal cut in one's life, creating a portal to a new time that also made the convert subject to new territorialities. Hence, Hovagim's conversion back to Christianity and his wearing of European clothes in order not to be recognized should be read within the radical changes to his temporal and territorial relations, that is, his effort to create a temporal and territorial difference between the person who converted to Islam and the one who returned from Aleppo wearing European clothes. Therefore, conversion not only meant changing one's religion or denomination, but also meant starting a new life with a new set of rights and responsibilities, new dynamics of time, and a new set of relations in a certain place. As will be seen in other cases in this chapter, it may even entail a change of place altogether. As the old life had to be annulled, it was easier to leave it behind and take up the different temporal and territorial relations in a whole new place.

Bandırma, 1848: "Either You Solve Our Issue, or My Name Is [Will Be] Ayşe"

In January 1848, five years after the tragic death of Hovagim, the Armenian clerics and *ishkhans* of Bandırma wrote a collective petition. This case is important on various levels, as it reveals local power dynamics and addresses Muslim versus non-Muslim relations. The document was signed by twenty-two people (nineteen stamps, three signatures) and written in Armenian by Arisdages Vartabed of Bandırma.[22] The petition was addressed to the Armenian patriarch, Madt'ēos Ch'ukhajyan Bolsetsi (1844–48).[23] According to the *Hayrenasēr* daily newspaper published in Smyrna, Bandırma had more than four hundred Armenian homes.[24] The petition details that a Rum man by the name of Triandafil(os) had left his wife and child in Ioanina's Grevena *kaza* seven years earlier and come to Bandırma as a result of his wife's prostitution. He had sent her neither letters nor money since coming to Bandırma, and his child had just died that same year, perhaps owing to his neglect. His having been away for seven years and his wife's turn to prostitution, if that accusation was a true one, were both likely mentioned because they could have been considered relevant reasons for his marriage to be annulled by the Armenian administration.

Hereafter in the document, he is called "the Greek" (*huyn*). For the past three years, Triandafilos visited the house of Nazlı, a native of Edincik, who is defined as "indecent/impudent" (*anbargeshd*) and whose husband, Fingo, had left her years before. One of Nazlı's two daughters, Hripsime, had an illicit relationship with Triandafilos, which implies her mother had likely enabled it. An illicit relation can easily be equated to adultery, not just by the Armenian and Greek communities but also by the Muslim population, which because of their hierarchical priority should also be considered a party to this issue, and as will be seen, was a decisive party indeed.

The "Muslims" (*aylazk*) of Edincik raided Nazlı's house, found Triandafilos hiding there, and punished him, though the document does not explain the method of punishment. They also sent Nazlı and her two daughters into exile. Both raiding the house and exile were territorial methods of penalizing the family. The house and the village are both territorially defined units, the former being part of the territoriality of the latter. In this case, it is clearly visible how the territoriality of the hierarchically superior group prevailed over the weaker ones, whose temporality was brought to an end in their native village. Needless to say, a reverse case of adultery in which a Muslim house could be raided by Christians cannot even be imagined. The leading representatives (known in Armenian as *ishkhans*) of the local Armenian and Rum *millets* as well as their clerics were aware of the incident, but none appears to have intervened. As will be seen in the rest of the petition, the issue was regarded as troublesome since it involved not only the Armenian and Rum *millets* but also various local power relations. While the Rum and local Armenian administrators remained passive, the local Muslim population intervened violently by raiding the house and punishing all parties involved.[25] Leslie Pierce states in her book concerning an earlier period (the sixteenth century) that "the state's role in the prosecution of adultery was theoretically ambiguous. On the one hand, the sovereign and his delegates could interpret their mandate to punish adultery (*zina*) offenses as being in the interest of society, allowing individuals themselves to take the initiative to prosecute *zina* and thereby define its scope as a socio-legal problem."[26] We see a similar situation in our case: the Muslim population of the district decided to raid Nazlı's home in order to find Triandafilos, and upon finding him punished everyone involved. Although we do not know how Triandafilos was punished, the exile of Nazlı's family shows who reigned over that time and territory.

As a direct result of this raid, Nazlı and her family could not find shelter anywhere. They were regarded as criminals in the eyes of the sovereign, and so nowhere was safe. The local Armenian administration took care of the situation and settled them in Bandırma's Nor village. Nazlı was a destitute woman, her husband had abandoned her, and she and her two daughters probably lived without a steady income. Her daughter Hripsime, who was a maiden (*guys*), had an affair with Triandafilos that went on for three years. The only solution to the problem was to have them married, but since one was Armenian Apostolic and the other Greek Orthodox, the marriage could be performed only after the conversion of one of the sides. It needed to be done quickly because as a case of adultery, the raid and exile were sources of life-threatening dangers.

Getting married was not easy for Nazlı and Triandafilos. The Armenian administration suggested that Triandafilos convert to the Armenian Apostolic confession and then marry Hripsime; otherwise, both of them had to be Islamized. The last part of the sentence, "otherwise you have to be Islamized" (*dajganal*), was used as a threat, and the petition admitted that "it was a half-way threat"[27] that became a source of trouble for all sides. Becoming Islamized would mean a break from their pasts and the loss of flock for both Armenians and Greeks. The signatories were said to have written to the patriarchate to get confirmation from the patriarch, but apparently, their petitions remained unanswered. Quite often, petitions sent from the provinces refer to numerous previous messages that had not been answered, as is the case here. In such cases, the longer a petition remained unanswered, the more difficult the problem became to solve. This in turn presented the sovereign with ideal opportunities to arbitrate power and decide according to its own interests, while keeping the roots of the conflict in the region so that the issue may bloom again in the future.

Nazlı and Triandafilos applied directly and indirectly to the local Armenian administration more than twenty times to get Triandafilos and Hripsime married without receiving an answer to their request. Finally, they started to threaten the Armenian administration with conversion to Islam. They used to appear in front of the church and shout, asking to get the marriage done or else they would convert. The petition stated that there was no way to control them: "There were neither prisons in the churches nor rooms with iron bars to lock them."[28] This means that practically everybody heard their pleas. Regardless of their real intention, Nazlı and Triandafilos may have thought of the conversion threat as the only way to be protected from a second raid until the issue was solved. While the Armenian administration waited for a response from Constantinople, Nazlı, her daughters, and Triandafilos were all in danger. According to the petition, Nazlı repeatedly shouted, "Either you solve our issue, or my name is Ayşe; I will convert to Islam with my two daughters and so will this Greek (*huyn*)."[29] After Nazlı's and Triandafilos's outbursts, the issue gained urgency for both the Armenian and the Rum administrations. In order to reduce tensions, the local Armenian administration renamed Triandafilos Garabet, which calmed the situation for a while, but it remained unsolved. The Rum and local Armenian administrations held several meetings and negotiated a solution. They seem to have worked harmoniously. Armenian and Greek clerics and *ishkhans* wrote a joint letter to the local Greek administration, asking the Greek Church to allow them to solve the issue by marrying Hripsime and Triandafilos/Garabet. This would happen either by converting Triandafilos/Garabet to Armenian Apostolic confession or Hripsime to Greek Orthodoxy. From the formulation used in the petition, it appears that the local Armenian administration was even willing to help Hripsime convert to Greek Orthodoxy. The local Rum *despot*, however, answered their request as follows: "They may convert to Islam, to Judaism, or Armenian Apostolicism."[30] The *despot* not only refused the request of the Armenian and Rum clerics and *ishkhans*, but also cast political aspersions on Triandafilos/Garabet and provoked the beg of Erdek to arrest him.

While looking for some documentation on the issue in the Ottoman archives, it occurred to me that the beg of Erdek refers to the *kaimakam* of Erdek, probably Mustafa Bey, who was appointed in 1849,[31] whose immediate predecessors were Kamil Efendi (1848)[32] and Emin Bey (1847).[33] With three *kaimakams* in just three years, it appears that even at the local level of administration in Erdek, temporal methods of governance were being utilized through the constant rotation of officials. It should be kept in mind that this area was densely populated by Rums and Armenians.

Upon the controversial answer of the *despot*, the local governor (*kaimakam*) asked the Armenian administration to submit Triandafilos/Garabet to his office because of the *despot*'s accusations. This development caused fear among the Armenian administration, and so they traveled in heavy winter conditions to Nor, normally a five-hour journey from Bandırma, to propose an Armenian man for Hripsime to marry in order to solve the case for good. However, Hripsime and her mother rejected this offer, so the administration wrote that there was no other way of fixing the problem except to allow her and Triandafilos/Garabet to marry. Here too, temporality plays a role, as the marriage occurred in private under the cover of darkness, perhaps a method of concealing it from the public until the criminalized nature of the relationship was resolved. The relationship already had the attention of local power centers, and the Armenian administration could not afford any more trouble from it. The administration explained to the patriarch that the threat of Triandafilos being summoned to the *kaimakam* was resolved by putting him under the protection of the Armenian *millet* through his conversion and marriage. This petition might never have been written had not the Ottoman local administration gotten involved in the case, as its purpose was to ask for the patriarchate's protection from the *kaimakam*.

The petition explained the local administration's actions by claiming that the conversion of the family to the Islamic faith would have been the worst-case scenario, and so they had to choose the lesser of two evils. It was repeatedly written that the community would have lost four or five people if the conversion to Greek Orthodoxy or Armenian Orthodoxy had not taken place. Moreover, it was mentioned that the Greek *despot* of the area had recently converted married Armenians to Greek Orthodoxy without even consulting the Armenian administration, despite there not being threats of raids or exiles in those cases. The members of the Armenian administration reportedly considered sending the family to the patriarchate in order to solve the issue but said the winter conditions made travel impossible. The petition clearly stated that the conversion of Triandafilos/Garabet was not something that the local Armenian administration in Bandırma wanted, but it was the only reasonable solution to the conflict. Interestingly, the Rum local administration did not seem interested in converting the family to Greek Orthodoxy. One reason may be that the Greek community was demographically in a superior position and apparently had better relations with the beg of Erdek, and so had no reason to get involved in a conflict where Muslim inhabitants of the region had already violently intervened. The second reason may lie in the statements at the beginning of the petition referring to Triandafilos's marital status. It's possible that the Rum administration might not have considered Triandafilos's marriage back in Ioanina to be annulled according to its ecclesiastical law, explaining why it didn't support the new marriage, even though it would have meant three more conversions to Greek Orthodoxy. In addition, the statement of the local *despot* and his accusation about Triandafilos/Garabet may indicate that the Rum administration preferred him to flee or go back to Ioannina. Another possibility is that the *kaimakam* and the *despot* may have had some issues to resolve, and this case was a good bargain between the two. By offering the *kaimakam* four people to be converted to Islam, the *despot* perhaps wanted to save his own skin. Therefore, it may well be the case that the Rum *despot* did not want to make life easier for Triandafilos and his new family, keeping the arbitrating power in his hand. As is seen, a case between the Armenian and Rum *millets* could easily attract the intervention of the local Ottoman administration, changing all power relations.

As will be further observed in the chapter on family law, this case also demonstrates how the entitlements of *millets* to apply their respective customary laws and regulations were not sufficient to solve all matters related to family law. The intervention of the local Muslim population and their claim to power over hierarchically weaker groups remained decisive and determined what actions the weaker groups had to take regardless of their *millet*'s laws. Raiding and causing the exile of a family are not simple acts of intervention. Apart from the unilateral violation of domestic boundaries, these acts have very strong temporal and territorial repercussions, criminalizing the members of a family in the eyes of their relatives and community, but more important of their respective administrations. It completely changed the family's life, tearing them out of their environment and forcing them to live under the constant threat of being exiled or raided again.

Antalya, 1871: Converting Married Armenians to Greek Orthodoxy

There were a number of cases from Antalya in 1871 of conversion to Greek Orthodoxy followed by marriage. A petition alerting the patriarch to these unexpected conversions was written in Armeno-Turkish and had six signatures.[34] The first paragraph of the *arz-ı mahzar* mentioned that the region was *hunasdan*, the land of the Rum,[35] and that signatories had "no patience anymore" for their "barbarisms." The story begins in 1870 when an Armenian from Denizli named Sarkis went to the Rum priest in Antalya and asked to be converted since he wanted to marry a Rum woman. The priest contacted his Armenian colleague and conveyed Sarkis's message. The Armenian priest convinced Sarkis not to convert and apologized to the Rum priest, saying that Sarkis had changed his mind. However, the story did not end there, as Sarkis instead went to Antalya to convert.

The second case mentioned in the petition is of a European (*frenk*) doctor who went to the Rum *despot* in Isparta to convert. The *despot* asked him to learn the rules of Greek Orthodoxy and baptized him a year later. Less than a year after the baptism, the European doctor moved from Isparta to Konya and became Muslim. As in the first case of Sarkis from Denizli going to Antalya to convert, the likely Catholic or Protestant European doctor first converted to Greek Orthodoxy in Isparta, and then later left for Konya to become a Muslim.

In a third case mentioned in the same petition, an Armenian from Erzurum arrived in Antalya asking to be converted to Greek Orthodoxy, and the local Armenians could not dissuade him. Here again, the changing of one's territoriality with the aim of severing all connections with the past and starting a new life in a new environment appears as a significant aspect of conversion. Once converted, their temporal dimension also changed, as the convert had to carry out the duties foreseen in the new religion, celebrate different religious festivities than before, and became subjugated to another realm of authorities and entitlements. Therefore, coming all the way from Erzurum to Antalya with the intention of conversion seems to be a significant indication of the converter's determination in itself, but also reflects the necessity of escaping the territoriality of one's former faith. After converting to Greek Orthodoxy, the Armenian man from Erzurum married a Rum woman with children. Hearing of this conversion and marriage, Sarkis mentioned in the first case returned, converted, and immediately married another Rum widowed woman with children. This was followed by the conversion of an Armenian from Burdur (written as Buldul) named Giragos, who was married and had children. The prominent Armenians of his area (called "*Ağalaremiz*" in the text) forbade this conversion, arguing that he was already baptized and married. They reportedly chastised the Rum priest, saying: "Baptize a Muslim [*aylazki*], Jew, or a pagan if you want to get merit in God's sight."[36] Despite this, Giragos managed to get converted. This was followed by two other unmarried male Armenians coming to Antalya from Constantinople apparently with the same intent of conversion. According to the note on the backside of the petition dated April 1872, it was decided to contact the Rum clergy to negotiate. Above this note, there is a summary of the cases described in the petition, including the fact that some of the converts were already married.

A conversion and subsequent marriage is in essence a divorce. A new set of rights were attained by conversion, and all prior responsibilities evaporated. After Giragos's conversion and second marriage to a widow with children, he was responsible to earn a living only for his new family, discharging him of any responsibility to his Armenian one. All the candidates for conversion in the Antalya cases were male, and almost all of them came from or went to a different place directly in relation to their conversion: Denizli, Konya, Burdur, Erzurum, or Constantinople. The Armenian administration in Antalya must have identified the trend and written this petition to the capital in order to hinder this practice from taking root. The petition makes their vulnerability clear by stating that there were even two unmarried Armenians from Constantinople who had come for conversion and the petitioners were sure that they would also be converted by the Rum. As noted in the marginalia, the petitioners hoped for direct contact with the Rum Patriarchate in the capital in order to get their issues resolved at the highest level of the hierarchy. The petition bears six signatures: Priest Kevork, Hovhannes Shahinyan, Minas Shahinyan, representative (*yerespokhan*) Haji Ohannes, Khachadur Tahmisjyan, and Agop Khachaduryan. That only four people other than the town clergyman and a representative of the local administration signed this petition about a relatively straightforward legal issue, which probably could have been resolved in the interest of the Armenian community, might be regarded as an indication of the weak presence of Armenians and their local administration in Antalya.

While there is a long Armenian history not far away in Cilicia, the nineteenth-century Armenian community of Antalya (Adalya) was a small one. As emphasized at the beginning of the collective petition, the region had a predominantly Rum population and therefore was defined as "*Hunasdan*" (Greece). This made the Armenian *millet* no match for the political and social influence of the Rum one. The petition mentioned the regional towns of Burdur and Isparta, places where the local Armenian administration was active with functional schools and churches. Antalya had an Armenian church as early as 1852.[37] At the beginning of the twentieth century, Antalya was part of the sanjak of Teke, which was under the jurisdiction of the vilayet of Konya together with Niğde, Burdur, and Isparta.[38]

We find other cases of apostasy in the minutes of the Armenian National Assembly, where the patriarchate sent two *takrirs* in March and August 1870 about cases of remarriage through apostasy. Amber, the wife of a certain craftsman of candleholders (*şamdancı*) Mihran, married a jeweler named Sukias in a ceremony conducted by a Rum priest. Considering the involvement of the Rum priest in the marriage, it is likely that Sukias was an Armenian who had already converted to Greek Orthodoxy, given that he had been referred to with an Armenian name in the document. The Rum Patriarchate was contacted to take the necessary steps for the annulment of this marriage and to confirm its illegal nature. However, the Rum and Armenian Patriarchates were apparently unable to resolve the case amongst themselves, and so a *takrir* was submitted to the police to take charge of it.[39]

Marc Baer highlights the gendered aspect of conversion, as it served as an "automatic divorce" for women and was a straightforward way to get rid of an abusive and undesirable husband.[40] In the cases analyzed here, though, we have a number of men coming from different parts of the empire to Antalya to convert and start a new life, even ones who weren't married. The documents at hand from Bandırma (1848) and Antalya (1871) use very similar expressions regarding the conversions. The Greek Orthodox administration is represented in each as being more powerful than the Armenian one. In the first case, conversion was used as a tool to stop a crime, the years-long illicit relations between unmarried people that had been de facto punished by the Muslim inhabitants. The conversion was followed by marriage, which boosted their safety and security as well as reestablished public order for all parties involved. In the second case, the conversion was utilized to start a new life with new rights and leave behind the responsibilities of their former life, starting from scratch in new towns and radically altering their territoriality.

Use of Common Spaces: Burial in Cemeteries

As shown in this chapter, the state of Armenian and Greek relations in the provinces depended on the center's relation to a given province, while at the imperial center they were instead constantly contested owing to the privileges that came with being in the center. The issue of burial space shared by Armenians and Greeks is perhaps one of the best examples demonstrating the impossibility of these groups to maintain the same temporality and territoriality in the imperial capital. It was a common practice to share a cemetery since space was limited in Constantinople. Often there were defined sections of the same area for each confession. In the nineteenth century, cemeteries were not just for burial, but also strolling areas or even places for entertainment: in 1852, an Armenian acrobat was allowed to erect a tent in the cemetery of Beyoğlu.[41] Two cemeteries at each end of the Grand Rue de Pera were long used as promenade grounds.[42]

In July 1864 the newspaper *Giligia* reported a case of conflict over a shared cemetery.[43] The Rum *millet* had claimed rights to the Armenian cemetery of Üsküdar for the past two years. The report noted that at the time of publication, the Rum administration had obtained a specific area from the Armenian cemetery and built a coffeehouse, which in turn had become the object of a lawsuit. While the case was in the courts, the newly buried corpse of an Armenian boy had been taken out of its grave on the evening of the burial and left in front of the coffeehouse. Unsurprisingly, the issue caused immediate aggravation and attracted public attention at the highest level. The next morning, the cemetery was filled with Armenian, Rum, and prominent Ottoman people, including investigators, high-ranking clerics, and security forces. The Armenians protested until the evening, and, through the intervention of the patriarch, the boy was reburied in his grave. In the next issue of *Giligia*, we read how Patriarch Boghos Taktakyan went to the Sublime Porte to discuss the issue with the grand vizier and the director of foreign affairs, but that the meeting did not have a favorable outcome. The Ottoman officials had urged the patriarch to stop the consumption of alcoholic beverages and coffee in the cemetery, and the grand vizier expressed his discontent with the reburial of the corpse in the same place.[44] In a couple of weeks, the same newspaper followed up with information about a newly established committee to pursue the case with the Rum *millet* regarding the issue of the coffeehouse. *Giligia* also published a follow-up about the exhumation and reburial of the corpse, stating that there were Armenians who had been placed in jail because of the case and that the patriarch was in negotiations with the Sublime Porte to set them free.[45] In September 1864, *Giligia* reported that all Armenians jailed because the Üsküdar Cemetery case had been released and added: "It was said that there was no imprisoned Rum either."[46]

A memorandum of the Political Assembly from 1865 stated that the issues related to cemeteries had become serious reasons for concern that resulted in the filing of lawsuits in both the provinces and the capital. The memorandum mentioned that almost all cemetery cases had been decided in a way that caused moral or economic damages to the Armenian *millet*. By the time this memorandum was published, the lawsuit against the Greeks regarding the cemetery in Üsküdar had been ongoing for four years. The case was arbitrated by the sheikh-ul Islam, who decided to give a small section to the Rum *millet*, a resolution that again disappointed the Armenians.[47]

I came across a second case related to the joint use of cemeteries, this time from Larende in Konya found in the patriarchate's memorandum from 1870–71. According to it, a conflict began when the Rum wanted to bury their dead in Larende's Armenian cemetery. While the Rum *millet* had already filed a case against Armenians in the local court, the memorandum emphasized that the issue should be solved between the two patriarchates, suggesting that the Rum *millet* withdraw the case. The *kapı kahyası*[48] had already been to the Rum Patriarchate and returned with its response, offering to leave the issue to the local Rum metropolitan and Armenian prelacy to make an on-site investigation and report the situation back to Constantinople. It was also stated that this decision should be communicated to "the people of Larende." Probably "the people" meant here were primarily Armenians, indicating that the cemetery conflict, as in the case of Constantinople, had received a great deal of public attention.[49]

The communal lawmaking of an individual *millet* quickly reached its limits in cases where another *millet* could likely become involved. In order to solve such issues as with the cemeteries, an intervention had to take place at the level of the patriarchs, after which a specialized council was established to work on the court case. In 1869, the patriarchate issued a special legal regulation exclusively about burials in Constantinople and the Bosporus villages. While the document is dated November 1869, it states there was a prior regulation published in February 1868 that was not correctly applied, making it necessary to issue a new one. The last article of this regulation seems to be related to the case from Üsküdar, stating that "without special permission of the Administration, disinterment of corpses is prohibited."[50]

The report of the patriarchate in 1876 mentions that the Armenian and Rum hospitals had a boundary issue that needed to be sorted out in terms of property rights. Apparently, both sides were not in favor of another conflict. As explained in the document, the hospital administration contacted the Rum Patriarchate and established a mixed council to sort out the legal rights of the properties remaining between the borders of the Rum and Armenian hospitals. Both hospitals are located in Balıklı, Istanbul, on either side of a road that passes between them today. The road probably did not exist in those days as a clear division between them. According to this document, the problem was resolved without conflict.[51]

Conclusion

This chapter showed the relations between the Rum and Armenian *millets* on the basis of primary and secondary sources. The selected cases were from Heraklion, Constantinople/Üsküdar, Konya/Larende, Bandırma/Edincik, Antalya, Samsun, Giresun, and Erzurum. The data I utilized were dated between the 1840s and the mid-1880s. In all Armenian sources, the Rum *millet* was represented as being in a more powerful or superior position. The only exception is the letter from prison sent by Nikolaos Polikhron Kabakaroghlu. I find the petition of Kabakaroghlu noteworthy, both in terms of its content, showing the possibilities of seeking justice for even a person at the lowest levels of the societal hierarchy, and in terms of its specific language form, a regional Turkish dialect written with the Greek alphabet. What makes this letter even more noteworthy if not unique is how it was successfully sent from prison to the Armenian Prelacy of Giresun, overcoming all mechanisms of control. Kabakaroghlu's effort in writing this petition, like that of Güldane of Sivas, Khatug of Çarşamba, or Nazlı of Bandırma, is a very empowering one. These are rare examples of primary sources showing us not just the agency of the most vulnerable and marginalized members of society, but also the existence and accessibility of primary sources belonging to them.

The second most important purpose of this chapter is to show how the Ottoman administration's tools of governance reached their limits when the groups faced significant oppression from the state. The case of Heraklion in Crete and the Rum *millet*'s compliments to the Armenian prelate Krikoris in Erzurum for defending their rights better than the Rum *despot* did depicts a situation opposite to the rest of the cases discussed here. While it was the Ottoman administration's method of governance to let conflicts fester over time and thus govern the groups by arbitrating power, this plan did not always work in circumstances where the local Christians faced similar oppression and therefore were supportive of each other.

I suggest reading the cases of conversion, all of which involve a geographical change by the converter, in line with Robert Sack's conceptualization of territoriality: "Territoriality is the backcloth of geographical context—it is the device through which people construct and maintain spatial organizations. For humans, territoriality is not an instinct or drive, but rather a complex strategy to affect, influence and control access to people, things and relationships."[52] Accordingly, it cannot be regarded as a coincidence or insignificant that in order to convert, these people took the great risk of traveling from Constantinople or Erzurum to Antalya at a time when even leaving one's village could be dangerous and required permission. Changing territorial relations and converting would result in a radical change to one's temporality as well. By changing their geographic space and later the legal realm to which they were subjected, these converters intended to change their lives and the power relations around them completely, establishing themselves anew in far-off cities and towns.

Again, following Sack's argument on territoriality as a component of power, a means of creating and maintaining order, and a way of experiencing and giving the world meaning,[53] my contention is that it is necessary to consider the *millets*' territorial regimes as well as those of Ottoman administrations in these terms. In the cases of shared cemeteries, we are able to clearly see the territorial regimes, the entitlements of the groups involved, and the arbitrating power of the Ottoman administration. The special regulations from 1869 that set the rules for burying corpses in the capital's cemeteries and villages of the Bosphorus can be read as the Armenian administration's territorial regulation in response to these conflicts or as a necessity stemming from them. Similarly, the opening of a coffeehouse within the territory of the Armenian cemetery and serving beverages or assuming ownership of a certain part of it can be read as the execution of the Greek administration's territorial power in the capital. Most important, the Ottoman regime of territoriality chose to condemn the efforts made by the Armenian Patriarchate to calm down the demonstrations by reburying the Armenian boy's disinterred corpse. The Ottoman administration's territorial regime picked the most brutal incident in the whole process to use against the weaker party, a choice overlapping with the Ottoman temporal and territorial methods of governance pursued throughout the provinces.

4

Juridical Entitlements of the Armenian Patriarchate

This chapter explores the wide range of juridical functions of the Armenian administration, detailing their significance in all matters of everyday life as well as their limits in the capital and the provinces. The content of the archival material presented here demonstrates the increasing centralization of the Armenian administration throughout Tanzimat. It is my contention that, the more Armenian administration in the capital turned into a point of reference for the provinces, the more cases were reported to Istanbul.

In the first part of this chapter, I will give priority to the cases that refer to institutional incarceration practices in the Surp Pırgiç Armenian Hospital and the Imperial Yarn Factory (*iplikhane* or *Riştehane-i Amire*), both institutions located in the capital. The cases that mentioned the Surp Pırgiç Armenian Hospital as an incarceration center are from Beşiktaş, Amasya, and Akşehir, while the ones related to the yarn factory are from Istanbul. These will be followed by cases of family law, including the annulment of a marriage in Constantinople, cases from Çarşamba of taking a second partner without the previous marriage being annulled, and the decision of a destitute abandoned woman from Sivas to save her life by remarrying without getting a divorce. Also included are cases highlighting the Armenian administration's notarial functions, such as facilitating the receipt of alimony and inheritance in Gallipoli and testifying to individuals' marital status in Divriği and Samsun. The cases related to family law both demonstrate a robust female agency in multiple respects from Armenian women in the provinces, despite their structural weaknesses at a time when they were often left alone while their husbands worked as *bantukhds* in the cities. The risks these women took and the solutions they found to defend themselves give us important hints regarding the functioning of Ottoman society.

The types of documents included in this section are collective petitions (*arz-ı mahzar*), personal petitions (*arz-ı hal*), interrogation records (*istintak*), records (*tahrir*), medical reports, and notarial attestations, often called *seneds*. I will define and discuss the nature of these documents in each case, which I chose based on the role and agency of the patriarchate, as well as that of the local power structures, their relations to the local officers, and, on a larger scale, the limits of the Armenian administration vis-à-vis the Ottoman administration. Another important point is that the documents examined here include almost every important detail that might have had an impact on the decision or assistance being requested of the patriarchate. Consequently, these documents are usually not brief, and in contrast to the *sicils*[1] or other Ottoman archival materials, they do not have long formulaic introductions and conclusions, but instead contain a body of text that should be investigated and understood in its entirety. They are generally written in a very precise style, irrespective of the language and language form used. The documents are written in a very detailed way using understandable, straightforward language. The reason for this can be explained by the fact that each document asked for the patriarchate's mediation and support or guidance (or both), and therefore the cases had to be explained to the capital in explicit detail. In the text of each case, the local administrations suggested best practices and solutions, especially in regard to both personal and collective petitions. Thus, these texts were constructed with a distinct intention to gain acceptance from the patriarchate or the Armenian central administration for their suggested solutions. Yet one has to keep in mind that the Armenian administration did not exist as a distinct body completely separate from the others. In many cases, the issues also involved other *millets* whose administrations might need to be contacted, or even the central Ottoman one itself, which may be regarded as one of the primary reasons for explaining the issue with precision. The Armenian Patriarchate was not only the central decision-making body for the Armenian administration but also an interface between the local Armenian and Ottoman administrations, be it in the capital or the provinces. The detailed and precise contents of these documents offer a unique chance to enhance our understanding of the social functioning of Ottoman society.

Surp Pirgiç Armenian Hospital as a Place of Incarceration

I will start with the cases that include or suggest incarceration practices, as they stipulated a territorial and temporal change in the lives of the ones who were found guilty. In particular, the role of Surp Pırgiç Armenian Hospital as a place of incarceration was revealed to me through formulaic expressions repeatedly used in the archival material referencing it. Before discussing the cases, it might be useful to take a look at the structure of the Surp Pırgiç Armenian Hospital and its variety of functions. According to a memorandum published in 1883, the hospital had seven sections; one was for sick people, and another was a Poorhouse for Men (*Angelanots' Arants'*) with disabled or ill males who were without family or unable to take care of themselves. There was a section that sheltered elderly men who had lost their mental abilities and were considered to be incurably mad. Another part called the Section for the Feeble-minded (*Abushanots'*) was for those who needed special conditions in order to recover from their mental and psychological problems. Further, children considered in need of discipline shared a floor with elderly men in a section called the Section for Dissolute Men (*Anaṛaganots'*). The Armenian Hospital had a special department for women called the Section for Women (*Gananots'*) that included sections for ailing women, women in need, elderly women, "mad" women, and female orphans. The existence of these sections is especially relevant for various cases in which the petitions suggest sending a person to the Armenian Hospital.[2]

There are also hints mentioning the Armenian Hospital as a place of imprisonment in literary sources. Zabel Yesayan's seminal work *The Gardens of Silihdar* (*Silihdari Bardēznerě*) is not only an autobiographical book on her life in Constantinople during the late nineteenth and early twentieth centuries but also one of the earliest Armenian literary works in which we find pieces of oral history, accounts from her grandmother of experiences from the first half of the nineteenth century. Considering the scarcity of these kinds of oral historical accounts, I found it relevant to mention them here. Her grandmother recalled specific incidents such as the banning of the Janissaries in 1826 and then continued with the emergence of the idea to establish an Armenian Hospital. Surp Pırgiç Armenian Hospital was founded in 1832, so we can date the period she discusses to be between those two years. According to her grandmother's account, the patriarchate had a prison (*zindan*). The streets and districts where the Armenian apostolics lived were controlled by guards of the patriarchate. Had they discovered an Armenian house cooking meat during Lent, they would occasionally send its owner to this prison, but usually only lashes (*falaka*) and a fine would be administered. She referred to two separate places, the prison of a church, without specifying which one, and the prison (*zindan* written as *zndan*) of the patriarchate. She also mentioned that those who were regarded as being feebleminded were kept under the church of Surp Hovhannes in Narlı Kapı. According to Yesayan's grandmother, those imprisoned under this church not only were chained but also carried shackles (*lale*) on their wrists and ankles.[3] There were guards who were responsible for keeping them silent by administering harsh beatings, a method that naturally had the opposite effect. The beatings caused the prisoners to shout and curse more, to the extent that their voices would be heard during the Sunday mass. Once, during an important religious Sunday celebration, their voices reached the ears of the *Amiras* and even the patriarch himself. After this outrageous incident, a discussion was held on how to get rid of these people. Kazaz Amira Bezciyan offered to establish an institution at a remote location in Yedikule to send them, which according to this literary source was the birth of the idea of founding the hospital.[4] Haseki Nisa Hospital was similarly used by the Ottoman administration as a Muslim women's hospital and prison for incarcerating prostitutes.[5]

Two Cases: Beşiktaş, 1856, and Amasya, 1859

The connection between Surp Pırgiç Armenian Hospital and incarceration mentioned in Yesayan's book can be traced in the Archives of the Patriarchate. In two different letters, I encountered the phrase "sent from zaptiah [*zaptiye*] to the Hospital," one written from Beşiktaş/Constantinople in 1856[6] and the other from the Armenian Hospital in 1859,[7] which implies that there was such a practice. Between 1840 and 1870, the zaptiah[8] was practically the empire's law enforcement organization, a combination of police and gendarmerie.[9] In the first case, the priest of Beşiktaş wrote to the patriarchate asking for clarification regarding the policy of incarceration regarding barber Sarkis, who was from his district of authority. According to the document, Sarkis was sent from the zaptiah to the Armenian Hospital for his crime.

The document was created to regulate the territorial and temporal conditions of Sarkis's penalization. The priest stated Sarkis had been "imprisoned" in the Hospital (*pandargyal e i hivantanotsn*), but that the patriarch decided to send him back home, most probably because the illness he was suffering from was incurable, but with the stipulation that Sarkis was to return to the hospital if he did recover. This clearly demonstrates that the hospital was partly used as a prison. Moreover, the state of his health, or better put the temporality of his illness, was combined with his place of incarceration. In this document, the priest seeks clarification of what should be done in case Sarkis died at home in chains, asking whether a zaptiah should be called to unchain the corpse so that it may be buried. This indicates to us that although the patriarch had the right to order Sarkis home, he did not have the right to have him unchained. The direct involvement of the zaptiah in this case and the cautious approach of the local cleric of Beşiktaş make me think that Sarkis's crime was not a petty one.

Another document containing the phrase "sent from zaptiah to the Hospital" is a correspondence from 1859 about a man named Hovhannes Dingilyan. Dingilyan had stolen money from the Coffer Room (*Sandık Odası*) of Taş Han in Amasya.[10] After bringing back the stolen money three days later, he was imprisoned for forty days and then set free by Kâmil Pasha. Shortly after, Kamil Pasha was removed from duty, and the person who replaced him imprisoned Dingilyan again. After four to five days in prison, Dingilyan was sent to Constantinople, for a reason not explained in the document, at which time he fell sick and was sent from the zaptiah station where he was being held to Surp Pırgiç Hospital. The document, found in Amasya's correspondence file, is written from Surp

Pırgiç Hospital addressed to a certain Mr. Telyan, and signed by Sarkis Bolnagyan. The statement seems to have been written to confirm the whereabouts of Hovhannes Dingilyan, which implies that the Armenian administration in Amasya asked for an inquiry about him. The document stated that he had been in the hospital for two months now. He may have been sent to the hospital because he was sick, or he might have pretended to be sick in order to be sent there. In any case, as no further information was given regarding his health situation and he had already been in the hospital for two months, perhaps he had been cured but continued to be kept in the Hospital as a criminal.

In both cases, it was suggested that the criminal be sent to another place for incarceration, and in both the zaptiah was aware of the fact that the Armenian Hospital was a place the people sent there could be located whenever necessary. In the following document from Akşehir, unlike the other two, the Armenian Hospital appears as a place of exile for the guilty party to be incarcerated.

Akşehir, 1856: A Case of Adultery, Incest, and Abortion[11]

A collective petition was written to the patriarchate from Akşehir in September 1856 suggesting exiling "the one" (*kimse*) by throwing the guilty party into *Pırgiç*, meaning Surp Pırgiç Armenian Hospital.

The collective petition opens by addressing the patriarch and authorities of the Armenian administration such as the National Assembly and *Amiras*.[12] The text then describes the problem at length, describing the perpetrator as Haji Hagop, son of tax collector Haji Eghia. He was described as the one "against our belief." The woman, who was referred to in the text as *dişehli*, was the daughter of Hagop's sister and most probably had been raped and impregnated by her uncle. She probably aborted the child, while accompanied by two other women. A Muslim midwife had been asked to carry out the abortion. The document names the crime as adultery (*zina*), not incest. The woman was married, and her husband had been away for two years. Upon hearing of this incident, her husband returned and filed a case at the local council, which then questioned the woman and her mother. Despite the harsh methods used by the interrogators to change her mind, even beating her, the woman insisted upon her testimony that the child was from her uncle. The language of the interrogators shows that they directly vouched for Hagop, and it was noted that they had told her: "We have never seen anything like this. This is your uncle, do not slander him." Despite the use of physical and verbal intimidation, she did not recant. Her husband and father-in-law asked the council to report the case to the patriarch to request his guidance, saying that they would not accept this "impure" (*murdar*) woman.[13] It was also stated that everybody had heard of the incident, and, had the case been brought to the Muslim (*aylazki*) court, five or six people would have been punished severely. Therefore, the solution offered by the petition was to send *the one* to Constantinople's Surp Pırgiç Hospital. While there are regulations for adultery, abortion, and incest, they are neither suggested nor mentioned in the text. Instead, the petition clearly suggests a temporal and territorial break for all sides, which could only be achieved by exiling the guilty one.

This Armeno-Turkish petition has nineteen signatures with seals and one without. Four signatories were priests (*k'ahana*), and eight were *mahdesi*.[14] The appellative *mahdesi* is used for those who have made the pilgrimage to Jerusalem. Hagop L. Barsoumian explains in detail the use of the title *mahdesi* in his book, that it was used by Christians, whereas Muslims utilized the term *haji*, though numerous documents demonstrate Armenians using both *haji* and *mahdesi* as titles. These were not only pilgrims but also prominent members of the community. Barsoumian mentions that women also used the title *mahdesi* in some instances.[15] By the end of the petition, we observe that the princes/rulers (*ishkhan*)[16] and clerics (*garkavor*)[17] of Akşehir's Armenian community were also involved in the juridical process.[18] We can assume from the use of the word *ishkhan* that the petitioners included people from the ruling class of Akşehir's Armenian *millet*. Therefore, the petition had the approval of both civil and religious elites at the local level, reflecting the makeup of local Armenian administrations prior to the ratification of the Nizamname.

The Armeno-Turkish petition shows a series of particular details in its language. Although the term *aylazki* is found in other documents, in this particular one there is a differentiation between the Muslims and those of other faiths, which is noteworthy. "*Aylazki*," meaning "anybody from another religious/ethnic group"[19] is used instead of Muslim, as the context of the user makes clear. Especially in the phrase "*akhir millete ve aylazkiye kepaze olduk*" (we are deeply disgraced by the Muslims and other *millets*), we see that the authors considered a difference between the "other *millets*" and the "*aylazki*" Muslims. In the same vein, "*aylazki şerahati*" refers to the Muslim/sharia court.

The importance of this case lies in the fact that the Armenian administration was worried about the consequences of it being brought before the sharia court, as it stated: "If the case were brought to Muslim (*aylazki*) court, it would be a catastrophe for five to six people."[20] It can be assumed that such a step would have devastating repercussions for the local Armenian administration of Akşehir, and therefore this petition came into being for two reasons, both because the woman would not recant and because the local Armenian administration was already fearful of its social and legal consequences, for which they had sufficient reason to be. As with the case in Bandırma, house raids, exiles, or other violent means could be applied by the Muslim inhabitants of the town.

The Armenian administration utilized the family law of the Armenian Church, whose rules on family relations were clearly codified. Since early times, regulations stipulated the prohibited degrees of kinship for marriage in great detail.[21] The first comprehensive legal regulations that the Armenian ecclesiastical law followed were the fourth-century laws of Basil the Great. According to these laws, a case of incest between a brother and sister is equated with the crime of murder and carries a punishment of four years of penitence crying outside the church, four years among the listeners, seven years among the listeners inside the church, and four years with the believers. After twenty years of penitence, the person would have the right to retake the sacramental bread. The illicit sex in this case between an uncle and niece must have been subject to a similarly severe punishment. If we follow the terminology used in the petition and consider the crime as adultery, Article 58 of Basil the Great's laws prescribes a punishment of fifteen years penitence for adultery, four years crying, five years among the outside listeners, four years among the inside listeners, and two years with the believers. However, the laws of Basil specifically qualify adultery as living with another man's wife, while a married man having illicit sex with another woman is categorized as debauchery.

The case at hand includes elements that could be categorized as all three crimes. In any case, the penalties laid down by ecclesiastical law had temporal and territorial dimensions that meant controlling the criminal by reminding the larger community about his crime over two decades by prohibiting the criminal to enter certain parts of the church. Hence, in the absence of prison as an institution, in terms of establishing a mechanism of control, time and territory were central to the logic of penalization. Rather than setting a penalty period to be served in situ, the petition suggests exiling the guilty one to the hospital in the capital. This implies that the local Armenian administration was not keen on having the guilty one in Akşehir anymore. Penalizing the criminal according to the existing laws mentioned above must have been considered counterproductive in this case, since it would be a constant reminder to everyone of the situation. Although we do not know exactly how they applied the ecclesiastical law, we can still assume that such a crime would not remain a secret, and indeed the petition mentions that both Muslims and other *millets* had heard about it. Exiling the guilty one meant a territorial and temporal cut for all sides, though perhaps less so for the woman. If we consider the woman as a victim of rape, impregnated by her uncle, and having endured the difficult process of abortion or killing of the infant, not to mention the interrogation process involving a certain degree of violence, her stigmatization would last her entire lifetime. Whether the woman's marriage would be annulled based on this crime would have to be decided by the Armenian administration or personally by the patriarch, given the complexity of the case.[22] As shown above, adultery does not have to mean the annulment of marriage according to ecclesiastical law, but in this case the husband's appeal was to end his marriage, setting him free to remarry. In the final analysis, the reason for asking the guilty one to be exiled reveals the limits of the juridical practices and entitlements of the Armenian local administration. They immediately reached their limits upon the involvement in this case of a Muslim, the midwife. Therefore, exiling "the one" would mean creating a tabula rasa for everyone.

This petition shows that not only the patriarchate in Constantinople but also local councils in the provinces were handling trials and making decisions by 1856, which is not only prior to the ratification of the

Nizamname-i Ermeniyan of 1863 but even before the first draft of the Nizamname in 1857. It would seem the ability to bring a case to the local Armenian administration's council must have been an even earlier practice. The husband and his father, who were the plaintiffs, requested this petition be made to Constantinople, meaning they knew that such a practice was already in place.

The Yarn Factory as a Place for Serving Sentences and Forced Labor

Constantinople, 1848: "Improper Behavior," "Violent Passion," and the Yarn Factory

Besides Surp Pırgiç Armenian Hospital, the other institution I came across while reading the documents was the yarn factory (*iplikhane*), more specifically the Imperial Yarn Factory (Riştehane-i/İplikhane-i Amire). As can be understood from its name, it was a factory that produced sails and ropes for the Ottoman Navy. Just like in the section above, here too I will delve into the meaning of a phrase that appears repeatedly in documents: "[to be] sent to the yarn factory." Donald Quataert mentions the *iplikhane* as a place that employed adults who had committed misdemeanors in the 1850s, referring to a single document from the Ottoman archives, dated 1855.[23] Yet, as seen in the following cases, the yarn factory was used as a prison and a place of forced labor much earlier.

The first document that I will examine is written in Armeno-Turkish and defined as a *sened*. As in other *seneds*, there is no addressee. It was signed by two guarantors and submitted to the patriarchate. In February 1848, a certain bookseller (*kitabcı*), Eghiazar, was sent to the yarn factory (*iplikhane*) for an undetermined crime. It was only mentioned that "in case he commits an improper action [*uygunsuzli*(u)ğ)k)], he would send himself back to the yarn factory."[24] This *sened* was submitted to the patriarchate to attest that Eghiazar would not commit the same crime again; otherwise, he would voluntarily go back to the yarn factory, give up his job at the bookstore, and give an alimony of forty *ghurush* to his wife. The last penalty makes me think they had separated because of the crime he committed, but she was not currently receiving alimony. "Improper action" would not be grounds for a marriage annulment, yet it seems that his wife was persuasive in her case, or perhaps this was not the first such crime he had committed. The document was signed by Eghiazar's son, Haji Apraham, also a bookseller, and a second person whose name is illegible.[25] The crime seems to have taken place at Haji Apraham's bookstore. Thus, in this case, the son of the criminal vouched for his father to be released from the *iplikhane*. Based on the involvement of his likely estranged wife and the offer of alimony as a penalty, I assume that the "improper behavior" may have been a sexual crime. Although the severity of the crime cannot be adequately determined, alimony may have been suggested as a deterrent factor because of the defamation, insult, or other negative effects his crime had on the social status of his wife.

The peculiarity of this document is that it refers to the yarn factory (*iplikhane*) as a prison as early as 1848. Reşat Ekrem Koçu's *İstanbul Ansiklopedisi* mentions the use of a yarn factory as a prison for artisans (*esnaf*), robbers, pickpockets, and those who behave improperly (*uygunsuz güruh*). The use of the word "*uygunsuz*" is noteworthy, as it is the same word used in this *sened*. Koçu adds that "falling into the yarn factory" (*iplikhaneye düşmek*) was a "catastrophe" (*felaket*).[26] He did not specify when the practice of using the yarn factory as a prison began. Additionally, we can see that those who fall into the yarn factory could not be easily released. For instance, in a document from the Ottoman archives dated 1841, a Greek boy named Istatako, son of Kostati from Monemvasia, was kept for six months in the yarn factory, and the Greek ambassador had to intervene to set him free.[27]

A collective petition was written on July 23, 1855, by the administrators of the Surp Kevork Church of Samatya in Constantinople, asking the patriarch to show his "mercy and kindness/graciousness"[28] to help release three convicted men, Tateos, Zamek, and Hampar, from the *iplikhane*. The crime is again not clearly defined; the only word that has a reference to the crime is *molut'iwn*, which can be translated as violent passion (defined as "azgınlık, kuduruş")[29] and may also include sexual crimes. As we have seen, the "improper behavior" mentioned above and "violent passion" demonstrate that the yarn factory was a place of incarceration for convicted and/or forced laborers.[30]

Referring to the yarn factory's function as a prison, Quataert gives examples of bakers who "sold short weight, as well as boatmen, grocers, stonemasons, and weavers with a sentence of one and two months."[31] No sexual crimes are mentioned. The documents analyzed here, however, at least imply sexual crimes. The severity of such crimes cannot be understood from these documents, as they were filed to rescue the criminals rather than to make a complaint. However, as is seen from these cases, there was clearly a practice of sending convicted men to work in the yarn factory as a penalty. Hence, it can be assumed that, while it may have been easy to "fall into the yarn factory," it seems to have been much harder to get out of it.

Naif Öztürk argues in a lengthy article on the establishment and development of the yarn factory that it was founded in order to self-sustain the Ottoman Army and Navy.[32] It was one of the rare institutions at the time representing Ottoman industrialization. Indeed, Öztürk's article frames this institution within Ottoman economic life, the need for industrialization, the amount of production, the type of products, the physical characteristics of the building, and so forth. However, its function as a place of incarceration or serving sentences is only mentioned twice, once in a full quote in the text and once in the footnotes. Öztürk does not refer to any archival documents regarding the yarn factory's function as a place to serve one's sentence, meaning he may not have found this function relevant to the industrialization of the Ottoman Empire. However, there is a direct nexus between unpaid labor and the industrialization of the Ottoman economy. For example, the same article mentions that from its inception in 1827, the yarn factory was financially difficult to sustain, giving incentives for unpaid work. Some more research on this institution reveals yet another function of the yarın factory, as Hagop L. Barsoumian refers to it in an entirely different context: "Thus, in 1836, by imperial order, thousands of Armenian youngsters, 'from eight to fifteen years of age,'[33] were collected from 'Garin [Erzurum] and Sepastia [Sivas], and other parts of Anatolia, to work in Constantinople at the iplikhane [spinning mill], the imperial shipyard, the factory manufacturing sails, and at [the foundry] forging hot iron; it was ordered that they be given only clothing and bread, and [no wage,] no salary.'" Barsoumian refers to two sources, the archives of the American Board of Commissioners for Foreign Missions and the *Badmu'tiwn Hayots'* by the patriarchate's former secretary-general Avedis Bērbēryan, who depicts the situation in detail.[34] In the continuation of the paragraph cited by Barsoumian, Bērbēryan gives the following information: "Up until this day,[35] the order is repeatedly implemented, collecting hundreds of children separating them from their families and fatherlands (*hayreneats*), having them walk thirty days barefoot and with torn clothes, many of them die as a result of the violence perpetuated by the officers and some convert to Islam, in the hope of freedom."[36]

Bērbēryan added that no one from the Armenian *millet* was able to stop this practice and estimated the number of children collected to be five thousand. One of the documents in the Ottoman Archives confirms that the practice of collecting Christian children from the provinces had been done even earlier in 1834. Saying that the number of Armenian children collected from Erzurum, Van, and Sivas was not sufficient, a firman was necessary to collect Rum and Catholic children from the areas of Ürgüp, Niğde, and Maden as well.[37] The firman ordered the collection of destitute children ("*bikes kalub da şunun bunun hidmetlerinde bulunanlardan ol miktar çocukların ahz-u tedariki ile Der-i Aliyeye sevk ve irsali babında lazım gelen fermanı*)."[38] Regardless of whether they were bought or captured, the practice bears a strong resemblance to slavery. Although a firman to collect children from other regions and other *millets* such as the Rum and Catholics would have been even more difficult to enact, it confirms that the children had already been collected from the eastern provinces. In his recent doctoral dissertation, Akın Sefer claims the reason the Imperial Arsenal (*Tersane-i Amire*) asked for Armenian children specifically can only be understood in terms of "encouraging the employment of children" as well as the greater ease with which the authorities could draft these children as opposed to adult subjects.[39] The last part of his argument indeed may hold true, since no Muslim family would give their children away to officers to be enslaved in Constantinople for Ottoman industrialization. Therefore, the significance of that greater ease with which the Ottoman authorities were able to "collect Armenian children" for decades must be questioned. In turn, the clear-as-day connection between industrialization and slavery should be reconsidered in light of these new findings.

The literature on slavery in the Ottoman Empire provides few hints to contextualize such cases. However, given the existence of *forsa*,[40] Christian captives and Muslim criminals forced to work in the dockyards and row on ships from the sixteenth century until the mid-nineteenth century, it may be said that the yarn factory likely followed those examples. Further, Ehud Toledano, in his book on the slave trade in the Ottoman Empire during the nineteenth century, points out that kidnapping was a method to collect slaves: "It was aimed at unprotected persons in an isolated position. . . . It frequently occurred on the eastern borders of Anatolia among the people of the Caucasus. The Laz were accused of abducting Georgian women and children while the men were serving in the Sultan's armies. . . . Circassians were often implicated in the abduction of free-born Muslim children."[41] As we see, Toledano references the fragile position of "unprotected persons" who could easily be kidnapped and enslaved. Although his accounts are mostly from the 1860s, the archival documents I examined above from 1834 include the targeting of unprotected, destitute, disabled, and Christian children.

Until its closure in the 1870s, the yarn factory was known for its coerced labor. Sefer rightly questioned the recruitment of non-Muslim workers to be "soldiers" as opposed to being drafted as laborers like many other provincial workers were.[42] Sefer wrote that out of a thousand workers, only 25 percent were listed as "naval troops," "boy soldiers of naval troops," or "boy soldiers of the reserve troops," and the other 75 percent were conscripted Christians from different parts of Anatolia.[43] Consequently, it can likely be assumed that there were children among the seventy-five percent of the yarn factories' conscripted Christian "workers." Indeed, Nazan Maksudyan draws attention to the high number of women, orphans, and children working in Ottoman industry.[44] The Armenian children collected from the provinces might not have originally been orphans, but became such after being taken away from their families. In addition, among the adults were Christians accused of crimes who were forced to work as a method of punishment.

Family Law

Constantinople, 1847: Marriage Annulment Based on Testified Impotence of Keseji Harut'iwn

In this part of the chapter, I will discern the applications of ecclesiastical law in light of the archival documents at hand. The first document that I will examine consists of two parts: a medical report and a judgment based upon it, both carrying the same date of August 12, 1847.[45] I will start from the second part, as it includes the reason for conducting the medical examination of a certain man, Keseji Harut'iwn, and the final judgment based on it. His wife of ten years complained that he was "unable to fulfill the rights required from the marital act."[46] The council decided to ask for an expert's opinion. Upon the request of the patriarch, three doctors examined Harut'iwn at a house in the district of Gedikpaşa. As a result, it was testified that he was healthy and had all his limbs; however, he was "unable" (*angarogh*) and therefore "not suitable" (*anharmar*) for the marital act. In other words, the medical report testified to Keseji Harut'iwn's impotence, which was used as evidence in his wife's case. Consequently, the council judged that the marriage could be annulled, allowing the woman to remarry.[47] This council must have been the Religious Council mentioned in the first chapter of this study. The word used for "decision" is *vjir*, which usually means "sentence" and clearly indicates a juridical decision. This proves that the council was entitled to make juridical decisions on family law as early as 1847.

The next document is the medical certificate of Keseji Harut'iwn's impotence. It is noted both in the marginalia of the medical report and in the decision itself that the "authentic translation" was included. However, there is only one medical certificate, and it is in Armenian. The names of the doctors indicate the reason for this remark. The doctors who examined Harut'iwn were Giovanni Romano from Genoa, Giuseppe Baroni from Sardinia, and Petraki, a surgeon (*cerah* written in Armenian letters).[48] The first two doctors were probably Levantine, while the last one Petraki might be Rum or a Catholic Armenian. The note about the "authentic translation" may mean that the doctors gave testimony of their expertise in another language, Italian, Greek, French, or Turkish, which was recorded by the Armenian priest Hovhannes sent by the patriarchate. It is noteworthy to also mention the content of the medical certificate. It starts with a statement that the signatories were called by the Armenian patriarch—the patriarch at the time being Madt'eōs Chukhajyan Gosdantnubolsetsi[49] (of Constantinople)—to a house in Gedikpaşa, and they affirmed the truthfulness of their testimony. "We examined a man by the name of Artin Khndam Khachaduryan from the Keseji artisans (*esnaf*). He has a healthy body (constitution/*gazmvadzk*) and should be twenty-eight years old. We saw that his natural limb was in complete form; however, it is deprived of any movement, it is completely impotent and improper for copulation."[50]

The medical report starts with a remark that the patriarch himself was personally involved in the case. Although Surp Pırgiç Armenian Hospital was already in service since 1834, Keseji Harut'iwn was not sent there for a medical report, nor were Armenian doctors called upon. The decision to investigate the case behind closed doors in a private house with "foreign doctors" carries a very subtle strategy, one that is both territorial as well as temporal. Through the choice of doctors, Keseji Harut'iwn was practically removed from the Armenian context. Hence, it can be assumed that this was also an attempt by both the council and the patriarch to protect Harut'iwn's reputation and his/their masculinity. The patriarch's choice of arranging this medical examination under these specific conditions is a good example of the unseen, elusive dimension of power embedded in communal spaces and times. Furthermore, while the wife's name is never given like the woman in the case of Akşehir, her agency to file a complaint regarding her husband's impotence is a noticeable one. Armenian ecclesiastical law defines the conditions under which annulment of marriage may be accepted. While the marital bond became considered to be unbreakable for the first time in the nineteenth century under the laws of Catholicos Kevork IV (1866–82),[51] there had been regulations for the annulment of marriage since the fifth century.[52]

One of the three conditions for annulment mentioned by Melik'-T'ankyan is "incurable diseases both physical and mental."[53] Hence, the committee might have regarded impotence as a physically incurable disease and therefore allowed the annulment of marriage on those grounds. The medical diagnosis opened the way to the marriage's annulment, giving the woman the possibility to enjoy a fulfilled marital life with someone else.

This case from 1847 demonstrates the systematic functioning of the Armenian Administration and its Religious Council established that same year. Melik'-T'ankyan gave an example from the end of the nineteenth century, stating that marriage annulments were subject to the confirmation of the catholicos in Echmiadzin. He referred to three cases of divorce from 1899 in which the patriarchate of Constantinople was asked to investigate, make decisions (*vjir*), and forward them to the Catholicosate of Echmiadzin.[54] In our case, while we again see the use of the word *vjir*, there is no mention of forwarding the decision to Echmiadzin. Therefore, it is not clear from what time all divorce decisions were required to be confirmed by the Catholicosate of Echmiadzin. In any case, the medical report of impotence was regarded as a solid reason for divorce that even the catholicosate could not refute or disregard.

It could be assumed that similar cases requiring a medical diagnosis for the annulment might have taken place before 1847 as well. For instance, incurable diseases like leprosy, and including mental illnesses, were regarded as relevant reasons for divorce that might have also required such medical attestations. This case also shows how the laws accepted throughout the centuries by the Armenian Church were points of reference for the Armenian Patriarchate in Constantinople.

In this intracommunal case, we observe that the limits of family law had to be extended by the patriarch himself and the right to have a fulfilled marital bond was maintained. Patriarchs were not independent agents operating in a vacuum, but on the contrary, since they were subjected to the confirmation of the Armenian administration, they had to take into consideration the structural inequalities and societal repercussions of each and every decision. In other words, the Armenian administration had to be attentive to the de facto situation, power relations, and legal regulations at hand for every case. They had to find the best way to execute legislative power in order to remain within the realm of legitimacy, even if it did not always adhere to the principles of ecclesiastical law.

Interrogation (Istintak) and Record (Tahrir) Documents from Çarşamba, 1869

The Archives of the Armenian Patriarchate contain a number of *istintak* documents from Çarşamba. *İstintaks* are interrogation records with a question-and-answer format. The documents are in Armenian, and the word *istintak* is written in Armeno-Turkish. They contain very detailed accounts of the cases, even more so than the petitions analyzed so far, providing even richer information on local provincial life than most other bureaucratic documents. Reading them as historical sources is quite different from that of court register books (*kadi sicili*), which from the earliest studies to the most recent have always been characterized as only containing the summary of a case. Ebru Aykut's article on women poisoning their husbands[55] and Milen V. Petrov's article on the court registers of the Vilayet of Danube both underline the importance of expanding our definition of court records beyond *sicils*, as they provide only summaries of the court cases and thus obscure important background information. The *sicils* have a number of limitations, including the density of formulaic language, the absence of direct quotes, and the shortage of information on the litigant's motivation or social background.[56] "Unlike virtually any other type of Ottoman legal source, the interrogation protocols are verbatim accounts of what was said during the investigative process. As such, these documents contain the first-person narratives of bona fide non-elite social actors, which have proven so elusive in other types of Ottoman sources including *sicil* records."[57] While Petrov's critique that *sicils* are not the only court records that should be researched, he only adds the insufficiently researched interrogation records of the Tanzimat period's Nizamiye courts. To my knowledge, there is no literature about the existence and importance of other vital sources, namely, the Armenian administration's interrogation records (*istintak*), or that of any other *millet*. Furthermore, his point referring to the detailed social background that can be read through *istintak* documents is also crucial for writing history from below.

As will be shown in this study, a detailed analysis of the interrogation records of Çarşamba not only provides the social background on the crime of a man having more than one wife or a woman living with a man as a second partner outside of marriage, but also reveals information about the legal practices of the Armenian administration in the provinces, the local use of language, the power relations between those of higher social status and the Armenian administration, claims of sexual rights, social mobility, and even the use of specific language patterns both in Turkish and in Armenian that have disappeared today. Hence, the interrogation records of Çarşamba contain completely new historical knowledge and are untapped sources not just on Armenian juridical practices but also on everyday life in the villages around Çarşamba. First and foremost, the very systematic method of questioning in the interrogation records (*istintaks*) indicates an existing practice of interrogation.[58]

In February 1869, six people were interrogated by the prelacy of Çarşamba. Four of the cases were interrelated and all of them involved the same type of issue, that of a woman living with a man who was not her husband or one who had not obtained a proper marriage annulment first. I will first examine the case of T'akvoroghlu Arakel and the second woman he brought into his home, Mariam, as they are not linked to the rest of the documents. In Arakel's interrogation record, we learn he was married to a woman by the name of Marinu, whom he left, claiming that she and her relatives were pressuring him to become Protestant. After leaving her, he returned and asked the local clerical leader to persuade her to reconcile, but Marinu did not accept. Arakel left his village Ghapughaya (Kapukaya) and took up with a woman named Mariam for two months. The record of interrogation makes clear that Arakel was an adulterous man, as he lived with another woman while married. The law of Basil (370–378) considers not just Arakel but also Mariam guilty of adultery for being the person with whom Arakel was committing adultery. Arakel declared that he would leave Mariam if his official wife wanted to return, clearly trying to find a way to avoid being punished for adultery. His punishment would include a fine, penitence, and perhaps even corporal punishment in the form of lashes. Furthermore, his fellow villagers might attack him because of his deed.[59] Therefore, it might be assumed that Arakel had left his village in order to avoid the scorn of his neighbors.

The second document is referred to as a *tahrir* of Mariam and is used as an attachment to the main *istintak*, that of T'akvoroghlu Arakel. She was asked only three questions, whereas Arakel had to answer thirteen. Mariam was asked why she left her village Choukhur (Çukur) and went to the village of Chakhmakh (Çakmak), apparently where she met Arakel. Going from one village to another was regarded as something suspicious in itself. She responded that she had gone there to collect a debt for her husband's business. She was asked how she met Arakel and who the matchmaker was. She answered by saying she did not know Arakel was married and that even his friend Tankaritoghlu Krikor, who was the matchmaker, did not mention Arakel being married. Mariam had been in Çakmak for three days when the matchmaker suggested she go to Arakel's house. The third question asked was whether anybody had officially married them. She responded negatively but added that she had slept with Arakel only once and was now pregnant.[60] Her *tahrir* does not make it clear why she chose to be with T'akvoroghlu Arakel. It can be assumed perhaps she was not happy in her marriage, but that was not a valid reason to annul it according to ecclesiastical law. Therefore, she might have used the opportunity to travel to another village in order to find a way to stay there. In her statement, she claimed that she did not know he was married and that nobody had informed her, implicating T'akvoroghlu Arakel and Tankaritoghlu Krikor with responsibility for the crime.

Mariam's presumed pregnancy clearly complicated Arakel's situation. In those days before the ability to test for pregnancy, it would provide her with more time to devise a strategy. As she might have faced backlash from the local community for having illicit sex and committing adultery, she needed a way out of the situation. Yet she knew that she was not alone in the crime; T'akvoroghlu Arakel committed the crime of adultery by living with another woman while married, and the matchmaker was also complicit in this crime. While the matchmaker knew that Arakel was married, he also knew the wife was no longer with him. Most likely, they thought the Protestantism of Arakel's wife would be an extenuating circumstance. Indeed, Protestantism might have been a strong argument for Arakel, as the Armenian Apostolic Church was adamantly against conversion. However, Arakel not only had a relationship with a married woman but also lived with her, which meant adultery for both sides. There were a number of possible penalties for adultery depending on the situation: fifteen years of gradual penitence, exile from the village, or beating.[61] As Mariam mentioned that the villagers were already marginalizing her, it could be argued that the village inhabitants de facto penalized the crime. Mariam was also committing adultery, but her claim of pregnancy made the situation much more complicated. Therefore, it is not a coincidence that Arakel readily offers to return to his wife in order to close the case altogether. Nonetheless, doing that would not be so simple if Mariam was indeed pregnant.

Arakel said that his wife was Protestant and so was her son, and he claimed that they both pressured him so much to convert that he was forced to leave the house. Both Arakel and Mariam left the area of authority of one place, that is, their villages, where they were most probably registered as inhabitants, and met in another village, where they were not locals. The territorial aspect here seems to play an important role. Although she had the alibi of going there to collect her husband's debt, it appears Mariam was escaping from him for an unknown reason. Both parties had illicit relations in another place, perhaps hoping to return to a zero point in time, a new beginning in a new place.

The remaining documents in this file are interconnected cases. The story starts with T'orosoghlu Harut'iwn. According to Harut'iwn's account, his wife, Anna, had a mental disease; he said that his wife had "developed a habit" (*khuy prnel*). He described this "*khuy prnel*" as something lasting two to three hours, after which she was able to get up and walk and keep the household again.[62] While this is most likely caused by some sort of psychological crisis, a physical one such as epileptic attacks cannot be ruled out. He said she had undergone these crises for seven or eight years. They did not go to a doctor, but they did see Christian and Muslim clerics to receive special prayers of healing (written as *nuskha/muska*). These crises stopped after a year, but then she started fainting. As the situation got worse, Anna was first sent to various relatives several times and then brought back. Regarding the "*khuy prnel*," it is possible that Anna was very unhappy with Harut'iwn, and, since there was no other way to get the marriage annulled, she may have performed a controlled hysterical crisis.[63] Indeed, cases have been reported in which women acted as if they were "bewitched" and were brought to the Muslim clerics (*hoca/hoja*) for healing. Since Anna and Harut'iwn did the same, we can assume that these crises were most probably psychological and that Anna's aim may have been to get an annulment of marriage on the grounds of being perceived to have an incurable psychological illness.[64] Therefore, the interrogators were trying to understand whether she was able to continue her marital life or not by asking Harut'iwn whether Anna was capable of continuing her daily life and housework in light of her condition.

Meanwhile, Anna's brother-in-law took her from her house because her family had heard that Harut'iwn had brought in another woman, Khatug. Khatug was married, but her husband was not in town, and she said she had been alone for one year when she met Harut'iwn. According to Khatug, who was questioned on the same day as Harut'iwn, February 3, 1869, she had sex with Harut'iwn when they went to work in the forest, and she became pregnant from it.[65] Probably pointing out this pregnancy, the interrogator mentioned that the villagers claimed Khatug had borne a "bastard," a child born out of wedlock who we understand from Harut'iwn's *istintak* had since died. During Harut'iwn's questioning, the interrogator asked him whether he knew that Khatug was a "prostitute"[66] and he answered "yes."[67] Apparently, their relationship continued for a while, and then Harut'iwn brought her into his household. He was aware of Khatug's marriage, but she did not know the whereabouts of her husband. He defended his decision by saying that he had no other choice and needed someone at home to serve him, his sick wife, and his mother, and that was the only reason he brought Khatug into the house. Moreover, he argued that his wife, Anna, and his mother wanted someone to serve them at home. Thus, he did not mean to have Khatug as his wife but as a domestic worker. Up to this point, Harut'iwn did not say anything about having sex with Khatug or wanting to get married to her. Accordingly, he rejected the claim he slept with her. The argument of psychological and incurable disease would help him in his situation, and therefore he was asked more than once by the interrogators what the nature of her disease was. However, he was still in the position of committing adultery, as he had brought another woman into his house. So was Khatug, as she was married and her husband was only away for one year. However, her situation was more complicated than that of Harut'iwn.

In Khatug's *istintak*, we read that she was married to Akil for eleven years without having children. When Akil returned to town after his one year away, he found Khatug pregnant and rejected her as his wife. When asked why she had gone to Harut'iwn, she used a quite interesting expression in Armenian, "*erig yertal uzetsi*," which literally translates as "I wanted to go [with] a man."[68] At the end of her interrogation, she used the same pattern in the following way: "I am five months pregnant, and it has been six months since I went [with] a man." Therefore, it is clear that Khatug was alone and wanted to have a man to take care of her and that Harut'iwn needed a domestic worker, a lover, or both. In any case, Akil's one year of absence was not long enough to apply for the marriage to be annulled. However, being married for ten years and not having children and then becoming pregnant by Harut'iwn would mean that Khatug was a fertile woman, but perhaps Akil was not a fertile man. This might have assisted her in terminating her marriage, but she had not done so when she had illicit sex with Harut'iwn.

As opposed to Harut'iwn's *istintak*, the *istintak* of Khatug, daughter of Magaroghlu Arakel, clearly stated that they had illicit sex, that the deceased child was from him, and that she was five months pregnant for the second time. Khatug's *istintak* is a very empowering one. She was aware of the fact that neither having illicit sex nor being pregnant was solely her problem, but also Harut'iwn's. Her self-awareness, self-esteem, and agency to make a decision that would cause her to be considered a "prostitute" in the eyes of the local Armenian administration must have had a good reason behind it. She might have considered her circumstances as a single woman in a time when women needed a man for protection and to take care of them, along with her wanting to have children, and found those factors to be more important than how society would see her. Legally, they both could have been penalized for their adultery, and in addition, Khatug could also be found guilty of prostitution, as the local administration had already labeled her as a "prostitute." This might have been the outcome of an investigation conducted prior to the interrogation by the members of the local administration. Being guilty of the crime of prostitution would mean banishment from the church altogether.[69] This ban would marginalize a woman within her community. It would leave her without protection and even open to the possibility of assault or rape attacks by other men. Therefore, it would have been crucial for Khatug to at least remain within Harut'iwn's home. By claiming her to be a domestic worker, Harut'iwn was trying to keep her in his house while covering for the adultery at the same time.

Molla Kesheshoghlu (Molla Son-of-Priest), an Unusual Name for an Islamic Cleric

Khatug and Harut'iwn were not married under any religious law. Khatug was asked in her interrogation whether they asked for a *molla* to marry them. She confirmed that they called a *molla* to their home to that end (*nikah ĕllal* was used in Armenian script), yet they changed their mind and sent him back. However, why call a *molla* to marry two Christians?

The word *molla*, used for a Muslim religious leader, is also used by the Gromtsis (people of Grom/Kurum). The Gromtsis were a silver-mining community living in the Kromni/Kurum region of eastern Pontus. Minas Pjshgyan mentioned them in his book *Badmut'iwn Bondosi Vor E Sew Dzov* (1819). He wrote that those people were "half and half," meaning that they were officially Muslim to the world but practicing Christians in private. "Inwardly they are Christian and outwardly they are Muslim. . . . This continues from father to child. Their Imam is like that too."[70] Pjshgyan's book was translated by Hrant Der Andreasyan in 1969 as *Karadeniz Kıyıları Tarih ve Coğrafyası*, wherein the same paragraph is found.[71] Der Antreasyan added that Ghugas Injijian's book *Ashkharakrut'iwn Ch'orsits' Masants' Ashkharhi*, published in 1806, mentioned the names of villages inhabited by Gromtsis.[72] Selim Deringil has written a quite informative chapter on "crypto-Christians" where he dwells upon the Kromni people and Stavriotes but unfortunately did not utilize the sources mentioned above.[73] In the chapter on crypto Christians, we learn from the book by Yorgo Andreadis, a descendant of a Gromtsi family, that their religious leaders used to be called *molla*.[74] Therefore, I assume that the *molla* mentioned in the *istintak* may be a clergyman from the people of Kromni. As

Pjshgyan also mentions, their imam was also "half and half," meaning that he would perform Christian marriage ceremonies as well as Muslim ones. Considering that he was called into an Armenian Apostolic house, he was supposed to perform an Orthodox marital ceremony. Although the Gromtsi inhabited the area between Trabzon and Gümüşhane,[75] they also migrated to surrounding areas after the mining company closed in 1857.[76] In the file of Çarşamba, I came across a document written by a Pontic Rum to the Armenian prelacy in Trabzon referring to "Gorum," another likely reference to the Kurum or Grom.[77] Therefore, I would not exclude the possibility that the *molla* in our case was Gromtsi, especially considering his surname of Kesheshoghlu (probably Keşişoğlu, meaning son of a priest). It can be assumed that Khatug and Harut'iwn may have thought that the only priest who could conduct this marriage was a Gromtsi *molla*. However, if *molla* means simply Muslim cleric, this would mean that they even considered to convert to Islam. The conversion, whether to Islam or to Greek Orthodoxy, was thought of as a way out of all other responsibilities for both Khatug and Harut'iwn. During the interrogation, while Khatug stated that they had called a *molla* to get married, when Harut'iwn was asked the same question, he rejected that claim.[78] Getting married would not be easy for someone who was already stigmatized as a "prostitute" like Khatug. One of the three conditions to get an annulment of marriage is being a prostitute. She might have not been able to get (re)married while being known as a prostitute. Had she been found guilty of the crime of prostitution, her husband could easily leave her. Yet this would leave her unable to remarry as she was stigmatized as a prostitute. Her double bind was that even if she had not been stigmatized for prostitution, she was to be guilty of committing adultery just like Harut'iwn. In either case, Khatug's situation was more fragile than that of Çelebi Harut'iwn.

To summarize, Khatug claims to have engaged in an illicit relationship with Harut'iwn and was pregnant by him for the second time, while Harut'iwn denies it completely.[79] Harut'iwn had taken his wife back home from her relatives in Göğceköy (Gövceköy), and the interrogators asked for precise information on this matter, such as the names of those who had been present and when exactly he brought Khatug into his home. The level of detail makes it obvious that the interrogators were well informed; they had questioned the village priest informally beforehand and may have even gotten information from local Armenians. They asked Harut'iwn whether the village priest warned him against his actions or not. He answered that Father Tateos and a certain Hagop, son of Hampig, had warned him, but he insisted that his mother and his wife needed to be taken care of and that Khatug was the domestic servant needed for the job. During her interrogation, Khatug was asked who her "worker" (*işci*) was. She responded: "My *işci* was Sara, a bride taken by Chavushoghlu."[80] However, what could *işci* have meant in this sequence of questions, immediately following the inquiry about an extramarital relation? From the context, I understand that *işci* meant the person who mediated between the two people, namely, the matchmaker.

An interrelated case to that of Sara was the one of Chavushoghlu Giragos from Ghapughaya (Kapukaya), who had been married for twenty-six years when his wife became disabled. Giragos testified that he had slept with a woman named Sara who had come to his house. Sara was also interrogated. Her interrogation, like Mariam's, was defined as a *tahrir.* According to her statement, Sara's husband had passed away four years prior, after which she found lodging at Harut'iwn's home, who she referred to as T'orosoglu Artin. She was let go from the home when another woman was brought into it (Khatug) because of the wife's illness. Sara gave a striking response when she was asked why she went to Chavushoghlu Giragos' house: "My husband Yeghia passed away four years ago. I was staying at my Çelebi T'orosoghlu Artin's house. This year my Çelebi brought another woman because his wife was ill and he kicked me out. . . . Seeing that my Çelebi brought a second wife, I followed Çelebi's pattern and went directly to the house of Chavushoghlu Giragos. . . . Up to today, we are husband and wife, we sleep together [*bargink gellankgor*]. I have not had my period for two months, and I might be pregnant."[81]

Sara was Khatug's matchmaker. Both women were de facto alone when they had sex with another man. Sara, a widow, had been kicked out of her *Çelebi*'s house, and hence was homeless. Khatug's husband had already been away for a year, meaning she needed somebody to provide for her. It seems that they helped each other in finding a house. As Sara was a widow, by law she was free to get married again.[82]

Was Sara working at Harut'iwn's house? If yes, it meant that the latter already had someone to serve his wife and mother and Khatug was not needed. Sara uses the title of *Çelebi* for him, one given to prominent Armenian personalities. A similar title, *Hoca*, was adopted starting from the fifteenth century, while *Çelebi* was used by "[Armenian] feudal nobility as well as those who had risen from the ranks of artisans in cities."[83] Thus, when Sara said, "I followed the example of my Çelebi, he took wife over wife [he brought a second wife into his house], and I went to the house of Chavushoghlu [Giragos] and settled,"[84] she was most probably pointing to T'orosoghlu Harut'iwn's prestigious status in order to protect herself. Sara's position was most precarious since there was no one who took care of her, but at the same time, she was free to be with a man. Harut'iwn preferred Khatug over Sara, probably because he knew that Khatug was pregnant.

The first question in each of these *istintaks* was always about the respondent's confession. It is asked in two ways: "What *millet* are you?" (*Inch' azk ēs?*) or "You are Armenian, what is your religion?" The answer in every case was "I am an Armenian, Apostolic."[85] *Azk/millet* was still defined by religious confession, and so just being Armenian was not sufficient for jurisdiction since a Catholic Armenian would be subject to a different legal framework. The interrogation continued with the marital status of the person, and, if married, their place of marriage, the identity of the godfather and priest, the number of years married, and the number of children. The subject matter followed these questions, namely, the reasons for bringing the second wife into his home and her identity. Since the subject matter was the same in all these cases, there was another interesting question asked exclusively to the women: "Who was your *işci*?" They too were responsible for the relationship. Indeed, if married people were introduced to each other, the subsequent adultery was also a crime for which the *işci* would be responsible.

This *istintak* file from Çarşamba allows for several remarks about the social life of the region in the second half of the nineteenth century. First and foremost, it is important to point out the precarious situation of women who remained without a male guardian or were sick. A woman without a male guardian faced the prospect of an unsustainable life and was probably reduced to a very precarious income or none at all. Giragos's wife was disabled and he had no children, which might be argued as extenuating circumstances for him, although having two wives in one house was strictly forbidden. Importantly, the records reflect very self-conscious, expressive, and empowered women. Khatug said that she wanted to have a man; Sara formulated very intelligently that she followed the example of her *Çelebi*; Mariam said that she was pregnant despite not being married. Those women, interrogated by the local Armenian administration, were well aware of who was primarily responsible for their situation, and their statements do not indicate any feelings of guilt.

The patriarchate and its prelacies in the provinces had been authorized to regulate marital issues for a long time. Arshag Alboyadjian points out an interesting provision found in an imperial permission (*berat*) given to Patriarch Nerses Varjabedyan in 1875 that did not appear in the previous ones issued in 1764 and 1831. Its sixteenth article stated that "marital issues including divorce and other cases relating to religion should be sorted out by the patriarch or his representatives according to ecclesiastical rule. No *kadi*, no *naib* should interfere." Article 17 very explicitly stated the following: "As the aforementioned religion forbids divorce and taking a second wife, or only allows marrying no more than three times after the death of the first wife, it should prevent and punish such cases. It is forbidden to enter the church for the ones who pretend to have a marriage, which was not considered legitimate in their ecclesiastical law, and for the ones who die in this position, their priests should decide about burial according to their religious practices. No *kadi*, no *naib* should interfere and make a judgment."[86] This *berat* came six years after these cases from Çarşamba. A *berat* should not just be considered a document that "gives rights and permissions" but often would merely recognize a right or existing practice.

Güldane from Evkere, 1860: "If You [Patriarch] Order to Separate Me from Haji Sarkis, My Blood and My Sins Be on Your Head"

Güldane, daughter of Haji Artin from Evkere (Efkere), which was under the authority of the *vijag* of Gesarya (Kayseri), wrote a rebellious petition to the patriarch in the capital showing her desperation and asking for his endorsement. Güldane had married a certain Krikor from Sarmısaklı fifteen years ago, but he left her and the village right after the marriage. He never returned, never wrote letters, and never sent money. In her Armeno-Turkish personal petition, Güldane mentioned she had to endure a number of life-threatening difficulties over all the long years of having nobody to take care of her, including going hungry and facing threats against her honor: "In a miserable situation of hunger, thirst, and nakedness, subjected to all kinds of attacks against my honor/chastity without anybody [to protect me] I live a wretched life (*Aç susuz ve çıblak gayet peruşan hali ile ve ırz babinde türlü mukhataralar içinde bu kadar müdetir kimim kimsem olmayıp sefil sergerdan kaldığımden*)."[87] As a result, Güldane decided to move into the house of Haji Sarkis on September 25, 1860. She wrote that she married Haji Sarkis and would no longer accept Krikor as her husband, even if he were to return. Clearly, with this petition she wanted her marriage to be annulled legally and her new relation to be recognized as a legal marriage. "I am writing this to you with tears in my eyes, should there be any trouble caused by my ex-husband, I would not cause any headache to anyone else, I'll be cutting my own rope putting an end to my words" (*kendi ipimi elim ile keserek soezü tükedeceyim*). Considering the very long time she spent living as a destitute woman, she might have had already petitioned for her marriage to be annulled, as seven years of absence was regarded as long enough to apply for one, but there is no mention of prior attempts. She signed the document together with two clerics and twelve witnesses. Her petition is a very powerful one, especially seeing it with the signatures of clerics and the many people who testified for her. Its language could be described as a cry to the patriarch to accept her decision in order to save her life. Güldane's petition is yet another proof of the impossibility of living in the villages of the provinces as a destitute woman, a situation that became all too common in the mid-nineteenth century primarily as a result of the process that turned Armenian peasants into migrant workers.[88]

Notarial Function of the Prelacies and Patriarchate

Notarial functions were under the authority of the Armenian administration. Those functions included being official witnesses, attesting and ascribing admissible testimony, testifying on debtor-creditor relations, inheritance, a person's marital status, and other matters. The systematized forms and contents of the documents in the Patriarchal Archive allow me to assume that the Armenian administration already had an existing practice of notarial functions, both through the Patriarchate of Constantinople and the Armenian churches or prelacies in the provinces. In this section, I will introduce some archival documents that acknowledge the notarial function of the churches, such as being an official witness and/or attesting legal testimony.

Gallipoli, 1858: Struggling for Alimony, Receiving an Inheritance

An Armeno-Turkish document from Gallipoli was sent by five men to the patriarchate on October 18, 1858, to testify that Mariam and her daughter, Pisdos, were the family of the late Khach'adur (Khach'ig in the text) who had abandoned them and never paid alimony.[89] The document explained that Mariam, daughter of Aghji (Ağcı)[90] Harut'iwn from Gallipoli and wife of Khach'ig from Beyoğlu, had come from Gallipoli to join Khach'ig in Constantinople nine years prior with their daughter, Pisdos. However, it seems that they could not get along with each other as a couple, and Khach'ig sent his wife and daughter back to Gallipoli. He never paid alimony, leaving the woman and child in severe poverty. In the meantime, Mariam went to the *kadı* court: "[She consulted] the mufti, and the judge and issued an alimony paper for the child" (*mühtüye, hakime danışıp cere kyahadı çıkarıyor çocuğun nafakası içün*).[91] She may have first attempted it within the Armenian legal mechanism but there is no trace of it. The letter only mentioned that she received a document of eligibility for eight years of alimony. Başak Tuğ makes mention of "deserted wives" who applied to the Muslim court for the annulment of their marriages in the absence of their husbands.[92] Mariam might have argued that her husband deserted her, as he sent neither money nor letters after their return to Gallipoli, and therefore asked for a "*cere kyahadı*" (*cere kağıdı*) for the "*nafaka*," both meaning alimony. The document stated that Mariam was the wife of Khach'ig ("*Khaçiyin kendi bsagavorudur*)."[93] Here again, "*bsag*" or "*bsagavor*" is the Armenian ecclesiastical terminology for the marriage or the one who is married, joined with the past form of "to be" in Turkish.

Mariam was severely indebted and suffered from numerous problems in daily life as a result. Meanwhile, Khach'ig must have passed away shortly before this document was written, as his mother contacted Mariam to come to collect her inheritance. There is an interesting sentence included in the document: "Even if Istanbul is big, the oral hearing must take place in the presence of our *Effendi*" (*şimdi Istanbol her nekadar genişise de, gene murafaaları Efendimizin huzurunda olur*).[94] This statement is further evidence that the patriarch himself used to participate in the oral hearings. The document was submitted to advocate for the rights of Mariam and her daughter and to ask for the patriarch's mercy by allowing her to escape severe poverty. The five male signatories included a priest and *Mahdesi* (pilgrim).[95] A note underneath the signatures mentions that Priest Kapriel from the patriarchate's main church attested that Mariam was Khach'ig's wife and Pisdos was their daughter. Hence, this notarial document sent from Gallipoli was testified to by the Armenian administration in Constantinople.

What makes this document different from many others is a note in Ottoman Turkish on the back of the paper. To be clear, the document utilizes the Turkish language written in Armenian characters on one side and Ottoman on the other. The rear text was written by the officers of the patriarchate to advocate for the rights of Mariam and her daughter, Pisdos, before the Ottoman administration, as it clarifies the situation to the Ottoman officials who would continue the bureaucratic procedure of inheritance. Copied documents are marked as "copy" (*badjen*), but this document is not marked as such. Therefore, the original must have been placed in the file, while Mariam might have received a copy to continue the process. On the rear, it was attested that Khach'ig son of Mehrab had passed away and Mariam's only daughter, Pisdos, had appointed Mgrdich' son of Ovannes as her representative for selling a plot of land that she had apparently inherited from her father. Interestingly, it is also mentioned that Pisdos had "repeatedly" (*defa'n*) appointed Mgrdich' as her representative.

This document shows that the Armenian administration executed various notarial functions both in Gallipoli and in the capital. In the main text, we have a notarial attestation that Mariam and Pisdos formed

Khach'ig's family, making them eligible for inheritance. On the back, we find another notarial testimony that appoints Mgrdich' as Pisdos's legal representative in order to sell the plot. Thus, although we have one document and three groups of testifiers, that is, those testifying for Mariam and Pisdos, Priest Kapriel testifying for the testifiers, and the patriarchate testifying to the appointment of Mgrdich' as Pisdos's legal representative, there were likely other stages in this case that were not mentioned. One stage must have been the case's hearing in Constantinople, in which Mariam and Pisdos were recognized as Khach'ig's family, and their right to inheritance was granted. Apparently, there was a stage where the inheritance was distributed and Pisdos inherited the plot of land. The next step must have been that she wanted to sell the plot and appointed Mgrdich' as her legal representative more than once. The reason for Mgrdich''s repeated appointment as her representative might mean that Pisdos was unable to keep up with the bureaucratic procedure, and so this note was written to enable her to obtain her inheritance. Therefore, the note must have been written to be shown to the relevant institution for the sale to proceed.

In this case, we have a woman who seeks redress and whose situation is recognized by the local priest and four others in Gallipoli and testified to in Constantinople. The signatories of this document were people who knew her or her husband and/or the poverty she lived in with her child and addressed this document to the patriarchate in support of her case.

In many cases where women were abandoned or deserted by their husbands, they were entitled to receive a monthly payment. Locating the man was of course crucial in forcing him to pay the monthly support to his family. *The Report of the Political Assembly of 1870–71* includes a similar case from the village of Vanig in Baghesh (Bitlis). Villager T'oros had abandoned his wife to settle in Mersin, leaving her destitute. A *takrir* of October 27, 1870, had ordered him to return to his hometown, and in the case his wife refused him, to send her a monthly payment. In some circumstances, if the case was finalized, or another bureaucratic step was taken, it was included in the report and noted underneath the decision. In this case, it was stated that "as a result of the *takrir*, an order addressed to the Adana governorate was received."[96] Therefore, in this case, we can assume that T'oros was forced to make the payment through not only the Armenian administration but the Ottoman administration as well. The next case detailed in the same report gives yet another example supporting the same principle and practice. Nishan Kanaryan had deserted his family in Agn and left for Italy. The patriarchate asked him to return home, and if he refused to do so he would be required to make a monthly payment to his family. Underneath the reply of the Sublime Porte included in the report it was stated that his whereabouts were unknown.

In all these cases, a legal annulment of marriage had not taken place and the family was left destitute, creating the conditions of a de facto divorce. All three of those husbands did not take care of their families, but had not applied for annulments either, likely because applying for one would have required the payment of alimony, or perhaps even harsher consequences in Khach'ig's case. To avoid such penalties, all three men simply left their families destitute. Armenian ecclesiastical law decreed in cases where the couple no longer lived together without a legitimate reason for separation, such as the man abandoning his wife, the property should be equally divided in order to financially secure the wife.[97] Therefore, in all three cases, ecclesiastical law attempts to punish the men for leaving the women destitute without reason. According to Melik'-T'ankyan, abandonment was a serious issue that not even penalties seemed to prevent.[98]

Khach'ig and Mariam's separation would today be termed as "irreconcilable differences" or "temperamental incompatibility," which was not a valid reason for an annulment. Of course, Khach'ig might have argued something else, for instance, that she returned with her child to Gallipoli by her own will. If the couple was willing to divorce, both sides must have jointly applied and made a reasonable case for it, but there was no guarantee it would be granted. Melik'-T'ankyan introduces cases, especially from the period of Mgrdich Khrimyan as catholicos of all Armenians in Echmiadzin (1893–1907), in which there was no valid reason per ecclesiastical law to grant a marriage annulment, but as both sides were becoming increasingly disadvantaged by the situation as time went on, it became preferable to grant the annulment than to prioritize the sanctity of the marital bond.[99]

Khatug and Sara from Çarşamba, like Mariam from Gallipoli and the woman from Akşehir, intervened in the existing legal and societal systems in the villages where they lived. By not changing their statements despite threats, by acknowledging their right to go with a man, by applying to the *kadı* court to obtain the right for alimony, by asking for a marriage annulment because of their husbands' impotence, or by perhaps pretending to be mentally ill or pregnant, they each advocated for their rights in their own ways. They formulated expressions of their agency and their own unique methods of resistance. Most of the time, this strong agency was the reason for the creation of these documents, opening up a new understanding before us and making their realities accessible through these valuable historical primary sources. They were each aware of their precarious, dependent, fragile, and threatened position within society, but refused to be submissive to it.

All of these cases involved a spatial change in some way or another, be it leaving one's own home or village or settling as a second wife in the house of a person with whom they had no prior legally binding marital bond. Even Anna, the wife of T'orosoghlu Harut'iwn, who was said to have some kind of incurable mental disease, left her house for certain periods to live with relatives. Allowances permitting someone to leave one's house, or village, or to settle somewhere else can happen based only on certain territorial and temporal regulations, both at the level of the Armenian and Ottoman administrations. The interrogators' logic read through the order in which the questions were asked demonstrates that these "moves" were not automatically permitted but subjected to mechanisms of control, and that those being questioned had transgressed them.

Kayseri, 1858; Divriği and Samsun, 1867; and Beykoz, 1865: Testifying to Marital Status, Providing Notarial Attestations

It was the duty of the local Armenian administrations to verify whether the man and woman who applied for marriage were actually eligible to marry. There were a series of checks that had to be done before getting married and therefore both sides had to inform their local administration in advance so that these investigations could be carried out. One of the most critical issues that had to be clarified was whether the couple had any kinship relations. Another was whether there were any obstacles to either of them getting married.

An Armeno-Turkish document was written in Constantinople in 1858 on the marital status of a certain Meshejioghlu Garabet from Kayseri.[100] The document stated that prominent Armenians from Kayseri living in Constantinople were asked about Garabet's marital status, to which they testified that Garabet was neither engaged nor married in the provinces. The document was signed by Mahdesi Manuk Manukyan, testifying that Garabet was single and that he could get married by showing it to his local administration.

The case of Nazlı, the daughter of Manendyan Krikor from Divrig (Divriği), was different. Apparently, Nazlı remarried Khach'adur Manukyan, who came from a *sarraf* (moneylender) family (mentioned as *Sarafents*), before obtaining the annulment of her first marriage. Therefore, a testimony signed by prominent Armenians from Divrig living in Constantinople stated that Nazlı was still the wife of T'oros, son of Vartan Ayvazyan from the same town, making her marriage to Manaukyan unlawful. There are fifteen signatures under the testimony, dated March 10, 1867,[101] and the document is addressed directly to the patriarch.

That same year on September 27, a certificate sent from Samson (Samsun) to Constantinople testified that Sirak from Ünya (Ünye), living in Samsun, had lost his wife a year before and had not remarried up to the day of the testimony, making him eligible for a second marriage.[102] The document, signed by Vicar (*Atoragal*) Mikael Tetleyan and priest Kevork Simonyan, was addressed to the patriarch of the time, Boghos Taktakyan.[103]

Armenian administrations both in the capital and in the provinces also served notarial functions for the members of their *millet*. On January 18, 1865, the local council of Beykoz testified that Gusina Kerovpyan, an inhabitant of Beykoz, had applied to the council to authorize Khach'ig Agha Papazyan as her representative in court.[104] The notarial attestation was sealed by the Armenian administration of Beykoz and signed by the head of the council and his deputy. It is important to mention that the local councils were established by order of the patriarchate in 1861. According to the order, every fifty houses were entitled to have a representative, who should be literate and over the age of twenty-five.[105] This testimony shows that those councils had been established and fulfilled notarial functions within the Armenian administration.

Conclusion

Throughout this book I analyzed multiple legal functions and juridical roles played by the Armenian administration, demonstrating how its entitlements were not limited to family law. It is important to note that while it is often mentioned that non-Muslim *millets* were entitled to apply their legal traditions according to their customary law, there is no literature on how family law functioned for Armenians at the height of Tanzimat. Second, the Archives of the Patriarchate show how the Armenian administration was directly involved in court cases related to land issues between Armenians and Kurds as well as debit-credit issues between Armenians and Rums, and was in close cooperation with Ottoman authorities. Hence, the increasingly centralized Armenian administration was actively involved in all matters of daily life, family law, provincial oppression, conflicts between the *millets*, and issues related to land and taxation.

Following the recurring formulaic expressions found in the documents led me to the first part of this chapter regarding institutions of incarceration, namely, the Armenian Hospital and the Imperial Yarn Factory. Both the Ottoman Archives and those of the Armenian Patriarchate, along with other primary and secondary sources, indicate there was a direct link between Ottoman industrialization, forced labor, and incarceration. Further, the Armenian Hospital also appears in these documents as a place of incarceration or exile. Further research is required on both the hospital and the yarn factory in order to understand more about their differences, such as for what reasons a convicted person would be sent to the hospital rather than the yarn factory. The nature of the crime and the involvement of a person from another faith may have played a role in this choice. However, the collection of Armenian children from the provinces makes one point abundantly clear: the yarn factory signified much more than a place where people were sent for minor crimes. It was an institution that set the pace of Ottoman industrialism, giving a rhythm and direction to it, and was fueled at least in part by Armenian forced labor.

In almost all the cases presented here, despite their structural weakness, Armenian women of the provinces did not abide by the territorialities and mechanisms of control imposed upon them, neither those of the Armenian nor Ottoman administrations. Leaving their villages when they were not allowed to, or deciding to live with another man when their husbands had left them without protection and money, were choices in determining their own destinies. Güldane's demand for help and the responses of the women in Çarşamba to their interrogators show powerful agency to advocate for their rights, be it to gain alimony or to have a male guardian.

In each chapter, I underlined the central role of the patriarch within the system of the Armenian administration, such as how the patriarch was actively involved in the juridical functions of the Armenian administration. Further, the patriarch had the authority and entitlement to create new legal practices based on existing legal norms and traditions. Thus, in many cases included in this study, when a personal or collective petition was sent to Constantinople to ask for the patriarch's order on an issue of family law, more often than not it was because a local Armenian administration was requesting the patriarchate's ad hoc support for a new practice that was usually against legal tradition. In other words, the lawmaking authority and entitlement of patriarchs were known and often applied for. Yet the patriarchs' decisions were very often contested by the adjustment they had to make in order to contend with the structural inequalities in a highly hierarchized societal order.

Conclusion

The decision to annihilate the Ottoman Armenians was a turning point in history. It marked their erasure from the empire's past, present, and future, which by extension includes today's Turkey. Intrinsic to physical annihilation is the annihilation of temporality, meaning once erased from their (home)lands, Armenian temporality also came to an end. In that sense, this book is an intervention reminding us of the existence of Armenian temporalities, matters of daily life, and the issues they had to confront both in Constantinople and the provinces. While it has been the merchants, *Amiras*, politicians, and intellectuals who usually represent mid-nineteenth-century Armenians in the historiography, Armenians were first and foremost peasants, villagers, migrant workers, and vulnerable women who inhabited very perilous positions in the provinces. The archival documents in this book offer a striking image of Ottoman life as multilayered and multidimensional in a way we have hardly ever seen before.

The first chapter is about the evolution of the Armenian administration throughout the nineteenth century. By closely reading the publications of the patriarchate and the Armenian administration, this chapter reveals the legal and administrative subjugation of Armenians to the Ottoman centralization process. The high expectations of egalitarianism deriving from the lofty ideals of Tanzimat were proven to be misplaced. While the centralization process entitled the patriarchate to find solutions to the problems of its *millet*, its authority was constantly contested and undermined by the Ottoman administration.

The Armenian Nizamname was a foundational text that set out the comprehensive mechanisms of administration while also reaffirming long-existing rights. Yet it was not a static text that completely standardized how the Armenian administration operated and its powers once and for all; instead, Armenian administration adopted other rules and regulations throughout its existence creating new positions or changing the duties of the Armenian administrative bodies. In order to understand the reasons for and nature of these changes, I followed the publications of the Armenian administration from the 1830s to the 1880s, tracing those structural and administrative reorganizations and adjustments. The Nizamname's ratification, its areas of authority, and its entitlements were constantly questioned and undermined by the Ottoman administration both on the local level and empire-wide, resulting in a constant struggle on the part of Armenian patriarchs and administrations to maintain it. Armenian Nizamname remains the most comprehensive and legitimate administrative text of reference even now when it comes to the elections of the patriarchs and other decisive matters of the Armenian administration.

This book sees Tanzimat first and foremost as a process of reconquest and restructuring through military operations. It also unpacks the undermining of Armenian institutions and their entitlements in the villages, towns, and cities outside the capital and of the Armenian administration at large. This loss of agency and authority created a structural unevenness amongst Armenians, as the changing local power relations left the Armenian population in the provinces and their institutions no choice but to constantly petition the central Ottoman as well as Armenian administrations for solutions to their ever-growing number of problems and oppressions. Through its centralization process, the Ottoman administration was forcefully integrating the autochthonous Armenian regions into the imperial capital, but at the same time was abandoning those Armenian inhabitants to the mercy of local power holders. Provincial oppressions resulted in Armenians banned from leaving their villages or buying provisions, condemned to famine, forced to pay high and unjust taxes, and subject to criminals and their own neighbors who could attack them with impunity. In other words, their fate and continued existence in those lands were no longer in the interest of the Ottoman administration. When this situation is considered in the context of the state already having consolidated alliances along its eastern borders and established full military and administrative control over the regions of Cilicia, the Sanjak of Iskenderun, and northern Mesopotamia, its post-Tanzimat initiatives such as the establishment of the Hamidiye Light Cavalry in the 1890s simply cannot be regarded as an unexpected or exceptional development. The Tanzimat-era violence of military conquests, exiles, and bureaucratic tools of governance was replaced by state-orchestrated and organized criminal gangs (*çetes*). Mass killing, mass migration, and mass destruction soon followed. Hence, the main motto of Tanzimat that heralded a new time marked by the security of life, property, and honor in actuality was one of insecurity of life, confiscation of properties, and increasing dishonor for Armenians, especially in the provinces.

The favored mode of governance during Tanzimat was to project the image of a progressive state, while in reality intentionally prolonging conflicts, leaving the complaints of its citizens unanswered, creating bureaucratic hurdles, and utilizing these troubles to collect valuable information. Based on the archival material discussed and analyzed in this book, it could be said that the nineteenth century was one in which a deep temporal and territorial gap was created between the Armenians of the capital and those of the provinces. The more the provinces were unable to make their voices heard as their problems accumulated, the more the authority and entitlement of the patriarchate as the central administration of all Ottoman Armenians were undermined. This unbridgeable gap, especially during the second half of the nineteenth century, can be read as the noncontemporaneity of the contemporaries in Harry Harootunian's conceptualization.[1] Accordingly, the living conditions in the provinces and the capital differed so greatly that the unevenness between them became irreconcilable. This is structurally represented in Khrimyan's term by his being a patriarch hailing from the heart of the provinces. He must have keenly felt and deeply understood this noncontemporaneity of being out of time and step with the Armenians in Constantinople, and indeed struggled mightily to properly address those differences institutionally within the administration. Therefore, I read Khrimyan's resignation as patriarch in 1873 as a turning point that hinted at the approaching dead end for Ottoman Armenians altogether.[2]

Despite constituting the empire's largest group of Christians, very little scholarly work has been done on the relations between Armenians and the Rum. The Ottoman administration's prioritization of the non-Muslim *millets* into a hierarchy played an important role in fuelling conflicts between them, such as over matters of conversion, the sharing of cemeteries, and land disputes. From the state's perspective, such turmoil was an effective tool of governance as it hindered the groups' possible collaboration. However, there were regions such as Heraklion and Erzurum where the Armenian and Rum administrations supported each other. Notably, both these regions were ones in which the state had long-running conflicts with the local populations. Relations between the Armenian and Rum *millets* were much more complicated in the capital, or places like Antalya and Bandırma where the Ottoman administration had comparatively better control. The detailed collective petitions sent from Bandırma and Antalya on complex cases of conversion reveal the various layers of power dynamics, territorial, and temporal rules as well as the functioning of local power relations in these core regions of the Empire. Yet the personal petition of Nikolaos Polikhron Kabakaroghlu to his regional Armenian administration asking for a trial to prove his innocence indicates the possibility of seeking justice at the intercommunal level.

All primary source material presented throughout this book allows me to draw another conclusion about the nature of the Ottoman bureaucratic system, which is that it was much more pragmatic, multilingual, and multigraphized than we would have known. Both the Ottoman Archives and the Archives of the Armenian Patriarchate are multilingual and multigraphized, and the documents clearly show that translation was part of their daily life.

The chapter on the juridical entitlements of the patriarchate along with the Armenian administration explores the variety of duties undertaken by the local and central administrations as well as their limits. The medical attestation that allowed the woman who applied for it to have her marriage annulled in 1847, the struggle of Mariam from Gallipoli to get her alimony and inheritance in 1848, the interrogation process in Çarşamba in 1868, and the patriarchate's notarial functions regarding the whereabouts or marital status of a given person are unique sources demonstrating how the Armenian juridical mechanism functioned in the Ottoman Empire. Furthermore, formulaic expressions in these documents unearthed another previously unknown layer of established practices, that of institutional incarceration at both the Armenian hospital and the yarn factory. Especially in the case of imprisonment in the yarn factory, there are clear implications of forced labor under very harsh conditions from the 1830s onward, not just for adults but also for Armenian children. These children were collected from the provinces to supplement the factory's production capacity, for whom it appears to have been a one-way ticket to hell. Slave laborers like them must have been a considerable driver of Ottoman industrialization in the nineteenth century, and thus it should be rethought in the light of the material presented here about the role of incarceration practices, forced labor, and slavery.

This book argues that Tanzimat set the rules of an engineered shift over decades during which Armenians became the weakest and most fragile *millet*, increasingly outcasts in the eyes of the Ottoman administration. Armenian men were gradually forced into the life of migrant workers, leaving their families behind to earn the money needed for the abusive and oppressive taxes imposed upon them. Thus, Armenian women were mainly left alone in the villages, adding a dimension of physical vulnerability to their existing social one. While Tanzimat has long been considered a period of "progress" and "reform" that afforded a system of rights for its citizens, when seen from Armenian sources a much different picture appears. Tanzimat in fact did not work for Armenians, nor does it seem to have ever intended to work for them either. The Armenian administration and the smallest unit of its society, the family, were both targeted throughout the nineteenth century to the point of utter sabotage. It is within such a framework that the sharp increase in forced Islamization and kidnapping of Armenian women in the villages late in the century should be understood. Doubtlessly, the process engineered during Tanzimat culminated in 1915 and its aftermath, engendering a temporal reversal, whereby the present was noncontemporanized.

For the Armenian administration in the capital, Tanzimat simultaneously denoted both centralization through the ratification of the Nizamname and the undermining of its authorities and entitlements whenever possible. Hence, the peripheries were becoming forcefully integrated into the center through structural and administrative changes that created an unevenness in Armenian temporal and territorial existence that was eventually to be extinguished utterly. Considering Tanzimat as a "failed reform attempt" because of wars and territories lost, or rising nationalisms, hides and ignores its foundational role in shaping the subsequent Hamidian period. This study instead emphasizes the era's central importance as a period of governmental continuance connecting the earlier and later periods. It was a time during which Ottoman administrative structures were reorganized and strengthened through the development of various tools and resources, including data collection, the know-how of Prussian Army officers, military conquests, and new alliances with certain groups in the provinces by which the state developed a reservoir of knowledge about its areas of least control. This information was supplemented with data collected by the Armenian local and central administrations about its population, monasteries, property, and what was gleaned from petitions and *takrirs* submitted by Armenians in service of the Ottoman centralization process and to assert their rights. Tanzimat's new administrative and structural mechanisms made the divisions between the *millets* sharper and more hierarchized along confessional and religious lines, reproducing a much more rigid system of superiority and inferiority to come. After seven decades of military and administrative interventions, along with constant structural, social, demographic, and ethnoreligious changes undertaken in the provinces, the Ottoman Empire and its administrative cadres chose to utilize this knowledge against its own population. And this is exactly what happened in 1915.

Appendix

Notes

Bibliography

Index

APPENDIX

Selected Documents from the Archive of the Armenian Patriarchate of Constantinople from Nubar Library, Paris

[illegible]

~~000012~~

1856 [illegible]

[illegible]

[illegible]

000013

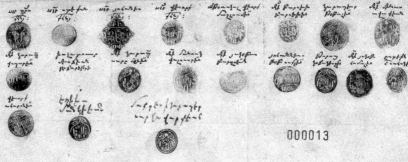

~~000001~~

[illegible]

[illegible] 12. Օգոստ 1847.

[illegible]

[illegible]

[illegible]
[illegible]
[illegible]

~~000002~~

[illegible]

[illegible]

1847

[illegible]

BN APC/CP12/106

1869. [illegible]
[illegible]

Հ. [illegible]
Պ. [illegible]
Հ. [illegible]
Պ. [illegible]
Հ. [illegible]
Պ. [illegible]
Հ. [illegible]
Պ. [illegible]
Հ. [illegible]
Պ. [illegible]
Հ. [illegible]
Պ. [illegible]
Հ. [illegible]
Պ. [illegible]
[illegible]
[illegible]
Հ. [illegible]
Պ. [illegible]
[illegible]
[illegible]
[illegible]
Հ. [illegible]
[illegible]

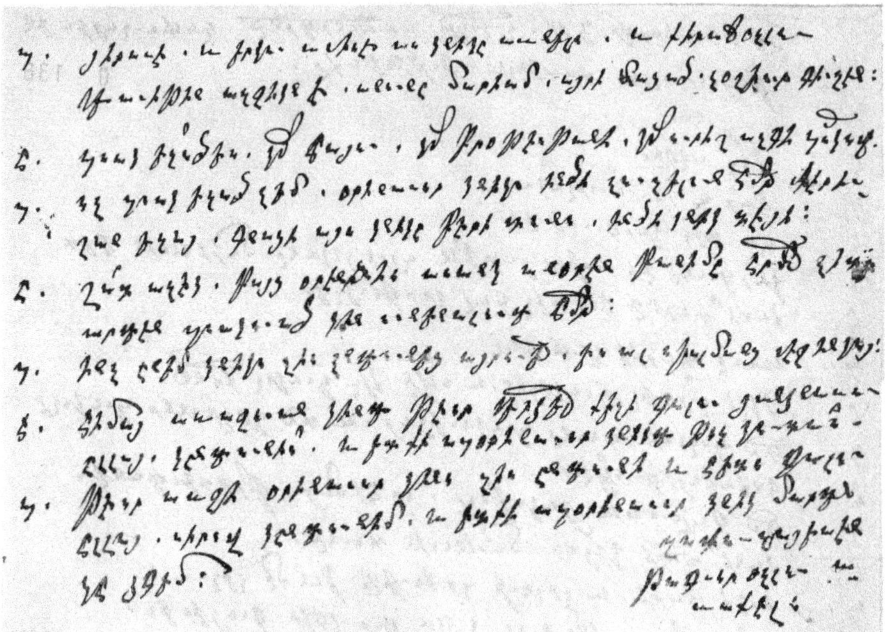

[illegible]

68 [illegible] 24:

[illegible]

[illegible]
[illegible]

Հ. [illegible]
Պ. [illegible]
Հ. [illegible]
Պ. [illegible]
Հ. [illegible]
Պ. [illegible]
Հ. [illegible]
Պ. [illegible]
[illegible]
Հ. [illegible]
Պ. [illegible]
Հ. [illegible]
Պ. [illegible]
Հ. [illegible]
Պ. [illegible]
Հ. [illegible]
Պ. [illegible]
Հ. [illegible]
[illegible]
Պ. [illegible]
[illegible]
Հ. [illegible]
Պ. [illegible]
[illegible]

Հ. [illegible]

Պ. այո՛, [illegible]

Հ. [illegible]

Պ. [illegible]

Հ. [illegible]

Պ. [illegible]
[illegible]

Հ. [illegible]

Պ. այո՛, [illegible]

Հ. [illegible]

Պ. [illegible]
[illegible]

Հ. [illegible]

Պ. [illegible]
[illegible]

[illegible]

Թագաւորութեան աստիճանը [illegible] [illegible] թագուհւոյն։
Իշխանութեան պատիւը [illegible] [illegible]։

Ե. [illegible] գիւղէն [illegible] ետք [illegible] [illegible] գիւղը։
Զ. [illegible] [illegible] [illegible] [illegible] [illegible] [illegible]
Է. [illegible] [illegible] թագաւորութեան [illegible] [illegible] [illegible]
[illegible] [illegible] [illegible] [illegible]։
Ը. [illegible] թագաւորութեան [illegible] [illegible] [illegible] [illegible] [illegible]
[illegible] [illegible] [illegible] [illegible] [illegible] [illegible] [illegible]
[illegible] [illegible] [illegible] [illegible] [illegible] [illegible]
[illegible] [illegible] թագաւորութեան [illegible] [illegible] [illegible]
[illegible] [illegible] [illegible] [illegible] [illegible] [illegible]
[illegible] [illegible] [illegible] [illegible] [illegible]։
Թ. [illegible] [illegible] [illegible]։
Ժ. [illegible] [illegible] [illegible] [illegible] [illegible] … [illegible]։

[illegible]
[illegible]։

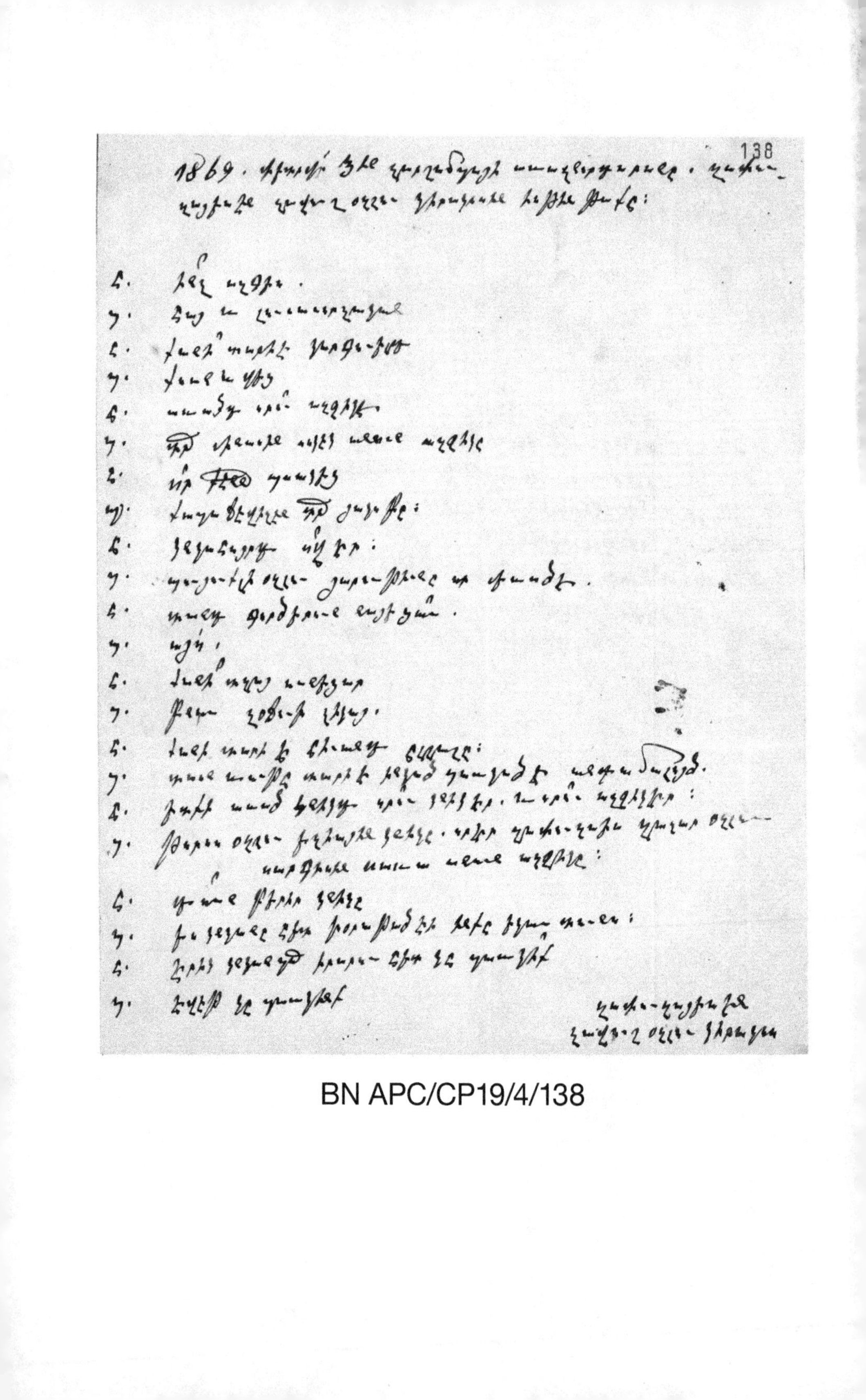

1869. [illegible]
[illegible]

Հ. [illegible]
Պ. [illegible]
Հ. [illegible]
Պ. [illegible]
Հ. [illegible]
Պ. [illegible]
Հ. [illegible]
Պ. [illegible]
Հ. [illegible]
Պ. [illegible]
Հ. [illegible]
Պ. [illegible]
Հ. [illegible]
Պ. [illegible]
Հ. [illegible]
Պ. [illegible]
Հ. [illegible]
Պ. [illegible]
[illegible]
Հ. [illegible]
Պ. [illegible]
Հ. [illegible]
Պ. [illegible]

[illegible]
[illegible]

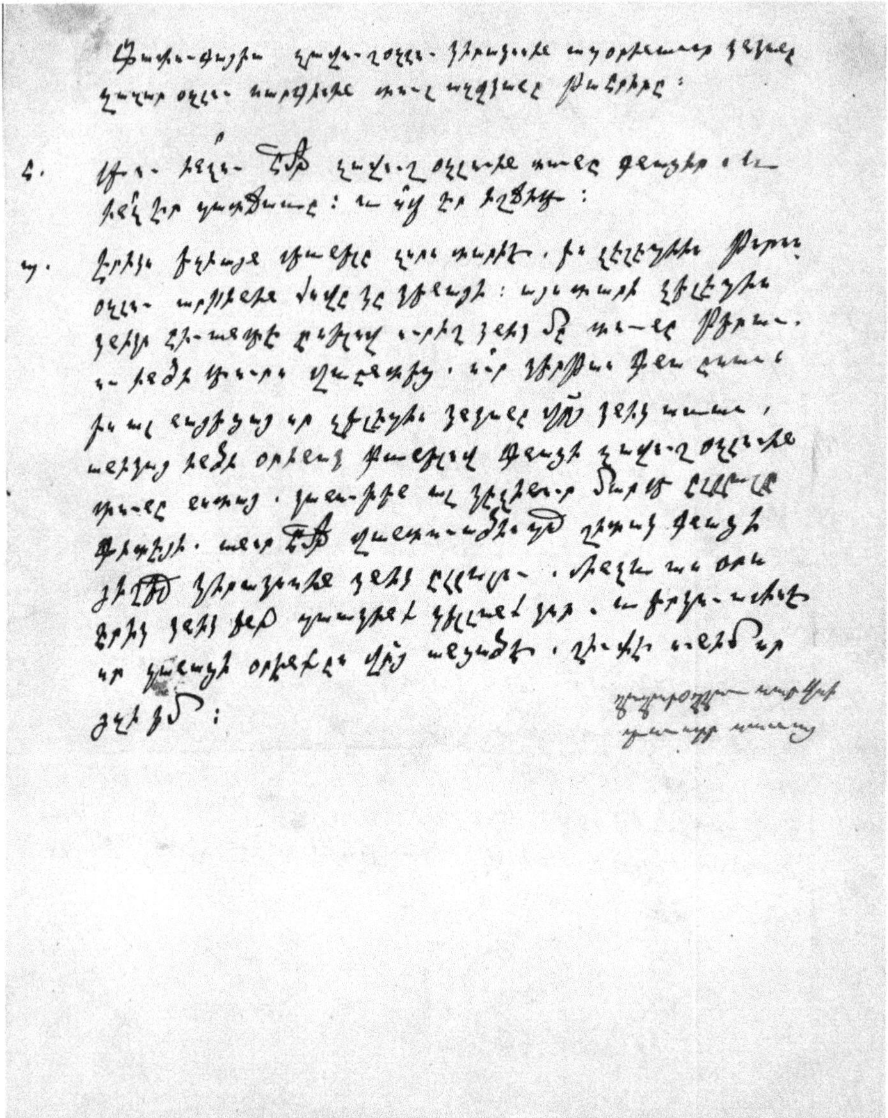

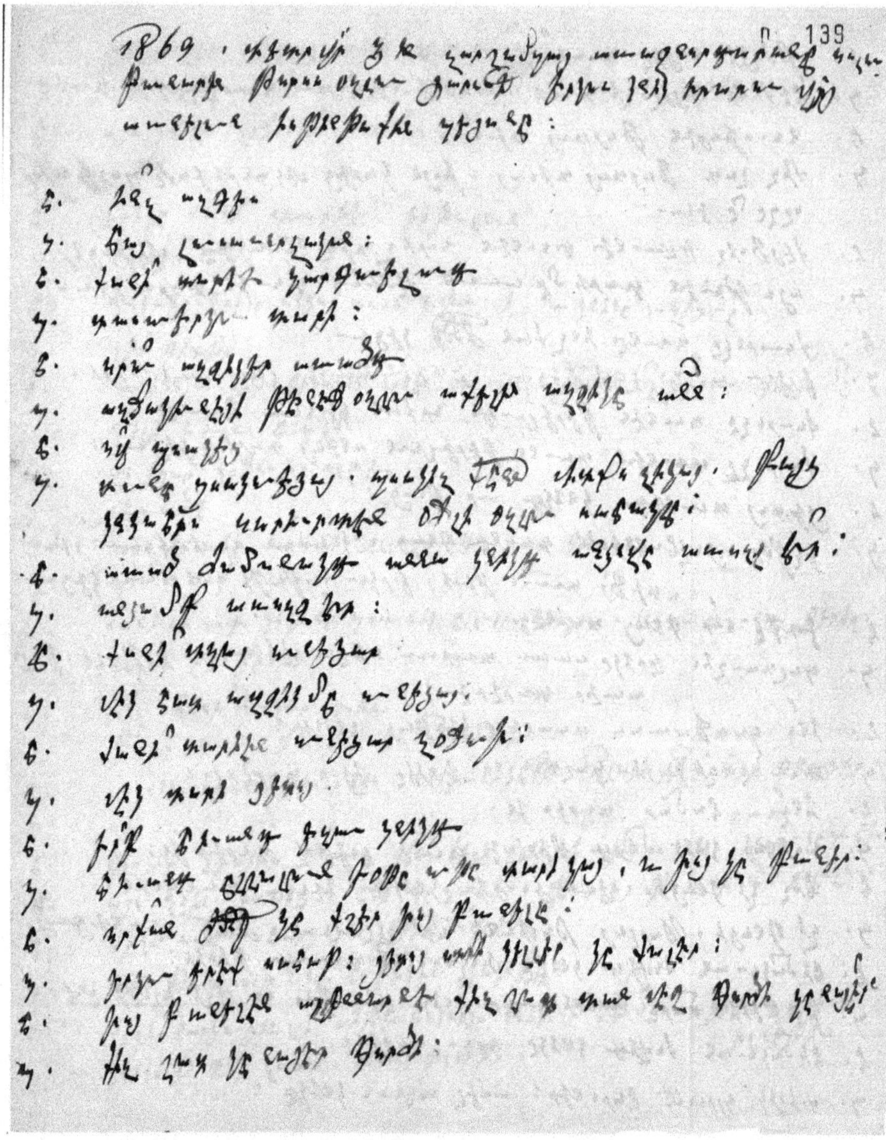

139

1869

BN APC/CP19/4/139

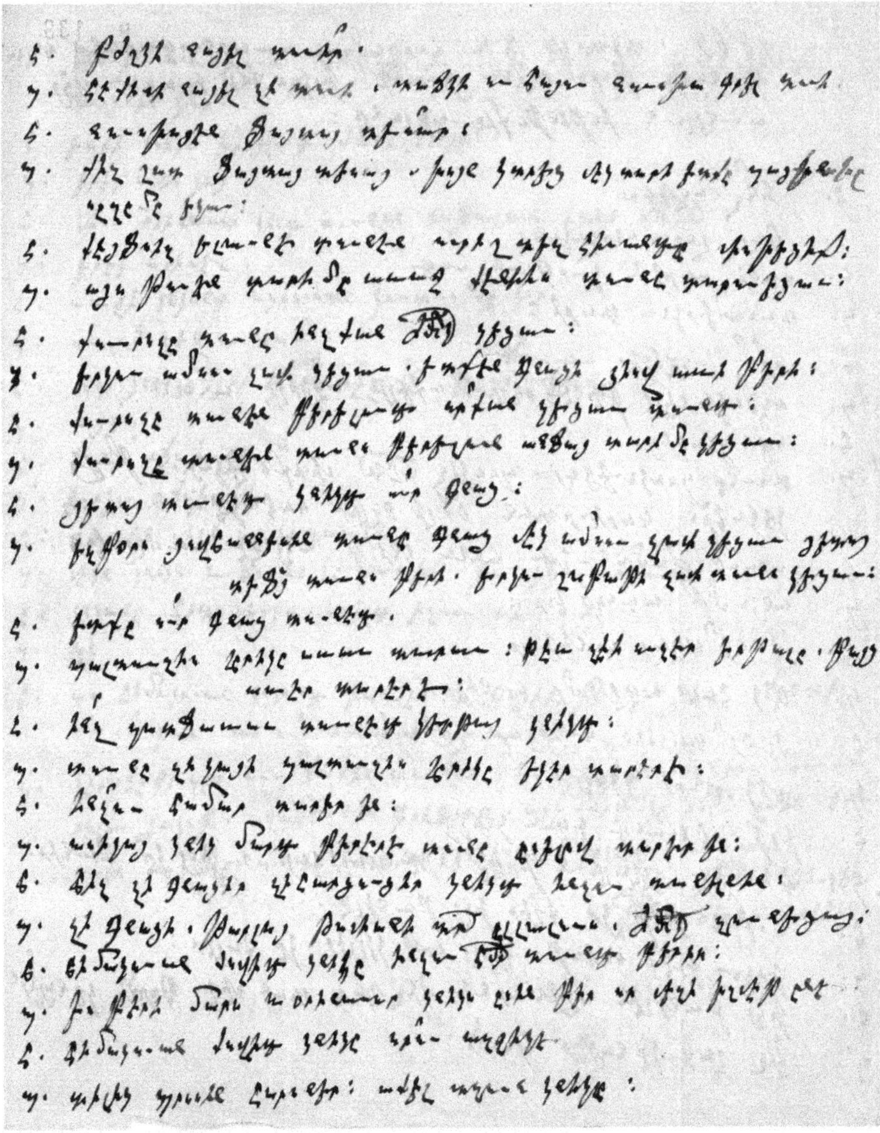

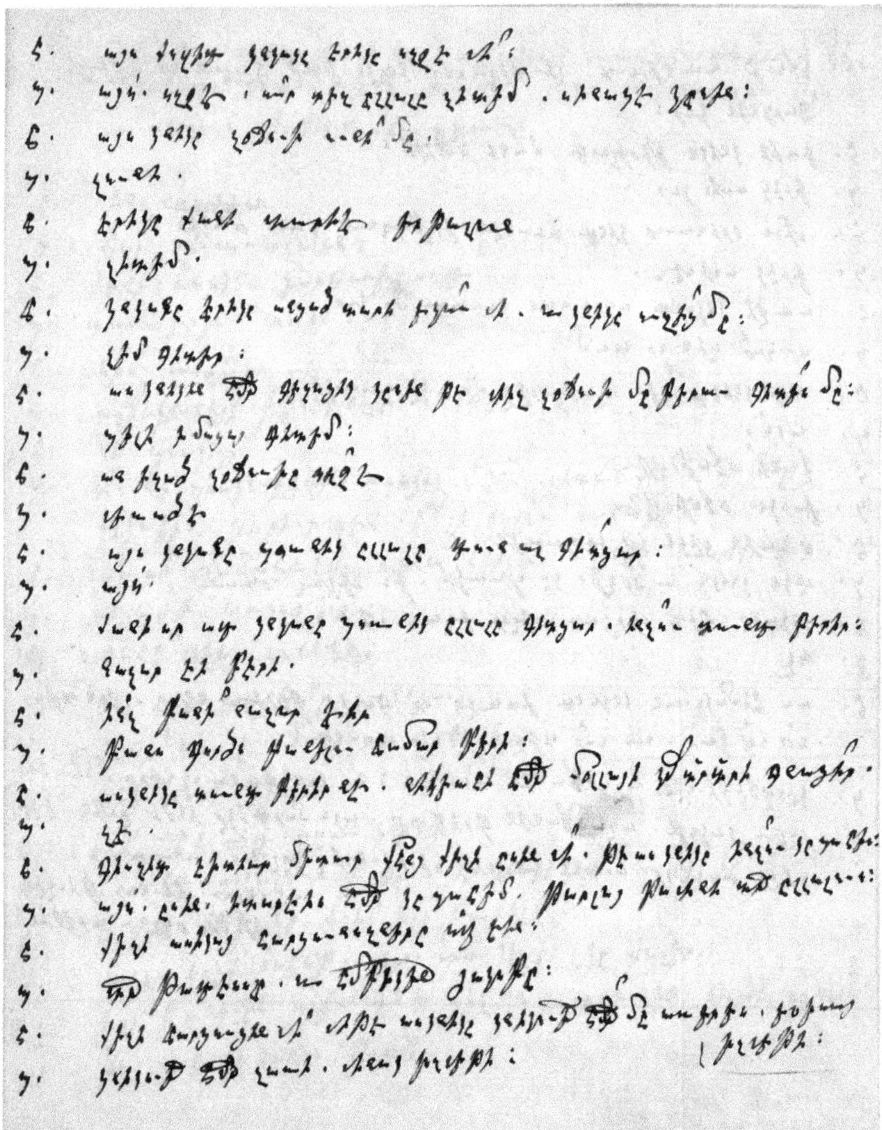
Հ. [illegible]
Պ. Այո՛. [illegible]
Հ. [illegible]
Պ. Չունիմ.
Հ. [illegible]
Պ. [illegible]
Հ. [illegible]
Պ. [illegible]
Հ. [illegible]
Պ. [illegible]
Հ. [illegible]
Պ. [illegible]
Հ. [illegible]
Պ. Այո՛.
Հ. [illegible]
Պ. [illegible]
Հ. [illegible]
Պ. [illegible]
Հ. [illegible]
Պ. [illegible]
Հ. [illegible]
Պ. [illegible]
Հ. [illegible]
Պ. [illegible]
Հ. [illegible]
Պ. [illegible]

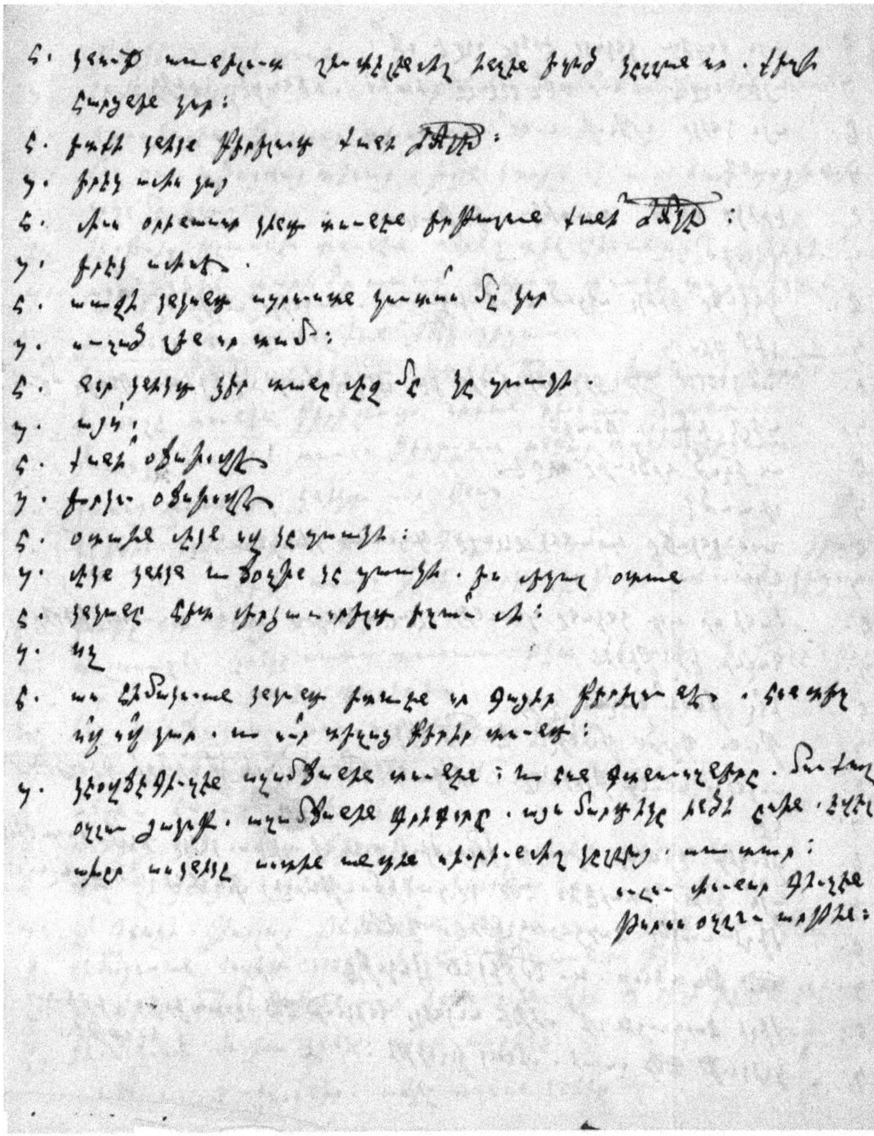

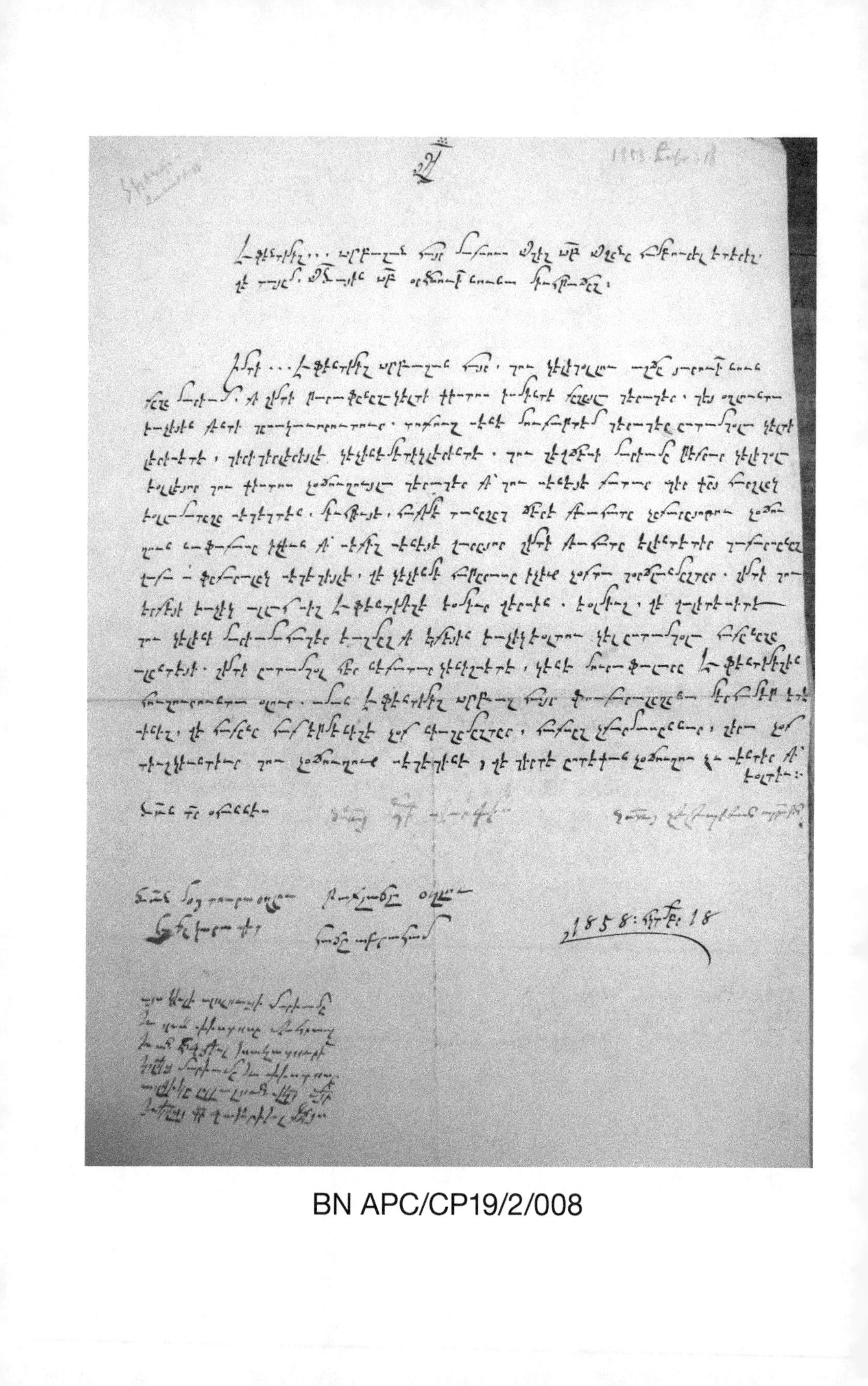

[illegible]

[illegible]

[illegible]

1858: [illegible] 18

[illegible]

BN APC/CP19/2/008

1858

15 [illegible]

قرتال قصبه‌سنده قرائی اجلا الحقیقه اولاد

حسن دربندم کائنه معلوم المقدار تارله

ایکی قطعه سند مقطوعه‌سنجه متصرف

اولدیغم خاچیک ولد مهراب خوبه اولوب

پیسروس نامنده بر نفر کبیره

قرنیه حاعدا اولوزی اولیمیوب

مرسوم الیکه الوبه بر صاته وتمه دوش

اولدیغی تقییه تقتمتنه ومرسوم تارلای حدلوی

علیه دن بالجمع وتارلوی متصرف اخره

بیع وفراغت ایتمه اوزره طرفمه

قالیانجی اوغلی مغاجی اوانس

ولد مقردیچ دخی بطریقخانه قره

وکیل نصب وتعیین ایلدم

اولوقه کیفیت معلوم اولمغه

اوزره اشبو علم وخبر وکیل

مرسوم یدینه ویرلدی

نامه حاکی

کندو عقارینی بعد الانتقال اخره

[illegible]

1865 · [illegible] 18 [illegible]

[illegible]

BN APC/CP/20/13

144

Πρὸς τὸν Θ. Πανιερώτατον τοῦ Ἀρχιεπισκόπου Νικομηδείας Κον Κον Στέφανον, Τοποτηρητὴν τῶν
Ἀρμενικῶν Πατριαρχείων

ιδ. ιδ.

ἐκ Κωνσταντινουπόλεως

1862 : յուլ. 2 : [illegible]
[illegible]
[illegible]
[illegible]
[illegible]

[illegible]

473

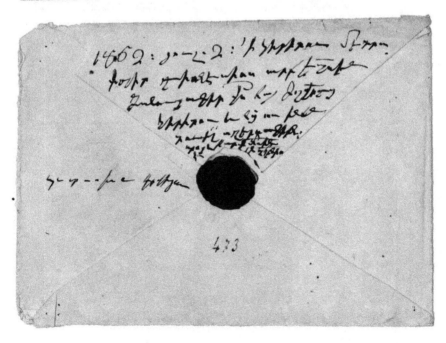

BN APC/CP12/8/144

Πρός τήν Α. Πανιερότητα τοῦ Ἀρχιεπισκόπου Νικομηδείας Κ.ου Κ.ου Στεφάνου Τοποτηρητήν τῶν Ἀρμενικῶν Πατριαρχείων

Πανιερώτατε!

Μετά τήν ἔρευναν τῆς ἐφέσεως μοι εὐμενοῦς ἐγγράφου τῆς, σπεύδω εὐσεβάστως νά τῇ ἐκδηλώσω, ὅτι οἱ ἐνταῦθα διαμένοντες Ἀρμένιοι καί ἐνίοτε ἐκτελοῦσαι εὐχετήρια ἀναφοράν, ἥν συνημμένως τῇ ἀποστέλλω, παραπονούμενοι δι' αὐτῆς κατά τοῦ ἱερέως αὐτῶν Κυρίου Παρασέθ, καθό μή ἐκπληροῦντος τά τῆς ἱερωσύνης αὐτοῦ καθήκοντα ἀκριβῶς, ἕνεκα τῆς συνεχοῦς ἀπουσίας του, καί καθό μή καλῶς συμπεριφερομένου πρός αὐτούς τε καί τήν γηραιάν μητέρα του. Ἐπειδή δέ διά τῆς ἀναφορᾶς των ταύτης ζητοῦνται οὗτοι, ἵνα καταστήσω τά παράπονά των γνωστά πρός τήν Ὑμ. Πανιερότητα, δέν χάνω διά τοῦτο, ὅπως τῇ ἀποστείλω τήν παροῦσάν μου, ἵνα εὐαρεστηθῇ νά λάβῃ πρόνοιαν περί τῆς διορθώσεως τούτων ὅπως οἶδε συμφερώ-

Ιερον δ' αυτούς. Ταύτα περί τούτου εις πληροφορίαν της, λαμβάνω δέ. Εν Ηρακλείω Κρήτης τη 24. Ιουνίου 1862.

Της υψηλοτάτης Εκλαμπρότητος

όλως πρόθυμος δούλος

θερμός ευχέτης

+ ο Μητροπολίτης Κρήτης

Διονύσιος.

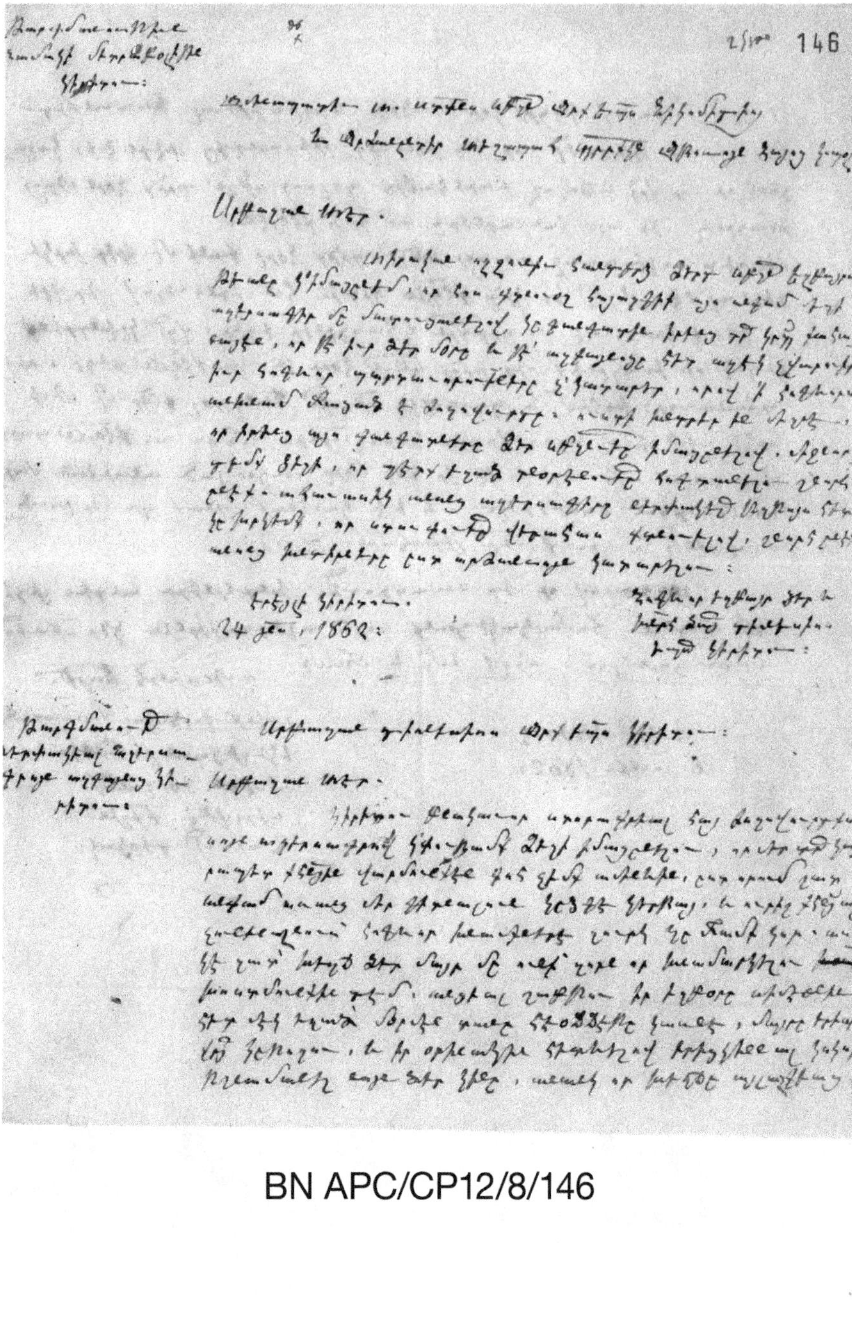

BN APC/CP12/8/146

[illegible]
[illegible]
[illegible]
[illegible]

[illegible]
[illegible]
[illegible]
[illegible]
[illegible]
[illegible]
[illegible]
[illegible]
[illegible]

[illegible]
[illegible]
[illegible]

[illegible]

[illegible]
6 [illegible] 1862.

[illegible]
[illegible]
[illegible]
[illegible]
[illegible]

Πρὸς τὴν Α. Σ. Πανιερότητα τὸν Μητροπολίτην Κρήτης Κύριον Κ.ον Διονύσιον

Ἴσον ἀπαράλλακτον ἐκ τῶν Ἀρχείων

Σεβασμιώτατε

Οἱ εὐσεβάστως ὑποφαινόμενοι Χριστιανοὶ κάτοικοι τῆς πόλεως Σητείας συνιστάμεθα νὰ ὑποβάλωμεν τῇ ὑμετέρᾳ Πανιερότητι, ὅτι οὐδόλως ἔσμεν εὐχαριστημένοι ἀπό τε τὴν διαγωγὴν καὶ συμπεριφορὰν τοῦ ἱερέως ἡμῶν Κυρ. Καραολῆ, διότι εἴδομεν ὅτι ἐκμεταλλεύεται τὴν ἄγνοιαν ἡμῶν τὴν θέσιν αὐτοῦ καὶ ὅτι ἕνεκα τῆς ἀπουσίας του ἡμεῖς δὲν δυνάμεθα νὰ ἐκπληρώσωμεν τὰ θρησκευτικὰ ἡμῶν χρέη· ἐπίσης ἐζήτησε, ἵνα ἀποσπάσῃ μετὰ τοῦ ἀδελφοῦ του Σωμακῆ ἀπὸ τῆς γραίας μητρός του τὴν κατοχὴν τὴν ἰδιόκτητον οἰκίαν της, τὴν ὁποίαν ἀδίκως καὶ παρανόμως ἤδη κατακρατοῦντες ἀρνοῦνται νὰ παραδώσωσιν εἰς αὐτὴν τὴν ἀπαιτουμένην [illegible], οὐ μόνον ἀγνωμονοῦντες πρὸς τὴν μητέρα αὐτῶν, ἀλλὰ καὶ παραδεχόμενοι τοὺς προπηλακισμοὺς ἢ μαστιγώσεις αὐτῆς ὑπὸ τῶν [illegible] ἤδη μὴ ἔχουσα [illegible] καὶ [illegible] καταφεύγει εἰς [illegible] ὅπως δι' ἐλεημοσύνης [illegible]. Ἀναφερόμενοι πρὸς τὴν ὑμ. Πανιερότητα τοῦ θρησκευτικοῦ

Προσάπτει καὶ πρόγραμμα τοῦ ἐνταῦθα σχολείου, ὅπερ
κατέθεσεν αὐτοῦ, ὅπως ἴσως ὑποσημείωσιν ἐπαρκῆ
νὰ γνωστοποιήσῃ τὰ κατὰ τοῦ εἰρημένου ἱερέως ἡμῶν
δίκαια παράπονά μας πρὸς τὸν ἐν Κωνσταντινουπόλει Σεβα-
στὸν ἡμῶν Πατριάρχην πρὸς ὃν καὶ ἄλλοτε ἀνα-
φέρθημεν. ἀλλὰ αἱ πρὸς αὐτὸν ἀναφοραί μας ὑπεξη-
ρέθησαν παρὰ τοῦ ἐκεῖσε διαμένοντος υἱοῦ του καὶ
παρεκρατήθη, ὅπως ἀθῷος καταστήσῃ τοῦτον τὸν εἰρημένον
ἱερέα ἡμῶν δι' ἄλλων κειμένων τὰ ἀναιτιολόγητα
πρὸς τὸ ὑψηλὸν τῆς ἱερωσύνης ἀξίωμα προσπίπτει, κα-
θόσον δὲν δυνάμεθα ν' ἀνεχθῶμεν ἐπὶ πλέον τὸ ἐν
ἐκείνοις ἔλλειψις τῶν χρεῶν του καὶ τὴν ἀφόρητον
πρὸς ἡμᾶς καὶ τὴν τάξιν κακίαν του συμπεριφορὰν καὶ ὅλως ἀσυγχώρητον διαγωγήν του περὶ οὗ δύ-
νανται ἐὰν ἐρωτηθῇ ἡ ὑμ. Παναγιότης, ἵνα ἐξετά-
σῃ καὶ πληροφορηθῇ πρὸς βεβαίωσιν τῶν λόγων μας.

Ἐλπίζοντες ὅτι ἡ δικαία ἡμῶν αἴτησις θέλει
εὐμενῶς ἀποδεχθῆ διατελοῦμεν

Ἐν Προύσῃ τῇ 6. Ἰουνίου 1863.

Τῆς ὑμ. Παναγιότητος εὐπειθέστατοι δοῦλοι

Ἰάκωβος Κωστάκης Τζελεπής
Θανάσης Γεώργιος Σαμαρτζόγλου
Κυριακὸς Παπαγιαννάκ
Σεραφείμης Παπαδάκης
Χρηστάκης Ράλλης

... 2.11.68

Ρουφεζίου ἐφένδημ

Πόρσινελέν σερί μακσχαρλά τζουριλμεσέ σαχλδουσουμεζλέν
χαυσάγη ἐληγιριμζε γιούσερι κληίμ βί χαλιμιν ἤραλέ ἐλγιο-
ρύμ Χρίςοι ἐφένδημιμζιν ἀσυνά. χαὶ ρισαάτζιξεν βιλιδλλε-
ρι ἀσαλίρ ἀγγή βί φεναρί κλτζε χοβεριά τζαριν ἤνιέλα
ραφαν τζογασλαρινί νάζαραν χίρ νέτελ κεργεζή χαὶ βί κα
ρίρ μηνασισ βί ἐμήρ σαχιτρ ἤρσαιννης ἐζαλημη μεζάλ ἐλδ
χοβερνέλα λεγημάμεγιν χιγλαί ὀλαζεαρηψιν μαλιμινζ ὀλσ
χίρ νάσιλ ἤνά σερί λακίν ἐλιρέκ σίρ ράχρη χαὶ σ
κωλαρσινι χ κηδεζε σέκ αισιρη λερεζγέ λιμκίρ ἐγλ
λή σιτημιν σίρ ἀχζέ σανά σαρζερί γιουλίρ χρηςό
ἐφένδημιζε μαγημ λίρ τζίκιν ἤγιηρμιν ἐζλί σινηλ
λαβα ὀλδυλαν σαζέ χ κιτζινιρκι σίρ γέγρη χαὶ σ
λερεζ χεραιὲλ ἐλμελί ἀγαχιν ριζαή βιἐφένδημιν ριζα
σι ὀλαμαγιζαγή λεμκίρ ὀλδυλαν ἐφένδημι ἀφζαγασί
χαλιμιν ἤραλι ἐγλεμεζι μαισδλαν ἀφεοχαλα τζισαρίλκ
λινή σκωλαρ ἐλγαλη ἀγλημι σίζ σόζ τζηκαλαι ζιξ
ζημ ζερίρ λαζηκί κηζηνλε κωλλησή κατα χιζ σίρ κονζ
χριςιανλαί ὀλμαγιζα σέκ ζερίρ λεριζγιν κηρηφλαρ ὀλ
χμιλαν νάσιλ κηδεζα μεχρίμιλιν σα χαλσίζ τζηχελερ βί
μασδλαν χιλιάσιγιν χαιμημιν χαὶ ἤγρισιλι σηδηρ
νιζ σασδλά χιλάζ ἐλμιζ νηγιαζινλάνδλίρ.

BN APC/CP12/8/136

σινημ σολά 284 κυρσί χαικημ δάρμαν σοχλαρ-
κασυγ ίλινιλίνσαγγρα κηλτίλαν σοκαλαγ λαγά σα-
γαγρη χαι λαγας ἰλμελι σοχτηπημιφ.
Κυριοίν μαιωχανασηλαν. Νικολαος Κολιχρον
2 γανραλγη λαρια 1868 Κασναραλλ ἰρόμ
Μηχεληνλεν

υπρεονλέ Ζραστξαγχ Διστώλ ξφενλη Μη
ζφοστολιουνά Ερμενιάν. σύση
σλά

Ερμενιαν μηχελη μενλιστή

[illegible]

[illegible]

000003

[illegible]

1848 [illegible] 27

[illegible]

000004

1848 [illegible]

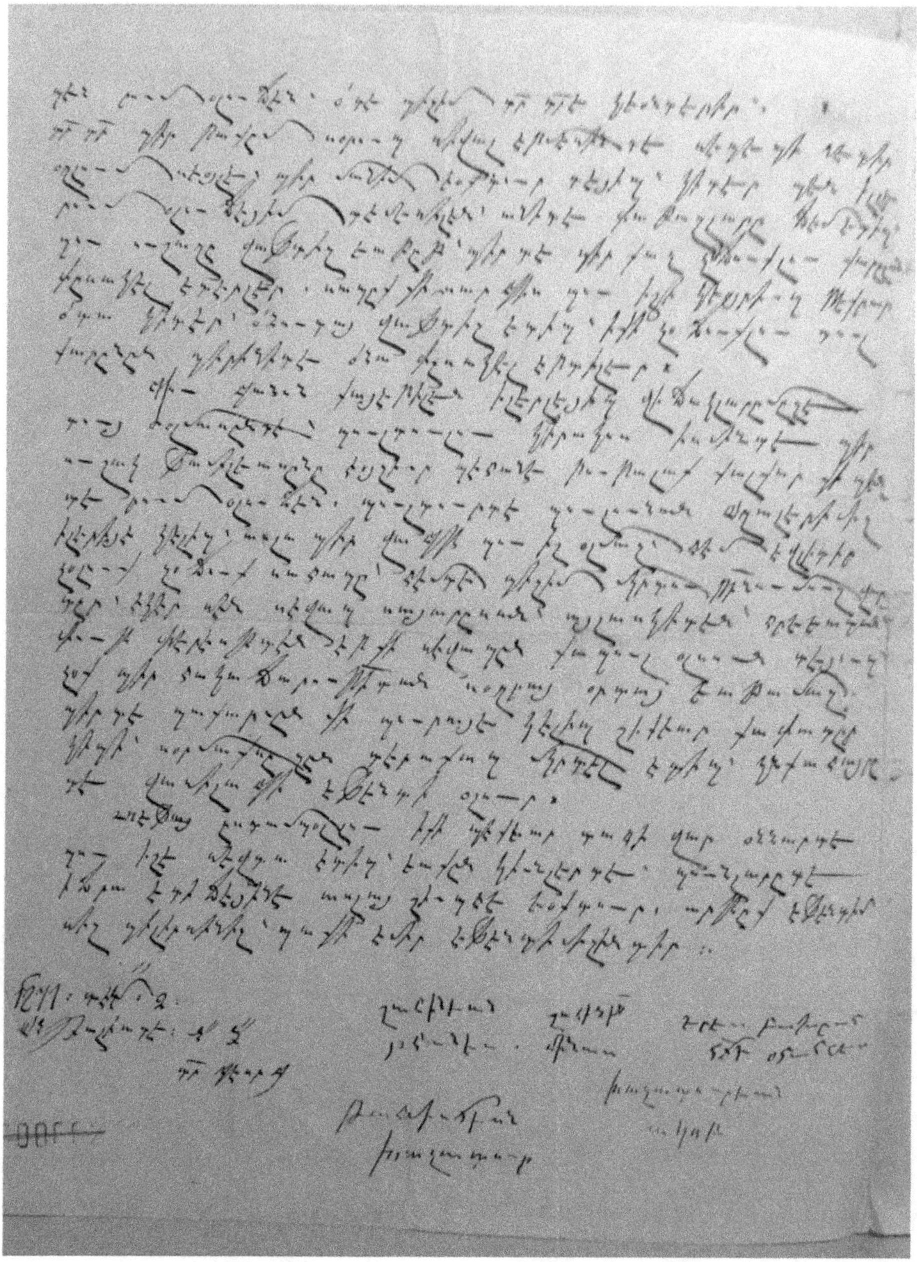

5 [illegible] 187[illegible]

[illegible]

[illegible] 36

[illegible]

000003

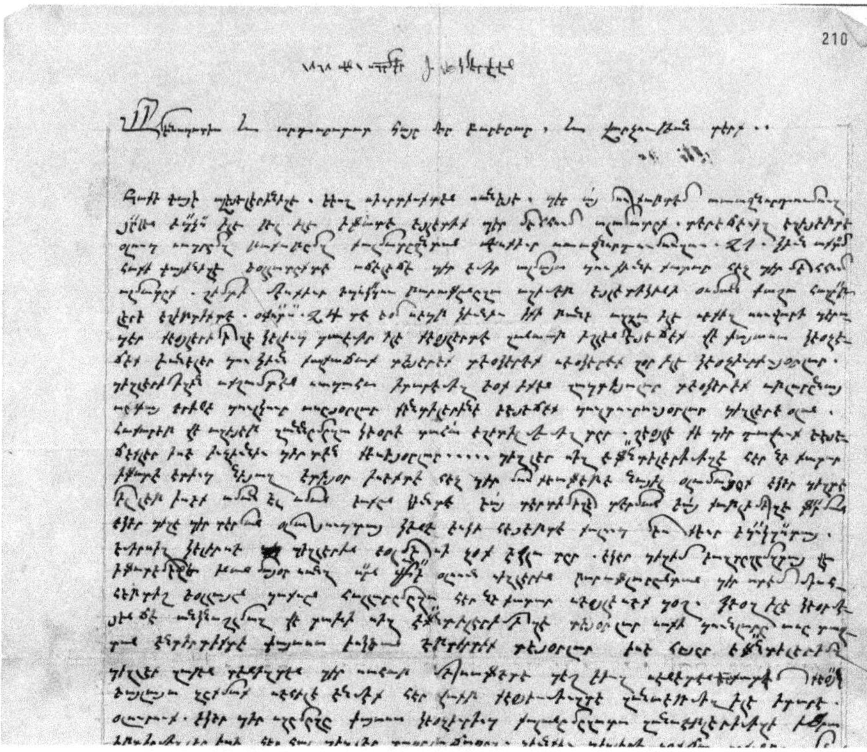

BN APC/CP19/10/210

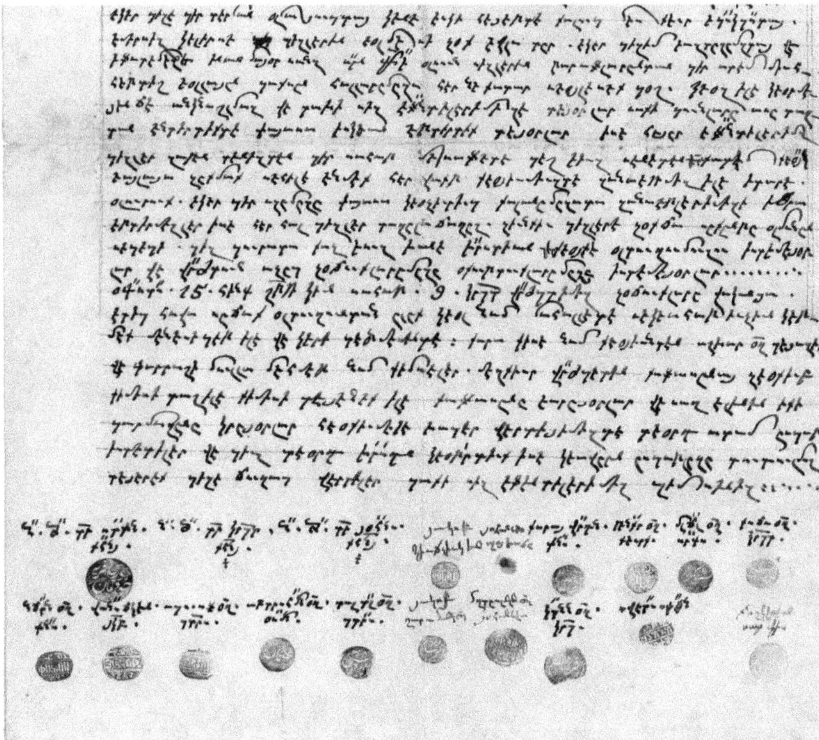

1868 [illegible] 11 [illegible]

[illegible]

[illegible]

[illegible]

00 009

[illegible]

[illegible]

1868 [illegible]

[illegible]

BN APC/CP20/10/009

[illegible]

[illegible]
[illegible]
[illegible]

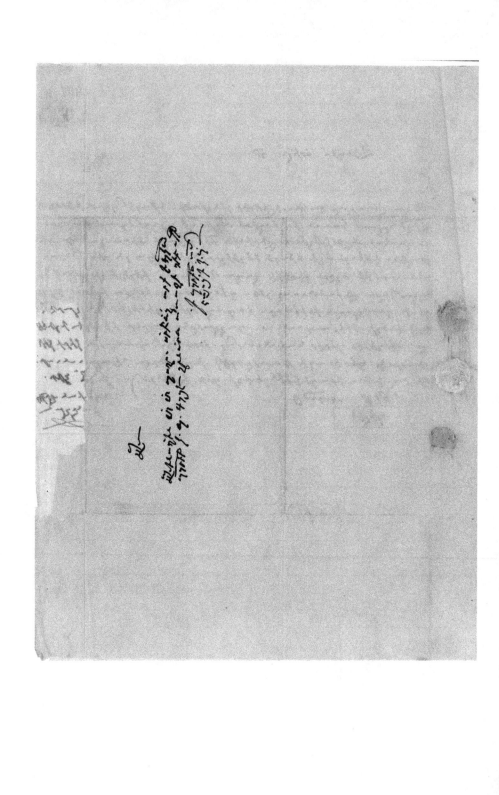

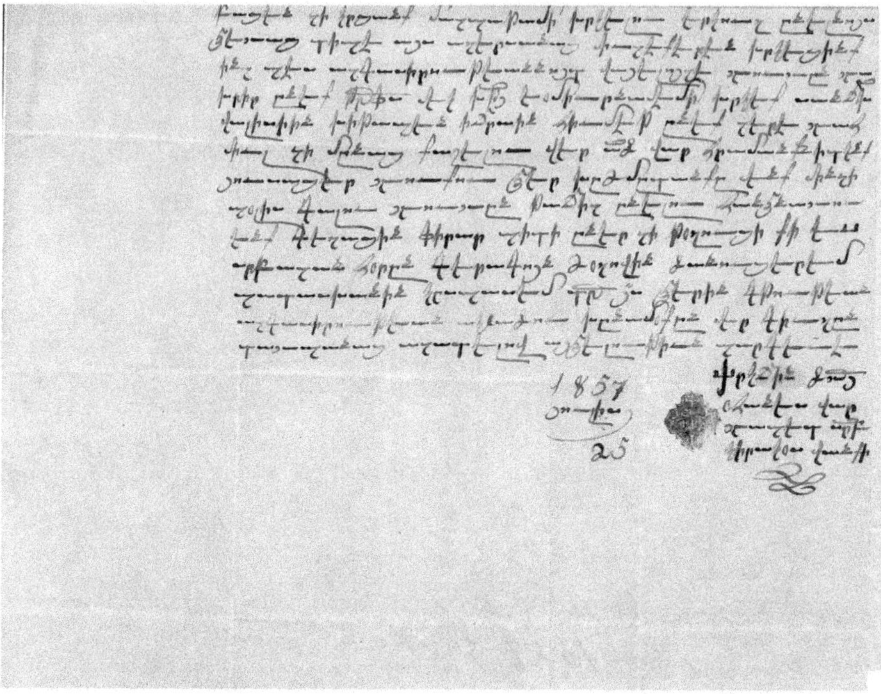
1857

25

[illegible]

[illegible]

[illegible]

[illegible]

[illegible]

1. [illegible]

2. [illegible]

3. [illegible]

4. [illegible]

5. [illegible]

---

6. [illegible]

---

7. [illegible]

---

8. [illegible]

---

9. [illegible]

---

10. [illegible]

---

11. [illegible]

---

12. [illegible] 10–12000 [illegible]

---

13. [illegible]

---

14. [illegible]

---

15. [illegible] 24 [illegible]

16. [illegible]

17. [illegible]

18. [illegible]

19. [illegible]

20. [illegible]

ա. [illegible]

բ. [illegible]

գ. [illegible]

[illegible]

[illegible] 7500 [illegible] 3000 [illegible] 3000 [illegible]

21 · [illegible]

22 · [illegible] 120 [illegible]

23. [illegible]

---

24. [illegible] 7000 [illegible] 15 [illegible] 30 [illegible]

---

25. [illegible]

---

26. [illegible] 12 [illegible] 7 [illegible]

---

27. [illegible] 6 [illegible] 5 [illegible]

---

28. [illegible]

29. [illegible]

30. [illegible]

31 [illegible]

32. [illegible]

---

33 [illegible] 18 [illegible]

---

34. [illegible]

[illegible] 34 [illegible]

1871 [illegible] 10

[illegible]

[illegible]

[illegible]

1. [illegible]

2. [illegible]

3. [illegible]

4. [illegible]

5. [illegible]

6. [illegible]

7. [illegible]

---

8. [illegible]

---

9. [illegible]

---

10. [illegible]

---

11. [illegible]

---

12. [illegible]

---

13. [illegible]

---

14. [illegible]

15. [illegible]

16. [illegible]

17. [illegible]

18. [illegible]

19. [illegible]

20. [illegible]

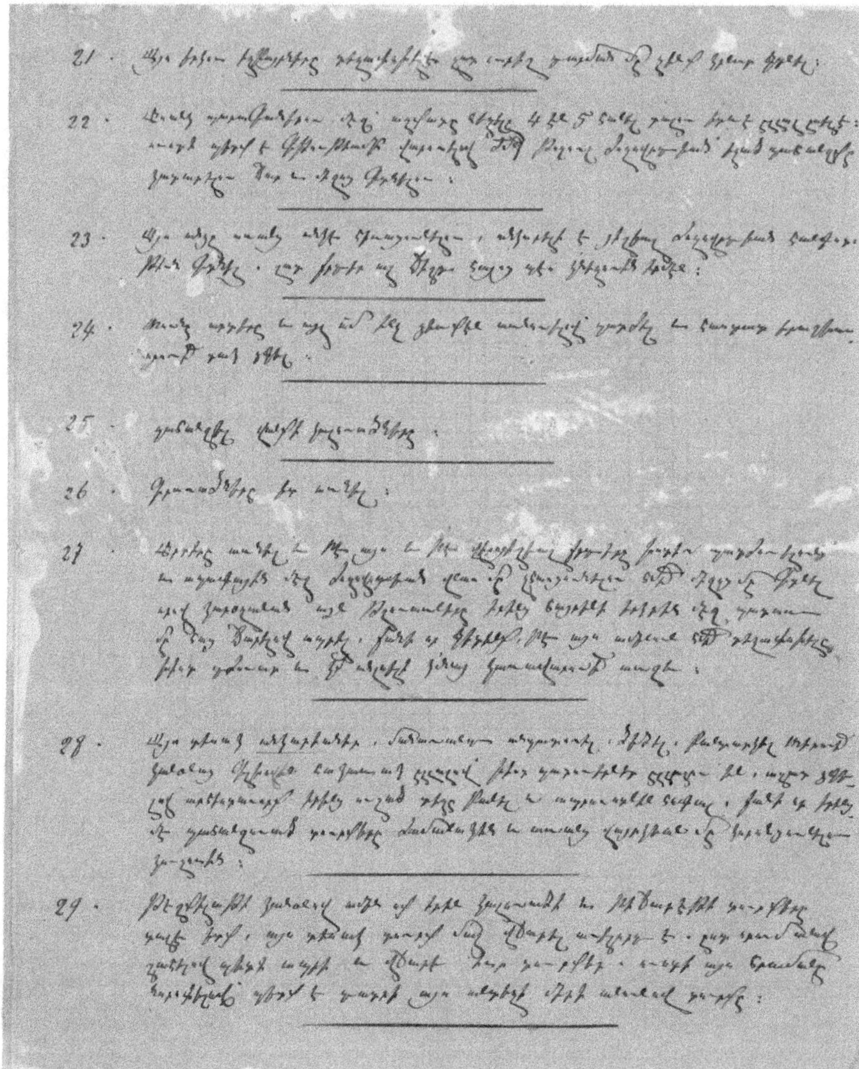

30. [illegible]

31. [illegible]

32. [illegible]

33. [illegible]

34. [illegible]

[illegible]

1871 [illegible] 10

[illegible]

[illegible]

5 Մայիս 1871 ։ Երզնկայի Առաջնորդ Վարդա-
պետ [illegible], Երզնկայէ
[illegible] ի պաշտպանութեան քաղա-
քական [illegible]
[illegible] ։

Թիւ 1285.

Notes

Introduction

1. Johannes Fabian, *Time and the Other: How Anthropology Makes Its Object*, 37–70.

2. The Ottoman Constitution was accepted in December 1876 (H., 7 Zilhicce 1293/G., Dec. 23, 1876) and suspended after the defeat of the Ottoman Empire by Russia in February 1878. On Ottoman constitutional thought and the role of Armenians and the Armenian Nizamname, see Aylin Koçunyan, *Negotiating the Ottoman Constitution 1839–1876.*

3. Dzovinar Derderian, "Nation-Making and the Language of Colonialism: Voices from Ottoman Van in Armenian Print Media and Handwritten Petitions (1820s to 1870s)," 12.

4. Massimiliano Tomba, *Marx's Temporalities*, 175. In the introduction of his recently published book, *Insurgent Universalities: An Alternative Legacy of Modernity*, Tomba also refers to the concept of temporal strata, *Zeitschichten*, and multiple layers of time, *Zeitebenen*, as suggested by Koselleck. See Reinhart Koselleck, *Zeitschichten: Studien zur Historik.*

5. "Tanzimat Fermanı," quoted in Halil İnalcık and Mehmet Seyitdanlıoğlu, eds., *Tanzimat: Değişim sürecinde Osmanlı İmparatorluğu*, 13–16.

6. The Armenian Patriarchate of Constantinople was an Ottoman institution, just as today it is an institution of the Republic of Turkey.

7. Avner Wishnitzer, *Reading Clocks Alla Turca: The Time and Society in the Late Ottoman Empire*, 19. Wishnitzer states that there has not been a single extensive study done on Ottoman temporality.

8. Armenian publications carry the Hijri and the Julian dates, and at times the Gregorian as well. A very early example is the publication of Injijian. See Ghugas Injijian, *Eghanag piwzantean* (Venedig: Dbaran Surp Ghazar, 1803), http://tert.nla.am/cgi-bin/koha/opac-detail.pl?biblionumber=8061&query_desc=kw%2Cwrdl%3A%20եղանակ.

9. Tomba, *Insurgent Universality*, 5.

10. Walter Benjamin, "Über den Begriff der Geschichte," in *Gesammelte Schrifte*, 697.

11. *Tışarı* (*dışarı*) or *taşra*. For more definitions of province and periphery, see Marc Aymes, *A Provincial History of the Ottoman Empire: Cyprus and the Eastern Mediterranean in the Nineteenth Century*, 3–8.

12. Robert David Sack, *Human Territoriality*, 19, 32–34.

13. See Uğur Bahadır Bayraktar, "Yurtluk-Ocaklıks: Land, Politics of Notables and Society in Ottoman Kurdistan, 1820–1890," 1; and Nilay Özok-Gündoğan, "Ruling the Periphery, Governing the Land: The Making of the Modern State in Kurdistan, 1840–1870," 161.

14. Ali Yaycıoğlu, *Partners of the Empire: The Crisis of the Ottoman Order in the Age of Revolutions*, 17.

15. Jun Akiba, "Preliminaries to a Comparative History of the Russian and Ottoman Empires: Perspectives from Ottoman Studies," 38. "Privileged provinces" include Egypt, Tunisia, Bulgaria, Eastern Rumelia, Bosnia, Samos, and Cyprus. Mount Lebanon and Crete are also categorized as such. Akiba notes that after 1898, Samos and Crete were autonomous procinces with Christian governments, Bulgaria was semi-independent, whereas Bosnia and Cyprus were under Austrian and British occupation, respectively.

16. Bayraktar, "Yurtluk-Ocaklıks," 27.

17. Akiba, "Preliminaries to a Comparative History," 39.

18. Yaycıoğlu, *Partners of the Empire*, 206.

19. Anna Vakalis, "Tanzimat in the Provinces: Nationalist Sedition (*fesat*), Banditry (*eşkıya*), and Local Councils in the Ottoman Southern Balkans," 19.

20. Roderic H. Davison, *Reform in the Ottoman Empire, 1856–1876*, 18.

21. Ömer Lütfi Barkan, "Türk toprak hukuku ve tarihinde Tanzimat ve 1274 (1858) tarihli arazi kanunnamesi," 415.

22. Musa Çadırcı, *Tanzimat döneminde Anadolu kentlerinin sosyal ve ekonomik yapıları*, 177.

23. Sezen Bilir and Alişan Akpınar, "Kürdistan eyaletinin kuruluşu," 21–22.

24. Çadırcı, *Tanzimat döneminde Anadolu*, 195.

25. Sack, *Human Territoriality*, 75.

26. Çadırcı, *Tanzimat döneminde Anadolu*, 195.

27. Karen Barkey, "In Different Times: Scheduling and Social Control in the Ottoman Empire, 1550–1650."

28. Richard Antaramian, *Brokers of Faith, Brokers of Empire*, 6–7.

29. Numerous criticisms have been published approaching Turkey's society as either a mosaic or an *ebru*. Yet there are still public opinion makers, organizations, and foundations that advocate the perception of society as resembling a mosaic structure, which presumably stands opposite to a society resembling marble. Marble is the metaphor used to envision a monoethnic society in Turkey. However, both those advocating for mosaic and those for marble had similar approaches when it came to the annihilation, exile, and eradication of autochthonous populations, and therefore both images, though in binary opposition, reproduce the mainstream. For the critique, see, for instance, Talin Suciyan, "Ebru, mozaik, Anadolu'nun rengi değilim ben," *Agos*, no. 787.

30. Antaramian, *Brokers of Faith*, 161–62.

31. Within the Ottoman bureaucracy, Nizamname meant literally regulation. Nizamname-i Ermeniyan was the legal and administrative text setting the rules and regulations for the centralized governance of *all* Armenians within the borders of the empire. However, as will be discussed in detail in the first chapter, neither were all Armenians willing to be subjected to a central authority, nor was the state willing to have a unified Armenian administration. Nizamname was referred to as the Armenian Constitution in Armenian, as it was the first comprehensive text carrying a constitutional nature. Throughout this book I will use both terms, in some cases with a slash, that is, the Nizamname/Constitution, to remind the reader of both terminologies and their differing meanings without being obliged to choose one or the other.

32. Artinian explained the establishment and development of constitutional administration around the Armenian Nizamname as follows: "An imperial edict was issued on 7 May 1847, ordering the millet to elect two separate and independent governing bodies, one for the civil and the other for the spiritual administration of the millet. . . . The Supreme Civil Council, which consisted of twenty lay members was to look after secular education, millet property, and justice. The Spiritual Council, comprised of fourteen clergy from Istanbul, was concerned with dogma, ordination of clergy, and religious education." See Vartan Artinian, *The Armenian Constitutional System in the Ottoman Empire, 1839–1863: A Study of Its Historical Development*, 73.

33. Masayuki Ueno devoted an article to clarifying the terminology of "privileges" in which he showed that the word was used in the text of the Reform Edict of 1856 as "clerical privileges." See Masayuki Ueno, "Religious in Form, Political in Content? Privileges of Ottoman Non-Muslims in the Nineteenth Century," 417–18. For the use of privileges and permissions, see Halil İnalcık, "Tanzimat nedir?," in *Tanzimat*, ed. İnalcık and Seydanlıoğlu; or for "ancient privileges," see Davison, *Reform in the Ottoman Empire, 1856–1876*, 114.

34. I am using the terminology of Tomba, *Marx's Temporalities*, 162. Tomba uses the term *violent synchronization of time* in the context of the emergence of the state as an institution to carry out the task of turning peasants into individual unorganized workers. However, some groups did not survive the process to become proletarians in the sense that Tomba described. By the mid-nineteenth century, Ottoman Armenians had already started becoming migrant workers. Derderian's doctoral dissertation has a chapter on Armenian migrant workers in which she mentions that the representation of *bantukhd* served to expand the discourse of colonization by creating hierarchies at the expense of the Armenians in the provinces, privileging Armenians in the capital, though it does not discuss what she means by colonization or how the process of privileging and suppressing is related to the creation of noncontemporaneities. For more, see Derderian, "Nation-Making and the Language of Colonialism," 245.

35. Ueno, "Religious in Form, Political in Content?," 422.

36. Tomba, *Marx's Temporalities*, 182.

37. See Zaven Der Yeghiayan, *Badriarkagan hushers: Vawerakirner ew vgayut'iwnner,* 403.

38. See Raymond Kévorkian, *The Armenian Genocide: A Complete History,* 5.

39. For more on Balakian, see Krikoris Balakian, *Hay koghkot'an: Truakner hay mardirosakrut'enē; Beṙlinēen tēbi Dērzor 1914–1920,* vols. 1–2; for the English translation, see Krikoris Balakian and Peter Balakian, *Armenian Golgotha.*

40. Kévorkian, *Armenian Genocide,* 5.

41. The specific characteristics of these languages and language forms shed light on local dialects and the systematics of the language forms in use, as well as provide interesting hints into the development of the languages. These documents enhanced my ability to work with various paleographic styles in a number of alphabets. I comment as much as this study allows on the characteristics of the languages found in the documents.

42. Aymes, *Provincial History of the Ottoman Empire,* 8, 177.

43. On *arz-ı hal,* see Mehmet İşpirli, "Arzuhal," in *TDV İslam ansiklopedisi* (Ankara: TDV, 1991), 3:447–48.

44. On *arz-ı mahzar,* see Mehmet İşpirli, "Mahzar," in *TDV İslam Ansiklopedisi* (Ankara: TDV, 2001), 27:398–401; and Halil İnalcık, "Şikayet hakkı: Arz-ı hal ve arz-ı mahzarlar," in *Osmanlı araştırmaları, VII–VIII,* ed. İsmail E. Erünsal, Christopher Ferrard, and Christine Woodhead (Istanbul: Enderun Yay., 1988), 33–54.

45. On *sened,* see Mehmet Boynukalın, "Senet," in *TDV İslam ansiklopedisi* (Ankara: TDV, 2009), 36:518–19.

46. On *tahrir,* see Mehmet Öz, "Tahrir," in *TDV İslam ansiklopedisi* (Ankara: TDV, 2010), 29:425–29.

47. See *Takvim-i Vekayi,* no. 1, Jan. 20, 1840 (H., 15 Zilkadde 1255/G., Jan. 8, 1840). After its sixth issue, it was published in Armenian with Julian and Hijri dates under the title of *Lroy Kir Medz Deruwtean Osmanean* in Armenian. For instance, see *Lroy Kir,* no. 19, Sept. 27, 1840 (H., 13 Shaban 1256).

48. *Hayastan* carried both the Hijri and the Julian dates.

49. All three only used the Julian calendar. For *Hayrenasēr,* see http://tert.nla.am/cgi-bin/koha/opac-detail.pl?biblionumber=6833&query_desc=kw%2Cwrdl%3A%20հայրենասէր; for *Ardzuig Darōnoy,* see http://tert.nla.am/cgi-bin/koha/opac-detail.pl?biblionumber=6720; and for *Zhamanag: Hantes Hayrenanuēr,* see http://tert.nla.am/cgi-bin/koha/opac-detail.pl?biblionumber=9463 (accessed Aug. 11, 2021).

50. These two used only the Julian calendar. For *Masis, see* http://tert.nla.am/cgi-bin/koha/opac-detail.pl?biblionumber=6904&query_desc=kw%2Cwrdl%3A%20masis (accessed Aug. 11, 2021). *Giligia* does not have online references within the Armenian National Library's database.

51. *Manzume-i Efkar* carried Hijri, Julian, and "Alafranga," the term for the Gregorian calendar in Turkish. For bibliographic information, see http://tert.nla.am/cgi-bin/koha/opac-detail.pl?biblionumber=7014 (accessed Aug. 11, 2022).

52. *Ceride-i Şarkiye* used both Hijri and Julian calendars. For bibliographic information, see http://tert.nla.am/cgi-bin/koha/opac-detail.pl?biblionumber=10096&query_desc=kw%2Cwrdl%3A%20Ճէրիտէ (accessed Aug. 11, 2022).

53. M. A. Paployan, *Hay barperagan mamuli madenakidagan hamahavak' ts'uts'ag (1794–1980)*; for publications in Istanbul and provinces, see 341–48; and for Aleppo and Jerusalem, see 353. According to Paployan's bibliographical study, just in the nineteenth century there were twenty-nine Armeno-Turkish newspapers, including *Takvim-i Vekai*, published in Istanbul.

54. Hasmik Stepanyan, *Ermeni harfli Türkçe kitaplar ve süreli yayınlar bibliyografyası*, 553–91. For Armeno-Turkish publications, see Alperd Khaṛadyan, Marko Mkhitaryan, and Linda Gevorgyan, eds., *Hay barperagan mamuli badmut'yun*. A. Khaṛadyan gave a separate list of periodicals in Armeno-Turkish published in Aintab (Antep), Adana, Bursa, Sivas, and Erzurum in the nineteenth century, seven in total. See Khaṛadyan, Mkhitaryan, and Gevorgyan, *Hay barperagan mamuli badmut'yun*, 625–43.

55. Regarding *Fr'at'* of Aleppo, it is important to mention that the newspaper was published by a prominent statesmen, Ahmet Cevdet, during his governorate in Aleppo. It was the official newspaper of his governorate and published bilingually in Turkish and Arabic. It also had an Armeno-Turkish section prepared by Manuk Karajyan. For more bibliographical information, see the website of the Union Catalogue of Armenian Continuing Resources, http://tert.nla.am/cgi-bin/koha/opac-detail.pl?biblionumber=12092&query_desc=kw%2Cwrdl%3A%20Frat (accessed Aug. 11, 2022).

56. Stepanyan, *Ermeni harfli Türkçe kitaplar*, 553–91.

57. Avedis Bērbēryan, *Badmut'iwn Hayots' sgsyal i 1772 ame P'rgchin minch'ev hamn 1860*.

58. For *Amiras*, see Hagop L. Barsoumian, *The Armenian Amira Class of Istanbul*.

59. Ōrmanyan had degrees in philosophy and theology and was an expert on ecclesiastical law. He served as a prelate in Erzurum in 1880 and later became the director of the seminary at the Monastery of Armash (Akmeşe today), one of the most prominent Armenian seminaries where numerous patriarchs and catholicoi had been educated. Born in 1842 in Istanbul, Ōrmanyan was not only one of the most charismatic and knowledgeable patriarchs, but also one of the most controversial. He was born into a Catholic Armenian family and had attended and served as a teacher at the Catholic Theological Seminary in Rome. Later he joined the Armenian Apostolic Church and made major contributions as a historian, patriarch, and leading political persona.

60. I thank Dr. Vartan Matiossian for bringing this source to my attention and Dr. Ara Sanjian for making it accessible to me.

61. In the second volume of his book, Melik'-T'ankyan mentioned that he was going to write a third volume about Armenian lawmaking, especially among the Ottoman Armenians, but unfortunately this project never came to fruition. I thank the librarians of the Armenian National Library, who were kind enough to conduct research into this

matter and assured me that a third volume was never written, nor are there manuscripts for a planned book.

62. On Ahmet Cevdet Pasha (1823–95), see Christoph K. Neumann, "Ahmed Cevdet Paşa." For more on Ahmet Cevdet, *Tezâkir*, and *Tarih-i Cevdet*, see Christoph K. Neumann, *Araç tarih, amaç Tanzimat: Tarih-i Cevdet'in siyasi anlamı.*

63. According to Davison, "The Armenian constitution, despite lacking clarity on some points and a lack of detail on the provincial organization, was a fairly sophisticated document setting up reasonably complex but workable machinery." Davison, *Reform in the Ottoman Empire*, 125.

64. Ahmet Cevdet, *Tezâkir 40–Tetimme*, 202–9. Ahmet Cevdet gave information on the Catholic Armenians and their population, signaling the differences and possible policies to be deployed.

65. As Thomas Kühn states, the Ottoman army conquered southwest Arabia between the 1840s and 1870s: "By 1873, soldiers and administrators had taken substantial steps towards organizing these territories as the new Province of Yemen, thereby continuing the efforts of the central government to extend its control over the empire's Arab borderlands between the Fizzan and the Shatt al-'Arab." See Thomas Kühn, "An Imperial Borderland as Colony: Knowledge Production and the Elaboration of Difference in Ottoman Yemen, 1872–1918," 5.

66. This is one of the most utilized methods up until today.

67. Karekin Srvantsdyants', "Aghers aṛ azkayin varchut'iwn," *Zhamanag*, no. 27, Jan. 4, 1864.

68. For instance, Roderic Davison's book makes one of those temporal leaps: "Mahmud's arm also reached out into the provinces. Military expeditions brought such regions as Kurdistan and Iraq once more under the control of Istanbul. By a combination of diplomacy and force the might of the *derebeyi*s was largely crushed. The most famous rebel, Ali Paşa of Yanina, was killed and his head displayed on a dish set out in the first court of the palace." Davison, *Reform in the Ottoman Empire*, 26. First Davison mentioned the 1840s defeat of the *derebeyis* in Kurdistan and Iraq and then without giving any further details jumped in time and space back to the 1820s rebellion of Ali Pasha of Ioanina. Besides their different time periods, the former was in the east, the latter in the west.

69. "The Tanzimat reforms were a sincere effort to win the hearts and minds of its non-Muslim subjects. . . . However with the loss of the most valuable Balkan provinces, the Hamidian state found itself obliged to fall back on its Muslim population. In this context the outbreak of Armenian nationalism in Anatolia, the last stronghold, was seen as a deadly threat. On the other hand, the Ottoman decision-makers faced intense pressure from the foreign powers. Although the Ottoman government retained ultimate political agency to the very end, foreign pressure was a constant reality in their political decision-making." Selim Deringil, *Conversion and Apostasy in the Late Ottoman*

Empire, 23. Here too Deringil utilizes the same kind of temporal leap Davison did. See note 68 above.

1. The Armenian Administration and Its Legislative and Executive Entitlements within the Ottoman Empire

1. Both Siruni and Alboyadjan were survivors who went into exile in Romania and Cairo, respectively, and continued to work and publish on the history of Armenians in the Ottoman Empire, leaving invaluable sources for future generations.

2. Artinian, *Armenian Constitutional System*, 38.

3. Bērbēryan, *Badmut'iwn Hayots'*, 500.

4. Hagop J. Siruni, *Bolis ew ir terĕ*, 3:99.

5. Artinian, *Armenian Constitutional System*, 40, 41–42.

6. Nerses Melik'-T'ankyan, *Hayots' Egeghets'agan irawunkĕ*, 731. On the establishment and closing of the Jemaran in 1841, see Hagop J. Siruni, *Bolis ew ir terĕ*, 2:310–24.

7. See Melik'-T'ankyan, *Hayots' Egeghets'agan irawunkĕ*. Ōrmanyan gives the date the Protestants were acknowledged as a *millet* as October 3, 1847. See Maghakia Ōrmanyan, *Azkabadum*, 3:3806.

8. Siruni, *Bolis ew ir terĕ*, 3:35.

9. Melik'-T'ankyan, *Hayots' Egeghets'agan irawunkĕ*, 731.

10. Varujan Köseyan, *Surp Pırgiç Ermeni Hastanesi tarihçesi*, 41.

11. Bērbēryan, *Badmut'iwn Hayots'*, 320–21; Artinian, *Osmanlı Devleti'nde Ermeni Anayasası'nın doğuşu, 1839–1863*, 86–87.

12. See Bērbēryan, *Badmut'iwn Hayots'*.

13. See Bērbēryan, *Badmut'iwn Hayots'*.

14. For the *Amiras*, see Hagop L. Barsoumian, *The Armenian Amira Class of Istanbul*.

15. Köseyan, *Surp Pırgiç Ermeni Hastanesi tarihçesi*, 41.

16. Arshag Alboyadjian, "Azkayin Sahmanatrut'iwnĕ: Ir dzakumĕ ew girarumĕ," 360. See also *Masis*, no. 251, Nov. 14, 1856.

17. Alboyadjian, "Azkayin Sahmanatrut'iwnĕ," 360.

18. Ōrmanyan, *Azkabadum*, 3:4017–19. For more, see Artinian, *Armenian Constitutional System*, 82.

19. Masayuki Ueno conducted an interesting study comparing the texts of the Nizamname from 1857 and 1860, but as the differences are not of direct concern to this study, I will not dwell on them here. For more, see Masayuki Ueno, "The First Draft of the Armenian Millet Constitution"; Alboyadjian, "Azkayin Sahmanatrut'iwnĕ," 390–422; and Ōrmanyan, *Azkabadum*, 3:4020–23.

20. Alboyadjian, "Azkayin Sahmanatrut'iwnĕ," 401–2.

21. Siruni, *Bolis ew ir terĕ*, 3:57, 58–59, 65.

22. Alboyadjian, "Azkayin Sahmanatrut'iwnĕ," 90.

23. Alboyadjian, "Azkayin Sahmanatrut'iwnĕ," 102.

24. Alboyadjian, "Azkayin Sahmanatrut'iwnĕ," 103–4, 134.

25. For the Catholicosate of Aghtamar, see Ōrmanyan, *Azkabadum*, 3:3959–62, 4113–15. For the Catholicosate of Sis, see Ōrmanyan, *Azkabadum*, 3:3957–59.

26. A *berat* in this context is a decree carrying the sultan's signature testifying or acknowledging rights and entitlements of the Armenian *millet*. For more on *berats*, see Mübahat S. Kütükoğlu, "Berat," in *Türkiye Diyanet Vakfı İslam ansiklopedisi* (Istanbul: TDV, 1992), 472–73.

27. Alboyadjian, "Azkayin Sahmanatrut'iwnĕ," 94–95.

28. *Deghegakir k'aghak'agan zhoghovoy getronagan varchut'ean ami ar azgayin ĕnt-hanur zhoghovoy, 1870–71*, 9.

29. *Manzume-i Efkâr*, no. 18, Apr. 3, 1866, quoted in Ueno, "Religious in Form, Political in Content?," 422.

30. Ueno, "Religious in Form, Political in Content?," 423.

31. *Masis*, no. 1285, Sept. 19, 1872, quoted in Ueno, "Religious in Form, Political in Content?," 427.

32. Ōrmanyan, *Azkabadum*, 3:3815.

33. Ōrmanyan, *Azkabadum*, 3:3980–82.

34. Bērbēryan, *Badmut'iwn Hayots'*, 433–34.

35. *Deghegakir k'aghak'agan zhoghovoy getronagan varchut'ean ar azkayin ĕnthanur zhoghovoy*, 49.

36. Ōrmanyan, *Azkabadum*, 3:4129–31. See also *Adenakrut'iwnk' azkayin ĕnthanur zhoghovoy 1866*, quoted in Ueno, "Religious in Form, Political in Content?," 421; and Siruni, *Bolis ew ir terĕ*, 3:78–79.

37. Artinian, *Armenian Constitutional System*, 78.

38. Masayuki Ueno refers to an Armenian periodical, *Meghu* (Dec. 31, 1856), to strengthen Vartan Artinian's argument that the first preparations for the Nizamname started even earlier than the proclamation of the Reform Edict: "Almost one and a half years ago the *millet* general assembly decided to organize a constitutional committee composed of both clergymen and laymen." See Masayuki Ueno, "First Draft of the Armenian Millet Constitution," 215–16.

39. *Masis*, no. 1273, Aug. 22, 1872, in Ueno, "Religious in Form, Political in Content?," 427.

40. Artinian, "Ek (Appendix) IX," in Artinian, *Osmanlı Devleti'nde Ermeni Anayasası'nın doğuşu*, 36. Written in Armeno-Turkish, it contains the original and ratified form of the Nizamname together with the Armenian-language one.

41. Artinian, *Osmanlı Devleti'nde Ermeni Anayasası'nın doğuşu*, 36.

42. Ōrmanyan, *Azkabadum*, 3:4018.

43. *Hamaraduut'iwn azkayin getronagan varchut'ean k'aghak'agan zhoghovoy 1874–75 ēw 1875–76 amats'*, 39.

44. Bērbēryan, *Badmut'iwn Hayots'*, 405, 406.

45. Artinian, "Ek (Appendix) IX," 20.

46. *Hamaraduut'iwn, 1874–75 ēw 1875–76*, 7–8.

47. Siruni, *Bolis ew ir terĕ*, 3:470.

48. Badrig Giwlbēngyan, appendix to *Ampoghchagan erger Khrimean Hayrigi*, 10–11.

49. *Azg* in Armenian does not easily translate to *nation* in English. While *nation* has a secular connotation, *azg* is based on religion or even confession. *Millet* can be considered as the preferred translation of the Armenian *azg* into Turkish. However, today it also has a secular connotation, although *millet* has always been defined based on religion and confession.

50. Giwlbēngyan, appendix, 13, 14.

51. Giwlbēngyan, appendix, 14.

52. *Hamaraduut'iwn, 1874–75 ēw 1875–76*, 7.

53. Giwlbēngyan, appendix, 15.

54. Siruni, *Bolis ew ir terĕ*, 3:472–75.

55. Although not mentioned in the Nizamname, the position of *kapı kahyası* might have previously existed but with a different job description.

56. *Deghegakir k'aghak'agan zhoghovoy getronagan varchut'ean ar azkayin*, 8.

57. *Hamaraduut'iwn, 1874–75 ēw 1875–76*, 7.

58. Dr. K. [Josef Koetchet], *Erinnerungen aus dem Leben des Serdar Ekrem Omer Pascha* (Sarajevo: Spindler und Löschner, 1885), 47–120, quoted in Davison, *Reform in the Ottoman Empire*, 138.

59. Artinian, "Ek (Appendix) IX," 4.

60. *Hrahank haraperut'ean aṙach'nortats' kawaṙagan varchut'eants' ĕnt deghagan garavariut'ean, vaverats'eal i gronagan ew k'aghak'agan kharn zhoghovoy getronagan varchut'ean*, 9.

61. Artinian, "Ek (Appendix) IX," 52.

62. *Hrahank vasn gazmu'tean kawaṙagan ĕnthanur zhoghovoy*, 1.

63. *Deghegakir k'aghak'agan zhoghovoy getronagan varchut'ean ar azkayin*, 25.

64. *Deghegakir k'aghak'agan zhoghovoy getronagan varchut'ean ar azkayin*, 24–36, 48, 49.

65. *Deghegakir k'aghak'agan zhoghovoy getronagan varchut'ean ar azkayin*, 5.

66. *Hrahank' harperut'ean aṙach'nortats'*, 4.

67. *Hrahank' harperut'ean aṙach'nortats'*, 4, 5, 8–9.

68. After April 1872, Khrimyan was advised to cease submitting official petitions but instead to go through Krikor Odyan. For more, see Ueno, "Religious in Form, Political in Content?," 426.

69. The administrative units mentioned are Mütessarıflık, the Kaymakamlık, and the Idare Meclisi in *Hrahank' harperut'ean aṙach'nortats'*, 5.

70. *Hrahank' harperut'ean aṙach'nortats'*, 5.

71. A series of juridical reorganizations were also undertaken, by which each *kaza* should have a *Meclis-i Deavi* court that would be responsible for minor crimes as well as trade cases when needed. In the *sanjaks Hukuk ve Cinayet Temyiz Meclisi*, courts were to be responsible for homicides, and a greater *Hukuk ve Cinayet Temyiz Meclisi* was to be established in the *vilayets* to deal with property issues. For more, see Ekrem Buğra Ekinci, *Osmanlı mahkemeleri*, 166, 172; and Çadırcı, *Tanzimat döneminde Anadolu kentlerinin*, 281.

72. Çadırcı, *Tanzimat döneminde Anadolu kentlerinin*, 255.

73. For more, see Çadırcı, *Tanzimat döneminde Anadolu kentlerinin*, 255.

74. Çadırcı, *Tanzimat döneminde Anadolu kentlerinin*, 257.

75. *Deghegakir k'aghak'agan zhoghovoy, 1870–71*, 29.

76. *Hrahank' harperut'ean aṛach'nortats'*, 8.

77. *Deghegakir k'aghak'agan zhoghovoy getronagan varchut'ean ar azkayin*, 8–9, 14.

78. *Deghegakir hamaraduut'ean getronagan varchut'ean vanoreits' khorhrtoy 1872–74 ami*, 1, 32–34.

79. *Deghegakir hamaraduut'ean, 1872–74*, 43.

80. Alboyadjian, "Azkayin Sahmanatrut'iwnĕ," 187–88.

81. Artinian, "Ek (Appendix) IX," 32, 52–53. This entitlement of the patriarchate to administer matters of family law was based on prior regulation. Alboyadjian compares three *Berat*s given by the sultans to Armenian patriarchs Krikor Basmadjian in 1764, Stepannos Aghavni in 1831, and Nerses Varjabedyan in 1875, all of which left matrimonial matters to the authority of the patriarchate. For more, see Alboyadjian, "Azkayin Sahmanatrut'iwnĕ," 96.

82. *Hamaraduut'iwn, 1874–75 ēw 1875–76*, 8.

83. *Deghegakir k'aghak'agan zhoghovoy, 1870–71*, 8, 3.

84. Artinian, "Ek (Appendix) IX," 32.

85. *Ōrēnk' azkayin varchagan gazmagerbut'ean, hasdadeal hazkayin erespokhanagan zhoghovoy ı nisd z. patsman 1880 ami*, 15, 16.

86. *Ōrēnk' azkayin varchagan gazmagerbut'ean*, 19.

87. Melik'-T'ankyan, *Hayots' Egeghets'agan irawunkĕ*, 67–82. He reviews not only the ecumenical meetings attended by the Armenian Church at Nicaea (AD 325), Constantinople (381), and Ephesus (431) and the decisions made at them, but also takes into consideration other councils that took place at Angora (Ankara, 313–35), Neo-Kesaria (Niksar, 314–315), Kankri (near Amasra, 340–370), Kesaria (Kayseri, date not given), Antioch (Antakya, 341), and Latakia (365). Melik'-T'ankyan also introduced and explained the thirty-four Apostolic laws based on tenth-century manuscripts from Echmiadzin and the Greco-Slavonic-Russian books from which Armenian ecclesiastical law adopted a total of eighty-five articles over the centuries. Melik'-T'ankyan, *Hayots' Egeghets'agan irawunkĕ*, 82–115.

88. Melik'-T'ankyan, *Hayots' Egeghets'agan irawunkĕ*, 319.

2. "Either Save Us from This Misery or Order Our Murder" (*Ya Derdimize Derman, Ya Katlimize Ferman*)

1. Nadir Özbek, *İmparatorluğun bedeli: Osmanlı'da vergi, siyaset ve toplumsal adalet (1839–1908)*, 34.

2. Wadie Jwaideh, *The Kurdish National Movement: Its Origins and Development*, 60–61.

3. Sack, *Human Territoriality*, 33–34, 52.

4. Dina Rizk Khoury, "Administrative Practice between Religious Law (Sharia) and State Law (Kanun) on the Eastern Frontiers of the Ottoman Empire," 312.

5. Practically the entire literature on Tanzimat refers to these aspects. The industrial and economic backwardness vis-à-vis Europe, loss of territories, and pressures from Russia, Britain, and France—referred to as the "Great Powers"—are given as reasons in almost all secondary sources. For instance, see Selim Deringil, *The Well-Protected Domains: Ideology and the Legitimation of Power in the Ottoman Empire, 1876–1909*; Şükrü Hanioğlu, *A Brief History of the Late Ottoman Empire*; Carter Findley, *Bureaucratic Reform in the Ottoman Empire: The Sublime Porte, 1789–1922*; Davison, *Reform in the Ottoman Empire*; and others.

6. Sabri Ateş, *The Ottoman-Iranian Borderlands: Making a Boundary, 1843–1914*, 56.

7. Ateş, *Ottoman-Iranian Borderlands*, 58. For more on Muhammed Pasha of Rawanduz, see Michael Eppel, "The Demise of the Kurdish Emirates: The Impact of Ottoman Reforms and International Relations on Kurdistan during the First Half of the Nineteenth Century."

8. Sinan Hakan, *Osmanlı arşiv belgelerinde Kürtler ve Kürt direnişleri (1817–1867)*, 86.

9. Hans-Lukas Kieser, *Der verpasste friede: Mission, ethnie und staat in den ostprovinzen der Türkei 1839–1938*, 64.

10. For more on Bedir Khan, see "Bedir Khan," in *Encyclopedia Iranica*, https://www.iranicaonline.org/articles/bedir-khan-badr-khan-d (accessed Aug. 21, 2021).

11. Jwaideh, *Kurdish National Movement*, 63, 67, 66–74.

12. Kieser, *Der verpasste friede*, 67.

13. See Helmut von Moltke, *Briefe Über Zustaende und Begebenheiten in der Türkei aus den Jahren 1835 bis 1839*, 6th ed. (Berlin: Mittler, 1893), 302, 369, quoted in Kieser, *Der verpasste friede*, 43–44.

14. Sack, *Human Territoriality*, 36.

15. Tuncay Baykara, *Anadolu'nun tarihi coğrafyasına giriş I: Anadolu'nun idari taksimatı*, 125.

16. Sack, *Human Territoriality*, 34.

17. Ateş, *Ottoman-Iranian Borderlands*, 319, 141.

18. Ateş, *Ottoman-Iranian Borderlands*, 216.

19. Ateş, *Ottoman-Iranian Borderlands*, 188. See also Candan Badem, *The Ottoman Crimean War (1853–56)*, 364.

20. As data collected in the region throughout the survey process between 1848 and 1852 was utilized by parties participating in the Crimean War, it was not a coincidence to come across the same names of military officers on duty during the war as those who had been active in mediation during the Erzurum Conferences (1847) and after it during the survey. The commission continued its work after the Crimean War. Ateş, *Ottoman-Iranian Borderlands*, 184, 188, 186.

21. Nuri Yavuz, "Fırka-i Islahiye ordusunun özellikleri ve faaliyetleri."

22. Ahmet Cevdet, *Ma'aruzat*, 113.

23. See Mehmet Akif Aydın, "Arazi kanunnamesi," 346–47, in Ömer Lütfü Barkan, "Türk toprak hukuku arihinde Tanzimat." The Cadastral Regulation (1849 Tapu Nizamnamesi) is also constitutive of the same process of property ownership and should be considered together with the Land Code of 1858.

24. Ateş, *Ottoman-Iranian Borderlands*, 186.

25. M. Macit Kenanoğlu, "Miri Arazi," in *TDV Islam Ansiklopedisi* (Istanbul: TDV, 2005), 30:159.

26. The first vilayet commonly considered to be organized or, better put, territorialized and temporalized under these regulations was Danube and was followed by Erzurum, Edirne, Bosnia, Aleppo, Syria, and Tripoli in Africa. For more, see Salaheddin Bey, *La Turquie à la l'exposition universelle de 1867* (Paris, 1867), 176–77, 192–93, 206, quoted in Davison, *Reform in the Ottoman Empire*, 158.

27. Davison, *Reform in the Ottoman Empire*, 168. From Davison's note I understand that the author of these articles dated 1868 and reprinted from *Impartial de Smyrne* was anonymous, and he presumed the author must have been a European. Davison informed his readers that the articles include sound criticisms of all phases of the law including election processes, courts, and Christian-Muslim equality.

28. Sack, *Human Territoriality*, 34.

29. For instance, Ortaylı referred to this period in the following way: "After the failed attempt to *control* [emphasis mine] the regions in Anatolia and Rumelia, which were governed by de facto autonomous *derebegs* . . ." The term *control* here actually means "military conquest." İlber Ortaylı, *İmparatorluğun en uzun yüzyılı*, 29.

30. Stephan Astourian, "The Silence of the Land," 62–64. For more, see Martin van Bruinessen, *Agha Shaikh and State: The Social and Political Structures of Kurdistan*, 222–34. See also Yener Koç, "Bedirxan Pashazades Power Relations and Nationalism (1876–1914)"; and Oya Gözel, "The implementation of the Ottoman Land Code of 1858 in Eastern Anatolia."

31. BOA HRT.h.308.0.0. H-28 Ramazan 1286.

32. BOA HRT.h.615.0.0. H-8 Safer1296. The map includes a note that Fischbach had attended the Ecole des Mines Vestphalienne.

33. BOA BEO 3591.269280.0. H-17 Cemaziyelahir 1327.

34. BOA Y.MTV.289.177.0. H-24 Cemaziyelahir 1324.

35. BOA HR.Th.61.80.0. G-17.2.1886.

36. BOA ZB.353.89.0. R-10-04-1325.

37. There are various publications by Helmuth von Moltke, who was likely the most famous of the Prussian Army officers operating in the Ottoman Empire. For instance, see Helmuth von Moltke, *Briefe über Zustaende und Begebenheiten in der Türkei aus den Jahren 1835 bis 1839* (Berlin: E. S. Mittler und Sohn, 1876).

38. For Karl Freiherr von Vincke's biography, see Herman von Petersdorff, "Vincke-Olbendorf, Karl Freiherr von," in *Allgemeine Deutsche Biographie* 39 (1895), 756–60, https://www.deutsche-biographie.de/pnd104047496.html#adbcontent.

39. Karl Freiherr von Vincke et al., *Memoir über die Construction der Karte von Kleinasien und Türkisch Armenien: In 6 Blatt.*

40. BOA, HRT.h. 408.01.-22. The file has twenty-two documents, including various statistical data, maps, and demographic information organized by region.

41. Ateş, *Ottoman-Iranian Borderlands*, 184–85.

42. BOA, DH.MKT. 2344.32. H-13 Muharrem 1318.

43. For the changing maps in the textbooks, see Benjamin C. Fortna, "Change in the School Maps of the Late Ottoman Empire."

44. Kemal Karpat, "Ifa and Kaza: The İlmiye State and Modernism in Turkey, 1820–1960," 31.

45. For more on the noncontemporaneity of the capital and the provinces, see Talin Suciyan, "Hagop Mnts'uri's *The Second Marriage*: Armenian Realities in the Pre- and Post-genocide Ottoman Empire and Turkey."

46. BN APC/CP1/13/052 (G., May 2, 1864).

47. BN APC/CP1/13/052.

48. BN APC/CP1/13/053. Kaghadia is a historic name used in the Armenian Patriarchate's Archive for the region of Angora/Ankara.

49. *Zhamanag*, no. 69, Sept. 4, 1865.

50. Garō Sasuni, *Badmut'iwn Darōni ashkharhi*, 226–29.

51. BN APC/CPGR/XIX/100. Letters and correspondence file of Khrimyan, Muş, Feb. 10, Apr. 6, 1864.

52. Salahaddin Bey, *La Turquie a L'exposition universelle de 1867* (Paris, 1867), 213; *Journal de Constantinople*, August 13, 1864, quoted in Davison, *Reform in the Ottoman Empire*, 151.

53. *Zhamanag*, no. 47, Oct. 10, 1864.

54. BN APC/CP22/5/19 (J., May 13, 1868/G., May 25, 1868).

55. For instance, see BOA MVL.716.28 (H., 30 Rejeb 1282/G., Dec. 19, 1865).

56. BN APC/CP22/5/20 (G., Sept. 7, 1868).

57. G., Aug. 23, 1868.

58. BN APC/CP20/11/011 (G., Sept. 5, 1868).

59. BN APC/CP20/10/009 (G., Aug. 21, 1868).

60. BN APC/CP20/10/009.

61. BN APC/CP20/10/009.

62. BN APC/CP20/11/007 (G., Aug. 21, 1868).

63. M. Safa Saraçoğlu, "Economic Interventionism, Islamic Law and Provincial Government in the Ottoman Empire," 75.

64. BN APC/CP19/10/210 (G., Sept. 13, 1868).

65. BN APC/CP19/10/210 (G., Sept. 5, 1868).

66. Cevdet, *Tezâkir 21–39*, 135, 107, 108, 219–26, 234–39.

67. Cevdet, *Tezâkir 21–39*, 68.

68. Astourian, "Silence of the Land," 71.

69. Orhan Kurmuş, "The Cotton Famine and Its Effects on the Ottoman Empire," 165.

70. *Manzume-i Efkâr*, no. 726, Aug. 14, 1868.

71. For more, see M. K. Nersisyan, "Zeyt'uni 1862 t'vagani absdamput'iwně," *Badmapanasiragan hantes*, no. 4 (1962): 59–68.

72. BOA A.MKT.MVL/85.92.1.1.

73. Cevdet, *Tezâkir 21–39*, 240.

74. "Kozan'ın zabt u ıslahından sonra müzakaresi hususuna karar verdirilerek nizam-namede bunlardan sükut olunmuş idi." See Cevdet, *Tezâkir 21–39*, 238.

75. Cevdet, *Tezâkir 21–39*, 238.

76. BN APC/CP19/10/210.

77. BN APC/CP19/10/210.

78. BOA DH.TMIK.S.14.21.2.1.

79. BOA DH.TMIK. S. .62.20.0. H-14 Muharrem 1324.

80. *Hamaraduut'iwn*, 44.

81. *Hamaraduut'iwn*, 27. For the famine in central Anatolia, see Özge Ertem, "Considering Famine in the Late Nineteenth Century Ottoman Empire: A Comparative Framework and Overview," 154.

82. *Hamaraduut'iwn*, 27.

83. For more, see Bruinessen, *Agha Shaikh and State*, 153.

84. *Manzume-i Efkâr*, no. 2647, H., Ramadan 16, 1291/J., Oct. 14, 1874/G. (Alafranga), Oct. 26, 1874. Zozan Pehlivan discusses the famines and droughts in the context of environmental crisis, climate change, and rising prices of grain in mid-nineteenth-century Diyarbekir. Based on the documents discussed here, the land and taxation policy of the period and the existence of "dozens of abandoned villages" could be read as interconnected realities and may also be linked to the military conquest in the region, especially in the case of newly established Vilayet of Diyarbekir. Zozan Pehlivan, "Abandoned Villages in Diyarbekir Province at the End of the 'Little Ice Age,'" 232.

85. Nadir Özbek, "The Politics of Taxation and the 'Armenian Question' during the Late Ottoman Empire, 1876–1908," 776.

86. Özbek, *İmparatorluğun bedeli*, 41.

87. Mehmet Polatel in his doctoral dissertation also mentioned the long-term legal and administrative battle in Çarsancak between peasants, *aghas*, and the state. Mehmet Polatel, "Armenians and the Land Question in the Ottoman Empire, 1870–1915," 93–94.

88. *Deghegakir K'aghak'agan Zhoghovoy, 1870–71*, 11, 9.

89. *Deghegakir K'aghak'agan Zhoghovoy, 1870–71*, 14.

90. Kēōrk Erewanyan, *Badmut'iwn Charsanjaki Hayots'*, 148–50.

91. For the Nizamiye courts, see Avi Rubin, *Ottoman Nizamiye Courts: Law and Modernity*; M. Macit Kenanoğlu, "Nizamiye mahkemeleri," in *TDV Islam Ansiklopedesi* (Istanbul: TDV, 2007), 33:187; Ekrem Buğra Ekinci, *Osmanlı mahkemeleri*, 205–16; and Davison, *Reform in the Ottoman Empire*, 255–56.

92. See Deringil, *Well-Protected Domains*, 46–47.

93. For post-1923, see Talin Suciyan, "Sanjak of Alexandretta," in *The Armenians in Modern Turkey: Post-genocide Society, Politics and History*, 77–82.

94. Sasuni, *Badmut'iwn Darōni Ashkharhi*, 255. See also Kiwd Aghanyants', ed., *Tiwan Hayots' badmut'ean, Kirk' 18: Harsdaharut'iwnner Dajgahayasdanum (Vawerakrer 1801–1888)*, 169–70. Khrimyan wrote in a letter to Srvantsdyants' that more than 680 *arz-ı hals* were submitted to the *Vali* (governor).

95. *Ardzuig Darōnoy*, no. 28, Oct. 15, 1864; no. 29, Nov. 1, 1864; no. 30, Nov. 15, 1864.

96. For more on the murder of Catholicos Bedros of Aghtamar, see Antaramian, *Brokers of Faith*, 77–82.

97. Antaramian, *Brokers of Faith*, 78. The governor of Van instead insisted upon Armenian involvement in the murder, casting suspicion on members of Van's Armenian elite, namely, Khachadur Shiroian and his allies.

98. Yaşar Tolga Cora, "Transforming Erzurum/Karin: The Social and Economic History of a Multi-ethnic Ottoman City in the 19th Century," 272. I thank Yaşar Tolga Cora for making his PhD thesis available to me. For more on these cases of murder, see Eyüp Şimşek, "Kırım Savaşı'nın Trabzon Eyaleti'ndeki sosyal etkileri," *History Studies* 5 (2003): 288; Stefo Benlisoy, "19. yüzyıl ortasında Osmanlı'da 'sorumlu' gazetecilik tartışması Anatoli ve Vatan kavgası," *Toplumsal Tarih* 236 (Aug. 2013): 52–53; and M. Kh. Ballar, "M. Ballaryani namagě K. V. Srvantsdyants'in," in *Tiwan Hayots' badmut'ean*, ed. Aghanyants', 258.

99. "Dispatch of the British Consul at Erzurum J. G. Taylor to Sir H. Elliot, dated October 3, 1872," in Reports by Her Majesty's Diplomatic and Consular Agents in Turkey Respecting the Condition of the Christian Subjects of the Porte: 1868–75, 74–76, quoted in Cora, *Transforming Erzurum*, 276.

100. *Ardzuig Darōnoy*, no. 30, Nov. 15, 1864.

101. *Giligia*, no. 44, Oct. 31, 1864.

102. This magazine, which has hardly ever been used as a primary source, published a considerable amount of news and analysis from the provinces, more so than any other periodical of that period.

103. Karekin Srvantsdyants', "Aghers ar Azkayin Varchut'iwn," *Zhamanag*, no. 27, Jan. 4, 1864.

104. Aghanyants', *Tiwan Hayots' badmut'ean*, 59–64. Some of these cases are included in Talin Suciyan, "Contesting the Authority of Armenian Administration at the Height of Tanzimat: A Case of Incest, Adultery and Abortion," 35.

105. Matenadaran, Register of Catholicosate, vol. 19, 146.219.146. This report was made to Patriarch Khrimyan in Istanbul.

106. K. S. Hovhannes Muradyan and N. Harut'iwn, "Kiwrteri kazanut'iwnnerĕ Mshoy tashdum," in *Tiwan Hayots' badmut'ean*, ed. Aghanyants', 59–64.

107. *Zhamanag*, no. 43, Aug. 15, 1864.

108. *Zhamanag*, no. 43, Aug. 15, 1864.

109. *Zhamanag*, no. 44, Aug. 29, 1864.

110. *Zhamanag*, no. 46, Sept. 26, 1864.

111. BN APC/CP12/1/075. On this document, see also Suciyan and Harootunian, "Abstracting the Peasant in Ottoman and Turkey's Historiography," 42–43.

112. Although not clarified in the text, their previous negotiation was probably with the local Ottoman administration. Another option may be that there had been negotiations in the capital on the issue that were discovered by the local Muslims. The document is in Armenian, but full of Armenian and Turkish local idiomatic words and phrases.

113. BN APC/CP12/1/075. "Zerre tahammül [no trace of patience in Turkish] chmnats."

114. Sack, *Human Territoriality*, 32, 39.

115. BOA A.DVN. 19–27. The Rum received permission as early as 1838 to call their communities by knocking on a piece of wood. See BOA HAT.777.36437.0 H-29 Zilhicce 1253. There is also an unscanned document in the Ottoman Archives that mentioned that *tahta çalmak* had to be done from within the church in order not to bother the Muslims. See BOA HR. MKT.2.81.0. H-5 Rebiülevvel 1260. Thus, as early as 1844 there were problems regarding calling communities to churches, while the calling of Muslims to a mosque was never an issue.

116. Mesrop V. Krikoryan et al., "Varaki miapanutean tughte," in *Tiwan Hayots' badmut'ean*, ed. Aghanyants', 74.

117. *Deghegakir k'aghak'agan zhoghovoy, 1870–71*, 9.

118. Raymond Kévorkian and Paul Paboudjian, *1915 öncesinde Osmanlı İmparatorluğu'nda Ermeniler*, 456, 457.

119. See Badem, *Ottoman Crimean War*, 338–39; and Karpat, "Ifa and Kaza," 32.

120. Çadırcı, *Tanzimat döneminde Anadolu kentlerinin*, 347.

121. BN APC/CCG 1/1/20. On this report, see also Suciyan and Harootunian, "Abstracting the Peasant Ottoman and Turkey's Historiography," 43–47.

122. *Deghegakir K'aghak'agan Zhoghovoy, 1870–71*, 34.

123. Özbek, *İmparatorluğun bedeli*, 41.

124. BN APC/CCG 1/1/24.

125. Çadırcı, *Tanzimat döneminde Anadolu kentlerinin*, 343, 345.

126. BN APC/CCG 1/1/20.

127. Çadırcı, *Tanzimat döneminde Anadolu kentlerinin*, 346.

128. BN APC/CCG 1/1/24.

129. BN APC/CCG 1/1/20.

130. BN APC/CCG 1/1/24.

131. BN APC/CCG 1/1/20.

132. BN APC/CCG 1/1/24.

133. Çadırcı, *Tanzimat döneminde Anadolu kentlerinin*, 344–45.

134. BN APC/CCG 1/1/20. See Çadırcı, *Tanzimat döneminde Anadolu kentlerinin*, 344. According to the regulation, each province had to establish a committee under the guidance of its governor consisting of three Muslim and three non-Muslim inhabitants. The members were appointed rather than elected.

135. BN APC/CCG 1/1/24.

136. BN APC/CCG 1/1/20.

137. Çadırcı, *Tanzimat döneminde Anadolu kentlerinin*, 343.

138. BN APC/CCG 1/1/24.

139. BN APC/CCG 1/1/20.

140. BN APC/CCG 1/1/24.

141. BN APC/CCG 1/1/20.

142. BN APC/CCG 1/1/24.

143. BN APC/CCG 1/1/21.

144. BN APC/CCG 1/1/24.

145. BN APC/CCG 1/1/21.

146. BN APC/CCG 1/1/24.

147. For more on Derviş Paşa, see Christoph Herzog and Barbara Henning, "Derviş İbrahim Paşa: Views on a Late 19th Century Ottoman Commander."

148. BN APC/CCG1/1/21.

149. Çadırcı, *Tanzimat döneminde Anadolu kentlerinin*, 320.

150. BN APC/CCG1/1/25.

151. BN APC/CCG1/1/21.

152. BN APC/CCG1/1/25.

153. BN APC/CCG1/1/21.

154. BN APC/CCG1/1/21.

155. BN APC/CCG1/1/25.

156. BN APC/CCG1/1/21.

157. BN APC/CCG1/1/25.

158. BN APC/CCG1/1/21.

159. BN APC/CCG1/1/22.

160. BN APC/CCG1/1/22

161. BN APC/CCG1/1/22.

162. BN APC/CCG1/1/25.

163. BN APC/CCG1/1/22.

164. BN APC/CCG1/1/25.

165. Known as Kuruçay today.

166. BN APC/CCG1/1/22.

167. BN APC/CCG1/1/22.

168. BN APC/CCG1/1/25.

169. BN APC/CCG1/1/22.

170. BN APC/CCG1/1/25.

171. BN APC/CCG1/1/22.

172. BN APC/CCG1/1/25.

173. BN APC/CCG1/1/22.

174. BN APC/CCG1/1/25.

175. BN APC/CCG1/1/22.

176. BN APC/CCG1/1/25.

177. For more, see T'ap'aṙagan [Kēōrk Halajian], *Tebi gakhaghan* (Boston: Hairenik, 1932), 21. Halajian wrote about the relations between Kurdish tribal chiefs and Armenians. According to him, for instance, Gulabi-zade Halil had sovereignty over ten thousand Kurds, and his son Gül Ağa had been Halajian's childhood friend (39). See T'ap'aṙagan, *Tebi gakhaghan*, 22–23.

178. BN APC/CCG1/1/23.

179. For instance, see BOA A.}MKT.MHM.6.68.0 H-08 Şevval 1264. The Reaya (non-Muslims) in Rumelia were forced into *angarya* by the landowners or BOA MVL.27.62.0. H-22 Ramazan 1264, the Armenian patriarch's request to stop the injustices including *angarya* committed by Saltoğlu El-Hac Mehmed Ağa in Elbistan. There are various complaints submitted from many parts of the empire against the practice of *angarya*.

180. BN APC/CCG1/1/25.

181. BN APC/CCG1/1/23.

182. BN APC/CCG1/1/25.

183. BN APC/CCG1/1/23.

184. For more, see chapter 1.

185. *Masis*, no. 1285, Sept. 19, 1872, quoted in Ueno, "Religious in Form, Political in Content?," 427.

186. Abdülkadir Özcan, "Zaptiye," in *TDV İslam Ansiklopedisi* 44 (2013): 128–30.

187. *First Report on Provincial Oppressions, Submitted to the Sublime Porte, in the Name of the Armenian National Assembly, April 11, 1872*, 1–8. I thank Efe Fırat from

Boğaziçi University for bringing the English translation of the patriarchate's report to my attention. Ronald Grigor Suny referred to the same translation in *They Can Live in the Desert but Nowhere Else: A History of the Armenian Genocide* (Princeton, NJ: Princeton Univ. Press, 2015), 387. The original is "Azkayin Zhoghovoy deghegakir kawaṛagan harsdaharut'eants' k'nnut'ean hantsnazhoghovoy," in *Adenakrut'iwn Azkayin Zhoghovoy* (Istanbul: Miwendisyan Dbakr, Oct. 8, 1871), 468–83.

188. *Manzume-i Efkâr*, no. 1724, Oct. 9, 1871.

189. For more, see the chapter "Report from Erznga."

190. *First Report on Provincial Oppressions*, 3.

191. *Azkayin Zhoghovoy Deghegakir Kawaṛagan*, 470.

192. *Azkayin Zhoghovoy Deghegakir Kawaṛagan*, 473.

193. *Hamaraduut'iwn, 1874–75 ew 75–76*, 26.

194. Çadırcı, *Tanzimat döneminde Anadolu kentlerinin*, 260.

195. *First Report on Provincial Oppressions*, 5 (emphasis in the original).

196. *Deghegakir k'aghak'agan zhoghovoy, 1870–71*, 29.

197. *First Report on Provincial Oppressions*, 6.

198. Nizamiye courts were established during Tanzimat to serve Muslims and non-Muslims alike to deal with issues that remained outside of the realm of sharia courts and the juridical systems of non-Muslims.

199. *First Report on Provincial Oppressions*, 7.

200. *First Report on Provincial Oppressions*, 8.

201. *Manzume-i Efkâr*, no. 1876, Mar. 15, 1872.

202. *Manzume-i Efkâr*, no. 1876, Mar. 15, 1872. and no. 1876, Mar. 16, 1872.

203. *Manzume-i Efkâr*, no. 1882, May 20, 1872.

204. *Manzume-i Efkâr*, no. 1876, Mar. 15, 1872.

205. *Manzume-i Efkâr*, no. 1877, Mar. 16, 1872.

206. Hans-Lukas Kieser, *Der verpasste friede*, 125.

207. *Hamaraduut'iwn, 1874–75 ew 75–76*, 44.

208. BOA Y.PRK.AZN.1–2.

209. M. Kh. Ballar, "M. Ballaryani namagě," in *Tiwan Hayots' badmut'ean*, ed. Aghanyants', 258.

3. Armenian-Rum Relations

1. Alboyadjian refers to such disputes dating back to the seventeenth century. See Alboyadjian, "Azkayin Sahmanatrut'iwně," 109–25. For the nineteenth-century confessional clashes, see chapter 1.

2. BN APC/CP12/8/144. This shows that it was not unusual to correspond in Greek and that although the signatories were Armenians, they likely knew the Greek language. Alternatively, the local Greek metropolitan may have had his scribe write their petition in Greek, knowing that it would not be a problem to read and translate the complaint in the capital.

3. BN APC/CP12/8/145. I thank Dimitri Theodoridis for helping me to compare the Greek version of this document, BN APC/CP12/8/144, with its Armenian translation.

4. Melik'-T'ankyan, *Hayots' Egeghets'agan irawunkě*, 1:93.

5. BN APC/CP12/8/146.

6. Ōrmanyan, "Appendix 5," in *Azkabadum*, 3:52.

7. The phenomenon of *bantukhd* was well known, as just a few years later in 1864 a novel by H. Kurkenyan published in serial form in Constantinople told the story of a *bantukhd*'s life. According to the advertisement, the fascicles of the novel were to be sold in all Armenian bookshops. *Zhamanag*, no. 40, July 4, 1864.

8. BN APC/CP22/2/025.

9. BN APC/CP19/4/076. It starts with "*Fazilet Efendim Mesrop Rupban Hazretlerine Trabizon Armenien Despot Hanesine*." The document was sent from Çarşamba and referred to Archbishop Mesrob as the "*Trabizon Armenien Despot Hanesine*." As will be seen in the next document, the Rum of the region used the term *despot hane*, which is how Rum local administrations are called. For Armenians, it was called *aṛachnortaran* (prelacy). The local Armenian administrations are referred to as *despot hane* quite often in the document.

10. P. K. Torlakyan, *Hay azkakrutyun ew panahyusutyun nyuter ew usumnasirutyunner 13, Hamshenahayeri azkakrutyuně*, 13–14. Torlakyan (born 1899) was a native of Gushana (Pınarlı), near Trabzon. I thank Yaşar Kurt for making this source available to me.

11. BN APC/CP12/8/136.

12. BN APC/CP12/8/136. *Metropolit* and *despot* are two clerical titles still used today for Rum clerics, and Kabakaroğlu uses them to refer to the Armenian prelate of Trabzon archbishop Mesrob Sukiasyan.

13. The reference must be to Payaslı İsmail Paşa who was the governor of Erzurum from May 1854 to April 1855, likely written before his appointment to Harput in April 1855. See Sinan Kuneralp, *Son dönem Osmanlı erkân ve ricali (1839–1922): Prosopografik rehber*, 85. In the Ottoman archives there is a document on his appointment to Harput, but the date was given as H. 29 Muharrem.1272, which would correspond to October 11, 1855. See BOA A.TŞF.21.63. In *Masis*, no. 181, July 14, 1855, a news item on Payaslı İsmail Paşa was published that stated as soon as he arrived in Harput, he rescued an Assyrian woman kidnapped by Kurds whom they were attempting to Islamicize. He returned the woman to her family and punished the kidnappers. It stated that by doing so he had won over the hearts of the Christian population in the region.

14. *Masis*, no. 174, May 26, 1855.

15. The date of Hovagim's conversion was given in Bērbēryan as four years before 1843, that is, 1839. See Bērbēryan, *Badmut'iwn Hayots'*, 515–16. For its detailed version, see http://www.digilib.am/book/3402/3953/24887/Պատմութիւն%20Հայոց. Reference

to it occuring on his business travel to Syria is only included in Deringil, *Conversion and Apostasy*, 69.

16. Deringil discusses this issue in the context of clashes between the progressive Tanzimat officials and the reactionaries. According to Deringil, Hovagim was beheaded because the "old guard won out." Deringil, *Conversion and Apostasy*, 69.

17. Ōrmanyan, *Azkabadum*, 3:3795.

18. Ōrmanyan, *Azkabadum*, 3:3797.

19. Bērbēryan, *Badmut'iwn Hayots'*, 515–16. For its detailed version, see http://www.digilib.am/book/3402/3953/24887/Պատմութիւն%20Հայոց.

20. Bērbēryan, *Badmut'iwn Hayots'*, 515–16.

21. Deringil refers to him as Avakim. Only once in a full quote is his name written as Hovagim. See Deringil, *Conversion and Apostasy*, 69–75.

22. BN APC/CP20/7/065. I mentioned this case, summarizing it shortly in Suciyan, "Contesting the Authority of Armenian Administration," 40.

23. Ōrmanyan, "Appendix 5," 52.

24. *Hayrenasēr*, no. 3, June 11, 1843. According to the news item, a new seminary was established, and a teacher was sent to Bandırma in 1843.

25. There is an anecdotal case published in *Manzume-i Efkar* according to which a Muslim man visited the house of a Muslim woman for a while, and the district inhabitants came together, negotiated the issue, decided to complain about this situation, and asked the *muhtar* (district/village headman) to warn her not to take any man into her house; otherwise, the case should be reported to the government. Regardless of its authenticity, the story points out there was a practice in place that did not include raiding the house and punishing the household members. *Manzume-i Efkâr*, no. 734, Aug. 24, 1868.

26. Leslie Pierce, *Morality Tales*, 357. For Zina in the sixteenth century, see also Colin Imber, "Zina in Ottoman Law."

27. BN APC/CP20/7/065.

28. BN APC/CP20/7/065.

29. BN APC/CP20/7/065.

30. BN APC/CP20/7/065.

31. BOA A.TŞF.7.51.

32. BOA I.MVL. 2320.

33. BOA A.TŞF.3.74.

34. BN ACP/CP1/15/089.

35. The same word *Hunasdan* names Greece in Armenian.

36. BN ACP/CP1/15/089.

37. Alboyadjian, *Badmut'iwn Hay Gesarioy: Deghakragan, badmagan ew azkakragan usumnasirut'iwn* (Cairo: Hagop Papazian Press, 1937), 883–91, quoted in Raymond

Kévorkian and Paul Paboujian, *1915 öncesinde Osmanlı İmparatorluğu'nda Ermeniler,* 177–78.

38. Alboyadjian, *Badmut'iwn Hay Gesarioy,* 883–91.

39. *Deghekagir K'aghak'akan Zhoghovoy, 1870–71,* 40, 33.

40. For getting an automatic divorce by converting to Islam, see Marc Baer, "Islamic Conversion Narratives of Women: Social Change and Gendered Religious Hierarchy in Early Modern Ottoman Istanbul."

41. BOA 8109, Meclis-i Vâlâ, İrade, Mar. 25, 1852, quoted in Masayuki Ueno, "Urban Politics in the 19th Century Istanbul: The Case of the Armenian Cemetery in Beyoğlu," 87.

42. Steven T. Rosenthal, *The Politics of Dependency Urban Reform in Istanbul,* 149. In 1853 the *Masis* newspaper reported about the discomfort caused by the existence of cafés near the Armenian cemetery in Pangaltı. According to the report, those cafés used the area as if it was their property, regarding it as a regular recreation site. The newspaper asserted that it was inappropriate to treat the area that way, and therefore the patriarch asked the Sublime Porte to handle the issue. See *Masis,* no. 16-65, Apr. 22, 1853.

43. *Giligia,* no. 28, July 11, 1864.

44. *Giligia,* no. 29, July 18, 1864.

45. *Giligia,* no. 35, Aug. 29, 1864.

46. *Giligia,* no. 37, Sept. 15, 1864.

47. *Deghegakir k'aghak'agan zhoghovoy,* 18–19. In the summer of 1865, one of the capital's worst cholera epidemics killed thousands of people, including many *bantukhds* and poor people, as they did not have access to basic sanitary needs and proper nutrition. The biweekly *Zhamanag* reported on the deaths and the religious ceremonies conducted by big crowds on the streets of Istanbul with the participation of clerics from all three religions, Muslims, Christians, and Jews. The churches were full from early morning to evening of people confessing their sins, doing penance, and receiving the sacrament. The biweekly also informed its readers about the complete disorder surrounding the burials. As a matter of fact, in most cases corpses were thrown into mass graves, and nobody knew the whereabouts of the deceased in the cemeteries. The biweekly reported that both Armenians and Greeks were very sloppy and inattentive to their burial rituals during the epidemic, and many Christians were buried without a proper funeral. While the news item in *Zhamanag* did not mention any conflicts during the epidemic between Armenians and Greeks, cemeteries continued to be a territorial unit in which they routinely came into contact. As mentioned in the memorandum of 1865, the Üsküdar court case was still not resolved at this time, which meant potential triggers for conflict remained during the epidemic. For more see *Zhamanag,* no. 68, Aug. 28, 1865.

48. For *kapı kahyası,* see chapter 1.

49. *Deghegakir k'aghak'agan zhoghovoy, 1870–71,* 18.

50. *Ganonatrut'iwn: Gosdantinobolsoy shrchagay tagherun ew Vosp'ori kiwgherun mech taghmants' veraperyal,* 5.

51. *Hamaraduut'iwn, 1874–75 ew 1875–76*, 39.

52. Sack, *Human Territoriality*, 216.

53. Sack, *Human Territoriality*, 219.

4. Juridical Entitlements of the Armenian Patriarchate

1. On Sicil, see Fahrettin Atar, "Şürut ve sicillat," in *TDV İslam ansiklopedisi* (Ankara: TDV, 2010), 39:270–73.

2. *Deghegakir S. P'rgich Azkayin Hiwantanotsi hokaparts'utean*, in Varujan Köseyan, *Surp Pırgiç Ermeni Hastanesi tarihçesi*, 69–73.

3. Zabel Yesayan, *Silihdari bardēznerě*, 190, 191. *Lale* is similar to *pranga*; both are forms of shackles. For the use of *pranga*/shackles, see Yasemin Saner, "Osmanlı'nın yüzlerce yıl süren cezalandırma ve korkutma refleksi: Prangaya vurma," in *Osmanlı'da asayiş, suç ve ceza*, ed. Noemi Levy and Alexander Toumarkine.

4. Yesayan, *Silihdari bardeznērě*, 192.

5. See Gülhan Balsoy, "Haseki Women's Hospital and the Female Destitute of Nineteenth-Century Istanbul."

6. BN APC/CP20/14/017.

7. BN APC/CP1/13/060.

8. This organization became the Zaptiye Nezareti after 1879. For more, see Noemi Levy, "19. yüzyılda Osmanlı'da kamu düzeni konusunda çalışmak: Bibliyografya üzerine bir değerlendirme," in *Osmanlı'da asayiş*, ed. Levy and Toumarkine, 63.

9. Çadırcı, *Tanzimat döneminde Anadolu kentlerinin*, 320.

10. BN APC/CP1/13/060.

11. On this petition, see Suciyan, "Contesting the Authority of Armenian Administration"; and Suciyan, "Kimsenin yüzünü görmedim: [Çocuk] dayımdandır: 1856'da Konya Akşehir'de Ermeni Kilisesi'nde çözülememiş bir dava."

12. The collective petition starts with "Judicious Holy Spiritual Father" (*Artaratad Srp[a]z[a]n Hayr Hokevor*) and continues with "kissing your holy feet." In the second line, it states that "our Holy *Efendi* and Amira *aghas* of our National Assembly" (*Bizim srapazan Efenedimiz ve Azkayin Joghovk Amira ağalarımız, efendilerimize*).

13. For *mundar* or *murdar*, see Etuart Hiwrmiwzyan, "Mundar or Murdar," in *Paṛkirk' hashkharaparē i krapaṛ*, 377. Here the Armenian equivalent of the word appears as *mndrel*, and its meaning in Turkish is *murdarlamak*, that is, to make something unclean, filthy, or stained.

14. BN APC/CP1/1/005.

15. Barsoumian, *Armenian Amira Class of Istanbul*, 29–31.

16. Suk'ias Sōmalyan, "Ishkhan," in *Hamaṛōd paṛaran i Hayē hankghiagan ew i Dajig / A Pocket Dictionary of the English Armenian and Turkish Languages*, 172.

17. Madat'ea Bedrosyan, "Garkavor," in *Nor paṛkirk' Hayeren-Ankliaren*, 332.

18. For more, see Barsoumian, *Armenian Amira Class of Istanbul*, 32.

19. For *aylazki*, see Mgrdich Avkeryan and Krikor Jelalyan, *Aṛtseṛn paṛaran haygazean lezui*, 34. See also Manuel Chakhchakhyan, *Paṛkirk' paṛpar Hay ew Idalagan*, 52. In the former, one of the synonyms is *akher milletden*, meaning "from another *millet*," while in the latter we also find the definition of the word in Italian: "Not Jew, . . . not Christian, . . . Muslim." In this text, *akher millet* and *aylazkinin* are used separately. Therefore, it is clear that they refer to different groups.

20. BN APC/CP1/1/005.

21. Melik'-T'ankyan, *Hayots' Egeghets'agan irawunkĕ*, 1:240–65. According to these laws, not only are relations between uncle and niece strictly forbidden, but so were relations among any relatives of at least six degrees, kinship through marriage, and even marriage between those with a family connection as a godparent. See Melik'-T'ankyan, *Hayots' Egeghets'agan irawunkĕ*, 2:248–65.

22. Melik'-T'ankyan, *Hayots' Egeghets'agan irawunkĕ*, 1:236–50, 245, 246, 243, 241, 244. According to Article 49, if the woman was raped, she could not be responsible for the crime. The laws accepted in the fifth century at the council of Shahabivan, near today's Beyazıd, prohibited marriage or adultery among close relatives. Melik'-T'ankyan, *Hayots' Egeghets'agan irawunkĕ*, 1:334.

23. Donald Quataert, "Manufacturing," in *An Economic and Social History of the Ottoman Empire*, ed. Halil İnalcık and Donald Quataert, 900.

24. BN APC/CP12/06/090.

25. BN APC/CP12/06/090.

26. Reşat Ekrem Koçu and Mehmet Ali Akbay, *İstanbul ansiklopedisi*, 1850. Stanford Shaw refers to the yarn factory in Eyüp as "Istanbul's principal political prison" without giving any source for this statement. See Stanford Shaw, *The Jews of the Ottoman Empire and the Turkish Republic*, 161.

27. BOA A. MKT.1631.

28. The original word used is *martasirut'iwn*, which can be translated as "humanity," as well as "kindness" or "graciousness." See Zakaria D. S. Papazyan, *Kordznagan pararan Hayeren-Anklieren*, 298. It also means "philanthropy."

29. Avkeryan and Jelalyan, "Molut'iwn," in *Aṛtseṛn paṛaran haygazean lezui*, 571. See also Madat'ea Bedrosyan, "Molut'iwn," in *Nor paṛkirk' Hay-Ankliaren*, 483.

30. BN APC/CP22/11/008. The signatories identified themselves as "the wardens of the St. Kevork Church of Samatya." The right corner of the paper is torn off, and therefore no signature or stamp can be seen.

31. Quataert, "Manufacturing," 900.

32. Naif Öztürk, "19. yüzyılda Osmanlı İmparatorluğu'nda sanayileşme ve 1827'de kurulan vakıf iplik fabrikası."

33. ABCFM, Mission to the Armenians, vol. 11, no. 114, Jan. 7, 1839, in Barsoumian, *Armenian Amira Class of Istanbul*, 132.

34. Barsoumian, *Armenian Amira Class of Istanbul*, 132. See also Bērbēryan, *Badmut'iwn Hayots'*, 261, 491.

35. This has to be before the publication of the book in 1871.

36. Bērbēryan, *Badmut'iwn Hayots'*, 261.

37. BOA, HAT 1321/51599-B. Akın Sefer utilizes the same document, but prefered to present it as undated. While the document does lack a typical Ottoman script date, it does contain one written in Arabic numerals, year H., 1250/G., 1834. While this date may have been added later, the document is not undated. See Akın Sefer, "The Arsenal of Ottoman Modernity: Workers, Industry and the State in the Late Ottoman Istanbul," 180.

38. BOA, HAT 1321/51599-B.

39. Sefer, "Arsenal of Ottoman Modernity," 181.

40. For *forsa*, see Nihat Engin, *Osmanlı Devleti'nde kölelik*, 167–70.

41. Ehud Toledano, *The Ottoman Slave Trade and Its Suppression: 1840–1890*, 17.

42. Toledano, *Ottoman Slave Trade*, 114. His answer to the question: "trauma triggered by rebellions, first by the Greeks in 1820s and then by the Egyptian governor Mehmed Ali Pasha in 1830s."

43. BOA.D.BŞM.TRE. d.15713 and BOA.D.BŞM.TRE.d.15716, quoted in Sefer, "Arsenal of Ottoman Modernity," 104–5.

44. Nazan Maksudyan, *Orphans and Destitute Children in the Late Ottoman Empire*, 95. On orphans working in the yarn factory, see also İnalcık and Quataert, *Economic and Social History of the Ottoman Empire*, vol. 2, *1600–1914* (Cambridge: Cambridge Univ. Press, 1997), 900; and Donald Quataert, *Ottoman Manufacturing in the Age of the Industrial Revolution*, 47, 175.

45. On this document, see also Talin Suciyan, "Testifying Impotence, Annulling Marriage."

46. BN APC/CP12/106.

47. The decision has fourteen signatures consisting of both married priests (*kahanay*) and celibate priests (*vartabed*), two of them from the Mother Church of the Patriarchate.

48. As there was a Catholic Armenian Çelebi by the name of Petraki, I cannot exclude the possibility that he was a Catholic Armenian. For Çelebi Petraki, see Barsoumian, *Armenian Amira Class of Istanbul*, 67.

49. Ōrmanyan, "Appendix 5: Armenian Patriarchs of Constantinople According to the Chronology of Ōrmanyan," in *Azkabadum*, 3:52.

50. BN APC/CP12/105.

51. Melik'-T'ankyan, "Bsagi ganonnerě 1875 tuin hradaragadz" [Marriage Laws published in 1875], in *Hayots' Egeghets'agan irawunkě*, 1:637–38, 2:271.

52. Melik'-T'ankyan discusses valid and invalid marriages based on the Shahabivan Laws of the fifth century, but the points he referred to are related only to marriages conducted illegally. One of the most comprehensive sets of regulations accepted during

the Shahabivan Council defines precise conditions for the annulment of a marriage to be permitted. This would include, for instance, a forced marriage, marriage among relatives, or marriage conducted secretly. All these were considered illegal; therefore, the marriage would not be valid if conducted under these circumstances. See Melik'-T'ankyan, *Hayots' Egeghets'agan irawunkĕ*, 2:268.

53. Melik'-T'ankyan, *Hayots' Egeghets'agan irawunkĕ*, 2:269. The first legally valid reason is prostitution. The second is incurable mental or physical disease, which according to the author included also having both female and male characteristics, and the third reason was the absence of the husband for more than seven years. See Melik'-T'ankyan, *Hayots' Egeghets'agan irawunkĕ*, 2:270–72.

54. Melik'-T'ankyan, *Hayots' Egeghets'agan irawunkĕ*, 2:272.

55. Ebru Aykut, "Toxic Murder, Female Poisoners and the Question of Agency at the Late Ottoman Courts, 1840–1908." For earlier periods and women poisoning their husbands, see Colin Imber, "Why You Should Poison Your Husband: A Note on Liability in Hanafi Law in the Ottoman Period."

56. Milen V. Petrov, "Everyday Forms of Compliance: Subaltern Commentaries on Ottoman Reform, 1864–68." On the limitations of *sicils*, see Haim Gerber, *State, Society and Law in Islam: Ottoman Law in Comparative Perspective*, 15, 43; and Dror Zeevi, "The Use of Ottoman Sharia Court Records as a Source for Middle Eastern History."

57. Petrov, "Everyday Forms of Compliance," 735.

58. In addition, I encountered *istintak* documents from Muş (1868) in Aghanyants', *Tiwan Hayots' badmut'ean*, 94–100.

59. Melik'-T'ankyan, *Hayots' Egeghets'agan irawunkĕ*, 1:243, 327.

60. BN APC/CP19/4/136.

61. Melik'-T'ankyan, *Hayots' Egeghets'agan irawunkĕ*, 1:246, 327.

62. BN APC/CP19/4/139.

63. For more on women pretenting to have hysterical crises, see Sabine Strasser, *Die Unreinheit ist Fruchtbar: Grenzüberschreitungen in einem türkischen Dorf am Schwarzen Meer*, 230–35.

64. Melik'-T'ankyan, *Hayots' Egeghets'agan irawunkĕ*, 2:269–70.

65. BN APC/CP19/4/137.

66. BN APC/CP19/4/139.

67. BN APC/CP19/4/139.

68. The Turkish translation would be *kocaya varmak*.

69. Melik'-T'ankyan, *Hayots' Egeghets'agan irawunkĕ*, 1:481.

70. Minas Pjshgyan [Bıjışkyan], *Badmut'iwn Bondosi vor e Sew Dzov*, 91.

71. Minas Pjshgyan [Bıjışkyan], *Karadeniz kıyıları tarih ve coğrafyası*, 59.

72. Ghugas Injijian, *Ashkharakrut'iwn ch'orsits' masants' ashkharhi*, 398–400.

73. Deringil, *Conversion and Apostasy*, 111–56.

74. Yorgo Andreadis, *Gizli din taşıyanlar* (Istanbul: Belge Yayınları, 1999), 66, quoted in Deringil, *Conversion and Apostasy*, 118.

75. Andreadis, *Gizli din taşıyanlar*, 14, quoted in Deringil, *Conversion and Apostasy*, 118.

76. Deringil, *Conversion and Apostasy*, 120.

77. BN APC/CP19/4/076.

78. BN APC/CP19/4/139.

79. BN APC/CP19/4/137.

80. BN APC/CP19/4/137.

81. BN APC/CP19/4/138.

82. Melik'-T'ankyan, *Hayots' Egeghets'agan irawunkě*, 1:243.

83. Hagop Anasian, *XVII dari azatakragan sharjumnern Arevmtyan Hayastanum* [Seventeenth Century Liberation Movements in Western Armenia] (Yerevan: n.p., 1961), 59, quoted in Barsoumian, *Armenian Amira Class of Istanbul*, 21.

84. BN APC/CP19/4/138.

85. See, for instance, BN APC/CP19/4/137 and BN APC/CP19/4/136.

86. Alboyadjian, "Azkayin Sahmanatrut'iwně," 96.

87. BN APC/CP12/5/059.

88. "After the first year of marriage our fathers would leave our mothers, going for *bantkhdel* [becoming migrant workers]. Many of us were not even born or just a couple of months old when our fathers left. And the *bantkhdut'iwn* [concept of migrant worker] was to be continued throughout their entire lifetime. They would return every four or five years, would stay for a year and then would leave again. From 20 to 60 years of age, out of 40 years our fathers would be present 5, or at most 10 years in the village. Our mothers would live 35 to 40 years of their lives alone in the villages." See Hagop Mnts'uri, "Mer mayrerě," 87.

89. BN APC/CP19/2/008.

90. *Ağcı* is a person who makes fishing nets.

91. BN APC/CP19/2/008.

92. Başak Tuğ, "Ottoman Women as Legal and Marital Subject," 365.

93. BN APC/CP19/2/008.

94. BN APC/CP19/2/008.

95. For *mahdesi*, see the explanation above.

96. *Deghegakir k'aghak'agan zhoghovoy, 1870–71*, 35.

97. Melik'-T'ankyan, *Hayots' Egeghets'agan irawunkě*, 2:267. At the same time, the author mentioned that the woman was asked to give the part she brought to the marriage to the local administration. According to him, this might have been thought of as a kind of penalty for the woman for not being able to keep the man in his marriage.

98. Melik'-T'ankyan, *Hayots' Egeghets'agan irawunkě*, 2:268.

99. Melik‘-T‘ankyan, *Hayots‘ Egeghets‘agan irawunkě*, 2:271.
100. BN APC/CP12/5/054.
101. BN APC/CP24/3/121.
102. BN APC/CP22/2/068.
103. Ōrmanyan, "Appendix 5," 52.
104. BN APC/CP20/13.
105. *Hrahank vasn gazmut‘ean*, 7.

Conclusion

1. Harootunian was inspired by Ernst Bloch, who wrote on the simultaneity of the nonsimultaneous (*Gleichzeitigkeit des Ungleichzeitigen*), as well as by Antonio Gramsci's noncontemporaneity of the contemporaneous, Marx's plural temporalities, and Peruvian philosopher Jose Carlos Mariategui's analysis of contemporaneous noncontemporaneity of indigenous people. For more on noncontemporaneity, see Ernst Bloch, "Summary Transition: Non-contemporaneity and Obligation to Its Dialectic," in *Heritage of Our Times*, 97–148; Vittorio Morfino and Peter Thomas, *The Government of Time: Plural Temporality in the Marxist Tradition*; and Harry Harootunian, "'In the Zone of Occult Instability': Some Reflections on Unevenness, Discordant Temporalities and the Logic of Historical Practice." The last article was delivered first as the annual Edward Said Lecture in Warwick University, United Kingdom, May 2019. I am thankful to Harry Harootunian for making his paper available and discussing its content with me.

2. For more on this, see Suciyan, "Hagop Mnt‘suri's *The Second Marriage*."

Bibliography

Unpublished Primary Sources

Matenadaran, Mesrob Mashtots Institute of Ancient Manuscripts, Yerevan Catholicosate Archive, vol. 19, 146.219.146

Nubar Library Archive of the Patriarchate of Constantinople, AGBU, Paris

Ottoman Archives (BOA), Istanbul, Turkey

Published Primary Sources

Aghanyants', Kiwd, ed. *Tiwan Hayots' badmut'ean, Kirk' 18: Harsdaharut'iwnner Dajgahayasdanum (Vawerakrer 1801–1888).* Tblisi: Dbaran N. Aghanyants'i, 1915.

Antranik. *Dersim seyahatnamesi.* Translated by Payline Tovmasyan. Istanbul: Aras Yayıncılık, 2014.

Bērbēryan, Avedis. *Badmut'iwn Hayots' sgsyal i 1772 ame p'rgchin minch'ev hamn 1860.* G. Bolis: Boghosi Kirijyan, 1871.

Çadırcı, Musa. *Tanzimat döneminde Anadolu kentlerinin sosyal ve ekonomik yapıları.* Ankara: Türk Tarih Kurumu, 1991.

Cevdet, Ahmet. *Ma'aruzat.* Edited by Yusuf Halaçoğlu. Istanbul: Çağrı Yayınları, 1980.

———. *Tezâkir 1-12.* Edited by Cavid Baysun. Ankara: Türk Tarih Kurumu Yayınları, 1953.

———. *Tezâkir 21–39.* Edited by Cavid Baysun. Ankara: Türk Tarih Kurumu Yayınları, 1963.

———. *Tezâkir 40–Tetimme.* Edited by Cavid Baysun. Ankara: Türk Tarih Kurumu Yayınları, 1991.

Deghegakir hamaraduut'ean getronagan varchut'ean vanoreits' khorhrtoy 1872–74 ami. G. Bolis: Dbakrut'iwn H. Kavafyan, 1874.

Deghegakir k'aghak'agan zhoghovoy getronagan varchut'ean ami ar azgayin ĕnthanur zhoghovoy, 1870–71. G. Bolis: Dbakrut'iwn H. Miwhendisyan, 1871.

Deghegakir k'aghak'agan zhoghovoy getronagan varchut'ean ar azkayin ĕnthanur zhoghovoy. G. Bolis: Dbakrut'iwn R. H. Kiwrkjyan, 1865.

Deghegakir S. P'rgich Azkayin Hiwantanotsi hokaparts'utean. G. Bolis: Dbakrut'iwn H. Kavafyan, 1883.

First Report on Provincial Oppressions, Submitted to the Sublime Porte, in the Name of the Armenian National Assembly, April 11, 1872. London: Gilbert and Rivington, 1877.

Ganonatrut'iwn: Gosdantinobolso shrchagay tagherun ew Vosp'ori kiwgherun mech taghmants' veraperyal. G. Bolis: n.p., 1869.

Hamaraduut'iwn azkayin getronagan varchut'ean k'aghak'agan zhoghovoy 1874–75 ēw 1875–76 amats'. G. Bolis: Dbakrut'iwn S. Mikaelyan, 1876.

Hrahank haraperut'ean aṛach'nortats' kawaṛagan varchut'eants' ĕnt deghagan garavariut'ean, vaverats'eal i gronagan ew k'aghak'agan kharn zhoghovoy getronagan varchut'ean. G. Bolis: Dbaran H. Miwhendisyan, 1873.

Hrahank vasn gazmu'tean kawaṛagan ĕnthanur zhoghovoy. G. Bolis: Dbakrut'iwn R.H. Kiwrkjyan, 1861.

Ōrēnk' azkayin varchagan gazmagerbut'ean, hasdadeal hazkayin erespokhanagan zhoghovoy ı nisd z. patsman 1880 ami. G. Bolis: Dbakrut'iwn Baronean, 1880.

Vincke, Karl Freiherr von, Friedrich Fischer, Helmuth von Moltke, and Heinrich Kiepert. *Memoir über die Construction der Karte von Kleinasien und Türkisch Armenien: In 6 Blatt*. Edited by Heinrich Kiepert. Berlin: Simon Schropp, 1854.

Newspapers

Ardzuig Darōnoy
Ceride-i Şarkiye
Hayrenasēr
Manzume-i Efkâr
Masis
Takvim-i Vekayi
Zhamanag: Hantēs Hayrenanuēr

Memoirs

Der Yeghiayan, Zaven. *Badriarkagan hushers: Vawerakirner ew vgayut'iwnner*. Cairo: Nor Asdgh, 1947.

Laurie, Rev. Thomas. *Dr. Grant and the Mountain Nestorians*. Boston: Gould and Lincoln, 1853.

Yesayan, Zabel. *Silihdari bardeznērě*. Vol. 1. Fascimile of the 1st ed. Antilias: Dbaran Giligio Gatoghigosut'ean, 1987.

Secondary Sources

Dictionaries

Avkeryan, Mgrdich', and Krikor Jelalyan. *Aṛtseṛn paṛaran haygazean lezui*. Venice: Surp Ghazar, 1865.

Balakian, Krikoris. *Hay koghkot'an: Truakner hay mardirosakrut'eně; Beṛlinēn tēbi Dērzor, 1914–1920*. Vol. 1. Vienna: Mkhitarian Press, 1922.

———. *Hay koghkot'an: Truakner hay mardirosakrut'enē; Beṛlinēn tēbi Dērzor, 1914–1920*. Vol. 2. Paris: Impr. Araxes, 1959.

Balakian, Krikoris, and Peter Balakian. *Armenian Golgotha*. New York: Alfred A. Knopf, 2009.

Bedrosyan, Madat'ea. *Nor paṛkirk' Hayeren-Ankliaren*. Venice: Mkhitareants' Dbaran, 1875.

Chakhchakhyan, Manuel. *Paṛkirk' paṛpar Hay ew Idalagan*. St. Lazarus, Venice: Dbaran Srpuyn Ghazaru, 1837.

Hiwrmiwzyan, Etuart. *Paṛkirk' hashkharapare i krapaṛ*. Venice: Surp Ghazar Dbaran, 1869.

Sōmalyan, Suk'ias. *Hamaṛōd paṛaran i Hayē hankghiagan ew i Dajig / A Pocket Dictionary of the English Armenian and Turkish Languages*. Venice: Surp Ghazar Dbaran, 1843.

Other Sources

Akiba, Jun. "Preliminaries to a Comparative History of the Russian and Ottoman Empires: Perspectives from Ottoman Studies." In *Imperiology: From Empirical Knowledge to Discussing the Russian Empire*, edited by Kimitaka Matsuzato, 33–47. Sapporo: Slavic Research Center, 2007.

Alboyadjian, Arshag. "Azkayin Sahmanatrut'iwně: Ir dzakumě ew girarumě." In *1910 Ěntartsag Ōrats'uyts' S. P'rgchean Hiwantanots'i Hayots'*, 76–528. Facsimile of the 1st ed. Istanbul: Korpus Kültür Sanat Yayıncılık, 2012.

Antaramian, Richard. *Brokers of Faith, Brokers of Empire*. Stanford, CA: Stanford Univ. Press, 2020.

Artinian, Vartan. *The Armenian Constitutional System in the Ottoman Empire, 1839–1863: A Study of Its Historical Development*. Istanbul: n.p., 1988.

———. *Osmanlı Devleti'nde Ermeni Anayasası'nın doğuşu, 1839–1863*. Istanbul: Aras Yayıncılık, 2004.

Astourian, Stephan. "The Silence of the Land." In *A Question of Geoncide Armenians and Turks at the End of the Ottoman Empire*, edited by Ronald Grigor Suny, Fatma Müge Göçek, and Norman M. Naimank, 55–82. Oxford: Oxford Univ. Press, 2011.

Ateş, Sabri. *The Ottoman-Iranian Borderlands: Making a Boundary, 1843–1914*. New York: Cambridge Univ. Press, 2013.

Aykut, Ebru. "Toxic Murder, Female Poisoners and the Question of Agency at the Late Ottoman Courts, 1840–1908." *Journal of Women's History* 28, no. 3 (2013): 114–37.

Aymes, Marc. *A Provincial History of the Ottoman Empire: Cyprus and the Eastern Mediterranean in the Nineteenth Century*. Translated by Adrian Morfee. London: Routledge, 2014.

Badem, Candan. *The Ottoman Crimean War (1853–56)*. Leiden: Brill, 2010.

Baer, Marc. "Islamic Conversion Narratives of Women: Social Change and Gendered Religious Hierarchy in Early Modern Ottoman Istanbul." *Gender and History* 16, no. 2 (2004): 425–58.

Balsoy, Gülhan. "Haseki Women's Hospital and the Female Destitute of Nineteenth-Century Istanbul." *Middle Eastern Studies* 55, no. 3 (2018): 289–300.

Barkan, Ömer Lütfi. "Türk toprak hukuku ve tarihinde Tanzimat ve 1274 (1858) tarihli arazi kanunnamesi." In *Tanzimat I Yüzüncü Yıldönümü Münasebetiyle*, 321–421. Istanbul: Maarif Matbaası, 1940.

Barkey, Karen. "In Different Times: Scheduling and Social Control in the Ottoman Empire, 1550–1650." *Comparative Studies in Society and History* 38, no. 3 (1996): 460–83.

Barsoumian, Hagop L. *The Armenian Amira Class of Istanbul*. Yerevan: American Univ. of Armenia, 2007.

Baykara, Tuncay. *Anadolu'nun tarihi coğrafyasına giriş I: Anadolu'nun idari taksimatı*. Ankara: Türk Kültürünü Araştırma Enstitüsü Yayınları, 1988.

Bayraktar, Uğur Bahadır. "Yurtluk-Ocaklıks: Land, Politics of Notables and Society in Ottoman Kurdistan, 1820–1890." PhD diss., Boğaziçi Univ., 2015.

Benjamin, Walter. *Gesammelte Schrifte*. Frankfurt: Suhrkampf, 1980.

Bilir, Sezen, and Alişan Akpınar. "Kürdistan eyaletinin kuruluşu." *Kürt Tarihi*, no. 3 (Oct. 2018): 21–24.

Bloch, Ernst. *Heritage of Our Times*. New York: Polity Press, 1991.

Bruinessen, Martin van. *Agha Shaikh and State: The Social and Political Structures of Kurdistan*. London: Zed Books, 1992.

Çadırcı, Musa. *Tanzimat Sürecinde Türkiye: Askerlik*. Edited by Tülay Ercoşkun. Ankara: İmge Kitabevi, 2008.

Cora, Yaşar Tolga. "Transforming Erzurum/Karin: The Social and Economic History of a Multi-ethnic Ottoman City in the 19th Century." PhD diss., Univ. of Chicago, 2016.

Davison, Roderic H. *Reform in the Ottoman Empire, 1856–1876*. New York: Gordian Press, 1973.

Demirci, Fatih. "Tanzimat'ın Erdemi: Özeleştiri ve adalet problematiğinin ihyası." *Muhafazakar Düşünce Dergisi* 15, no. 4 (2008): 173–92.

Derderian, Dzovinar. "Nation-Making and the Language of Colonialism: Voices from Ottoman Van in Armenian Print Media and Handwritten Petitions (1820s to 1870s)." PhD diss., Univ. of Michigan, 2019.

Deringil, Selim. *Conversion and Apostasy in the Late Ottoman Empire*. New York: Cambridge Univ. Press, 2012.

———. *The Well-Protected Domains: Ideology and the Legitimation of Power in the Ottoman Empire, 1876–1909*. London: I. B. Tauris, 1999.

Ekinci, Ekrem Buğra. *Osmanlı mahkemeleri*. Istanbul: Arı Sanat, 2004.

Engin, Nihat. *Osmanlı Devleti'nde kölelik*. Istanbul: Marmara Üniversitesi İlahiyat Fakültesi Vakfı Yayınları, 1998.

Eppel, Michael. "The Demise of the Kurdish Emirates: The Impact of Ottoman Reforms and International Relations on Kurdistan during the First Half of the Nineteenth Century." *Middle Eastern Studies* 44, no. 2 (2008): 237–58.

Erewanyan, Kēōrk. *Badmut'iwn Charsandjaki Hayots'*. Beirut: Dbaran Donikyan, 1956.

Ertem, Özge. "Considering Famine in the Late Nineteenth Century Ottoman Empire: A Comparative Framework and Overview." *Collegium: Studies across Disciplines in the Humanities and Social Sciences* 22 (2017): 151–72.

Fabian, Johannes. *Time and the Other: How Anthropology Makes Its Object*. New York: Columbia Univ. Press, 1983.

Findley, Carter. *Bureaucratic Reform in the Ottoman Empire: The Sublime Porte, 1789–1922*. Princeton, NJ: Princeton Univ. Press, 1980.

Fortna, Benjamin C. "Change in the School Maps of the Late Ottoman Empire." *Imago Mundi* 57, no. 1 (2005): 23–34.

Gerber, Haim. *State, Society and Law in Islam: Ottoman Law in Comparative Perspective*. Albany: State Univ. of New York Press, 1994.

Giwlbēngyan, Badrig. *Ampoghchagan erger Khrimean Hayrigi*. New York: Gochnag Dbaran, 1929.

Gözel, Oya. "The implementation of the Ottoman Land Code of 1858 in Eastern Anatolia." Master's thesis, METU, 2007.

Haboona, Hirmis. *Assyrians, Kurds, and Ottomans: Intercommunal Relations on the Periphery of the Ottoman Empire.* Amherst, NY: Cambria Press, 2008.

Hakan, Sinan. *Osmanlı arşiv belgelerinde Kürtler ve Kürt direnişleri (1817–1867).* Istanbul: Doz Yayıncılık, 2007.

Hanioğlu, Şükrü. *A Brief History of the Late Ottoman Empire.* Princeton, NJ: Princeton Univ. Press, 2008.

Harootunian, Harry. "'In the Zone of Occult Instability': Some Reflections on Unevenness, Discordant Temporalities and the Logic of Historical Practice." In *Archaism and Anachrony: Reflections on the Question of Historical Time and Uneven Development.* Durham, NC: Duke Univ. Press, forthcoming.

Herzog, Christoph, and Barbara Henning. "Derviş İbrahim Paşa: Views on a Late 19th Century Ottoman Commander." In *Occasional Papers in Ottoman Biographies,* edited by Christoph Herzog, 1–21. Bamberg: OPUS, Otto-Friederich Universitaet, 2012.

Imber, Colin. "Why You Should Poison Your Husband: A Note on Liability in Hanafi Law in the Ottoman Period." In *Studies in Ottoman History and Law,* 255–61. Istanbul: Isis Press, 1996.

———. "Zina in Ottoman Law." In *Studies in Ottoman History and Law,* 176–206. Istanbul: Isis Press, 1996.

İnalcık, Halil, and Donald Quataert, eds. *An Economic and Social History of the Ottoman Empire.* Cambridge: Cambridge Univ. Press, 1994.

İnalcık, Halil, and Mehmet Seyitdanlıoğlu, eds. *Tanzimat: Değişim sürecinde Osmanlı İmparatorluğu.* Ankara: Phoenix Yay. 2006.

Injijian, Ghugas. *Ashkharakrut'iwn ch'orsits' masants' ashkharhi.* Vol. 1. Venice: Surp Ghazar, 1806.

Issawi, Charles, ed. *The Economic History of the Middle East, 1800–1914: A Book of Readings.* Chicago: Univ. of Chicago Press, 1966.

———. *An Economic History of the Middle East and North Africa.* New York: Columbia Univ. Press, 1982.

Jwaideh, Wadie. *The Kurdish National Movement: Its Origins and Development.* Syracuse, NY: Syracuse Univ. Press, 2006.

Karpat, Kemal. "Ifa and Kaza: The İlmiye State and Modernism in Turkey, 1820–1960." In *Frontiers of Ottoman Studies.* Vol. 1, *State, Province, and the West,* edited by Colin Imber and Keiko Kiyotaki, 25–42. London: I. B. Tauris, 2005.

Kévorkian, Raymond. *The Armenian Genocide: A Complete History*. London: I. B. Tauris, 2011.

Kévorkian, Raymond, and Paul Paboudjian. *1915 öncesinde Osmanlı İmparatorluğu'nda Ermeniler*. Istanbul: Aras, 2012.

Khaṛadyan, Alperd, Marko Mkhitaryan, and Linda Geovorgyan, eds. *Hay barperagan mamuli badmut'yun*. Cairo: H. H. Kidut'yunneri Azkayin Agatemia Badmut'yan Insdidud, 2006.

Khoury, Dina Rizk. "Administrative Practice between Religious Law (Sharia) and State Law (Kanun) on the Eastern Frontiers of the Ottoman Empire." *Journal of Early Modern History* 5, no. 4 (2001): 305–30.

Kieser, Hans-Lukas. *Der verpasste friede: Mission, ethnie und staat in den ostprovinzen der Türkei 1839–1938*. Zurich: Chronos Verlag, 2000.

Koç, Yener. "Bedirxan Pashazades Power Relations and Nationalism (1876–1914)." Master's thesis, Boğaziçi Univ., 2012.

Koçu, Reşat Ekrem, and Mehmet Ali Akbay. *İstanbul ansiklopedisi*. Vol. 4. Istanbul: Istanbul Anskilopedisi Neşriyat Koll. Şti., 1960.

Koselleck, Reinhart. *Zeitschichten: Studien zur Historik*. Frankfurt: Suhrkamp, 2003.

Kühn, Thomas. "An Imperial Borderland as Colony: Knowledge Production and the Elaboration of Difference in Ottoman Yemen, 1872–1918." Borderlands of the Ottoman Empire in the 19th and Early 20th Centuries. *MIT Electronic Journal of Middle East Studies* 3 (Spring 2003): 4–16.

Kuneralp, Sinan. *Son dönem Osmanlı erkân ve ricali (1839–1922): Prosopografik rehber*. Istanbul: Isis, 2003.

Kurmuş, Orhan. "The Cotton Famine and Its Effects on the Ottoman Empire." In *The Ottoman Empire and the World-Economy*. Edited by Huri İslamoğlu-İnan, 160–68. Cambridge: Cambridge Univ. Press, 1987.

Levy, Noemi, and Alexander Toumarkine, eds. *Osmanlı'da asayiş, suç ve ceza*. Istanbul: Tarih Vakfı Yurt Yayınları, 2008.

Makdisi, Ussama. *The Culture of Sectarianism: Community, History and Violence in the Nineteenth Century Ottoman Lebanon*. Berkeley: Univ. of California Press, 2000.

Maksudyan, Nazan. *Orphans and Destitute Children in the Late Ottoman Empire*. Syracuse, NY: Syracuse Univ. Press, 2014.

Melik'-T'ankyan, Nerses. *Hayots' Egeghets'agan irawunkě*. Vol. 1. Shushi: Dbaran Eghisapet M. Mahdesi Hagopyan, 1903.

———. *Hayots' Egeghets'agan irawunkě*. Vol. 2. Shushi: Arakadib Der Sahagyani, 1905.

Mnts'uri, Hagop. "Mer mayrerě." In *Kiwghě gabri im mech's*. Istanbul: Aras, 2005.

Morfino, Vittorio, and Peter Thomas. *The Government of Time: Plural Temporality in the Marxist Tradition*. Leiden: Brill, 2018.

Neumann, Christoph K. "Ahmed Cevdet Paşa." In *Encyclopaedia of Islam*, edited by Kate Fleet et al. http://dx.doi.org/10.1163/1573-3912_ei3_COM_22786.

Ōrmanyan, Maghakia. *Azkabadum*. Vols. 1 and 3. Antilias: Catholicosate of Cilicia, 2001.

Ortaylı, İlber. *İmparatorluğun en uzun yüzyılı*. Istanbul: Hil Yayınları, 1993.

Özbek, Nadir. *İmparatorluğun bedeli: Osmanlı'da vergi, siyaset ve toplumsal adalet (1839–1908)*. Istanbul: Boğaziçi Ünversitesi Yayınları, 2015.

———. "The Politics of Taxation and the 'Armenian Question' during the Late Ottoman Empire, 1876–1908." *Comparative Studies in Society and History* 54, no. 4 (2012).

Özok-Gündoğan, Nilay. "Ruling the Periphery, Governing the Land: The Making of the Modern State in Kurdistan, 1840–1870." *Comparative Studies in South Asia, Africa and the Middle East* 34, no. 1 (2014): 160–75.

Öztürk, Naif. "19. yüzyılda Osmanlı İmparatorluğu'nda sanayileşme ve 1827'de kurulan vakıf iplik fabrikası." *Vakıflar Dergisi* 21 (1990): 23–80.

Papazyan, Zakaria D. S. *Kordznagan paṛaran Hayerēn-Anklierēn*. G. Bolis: H. Madt'ēōsyan, 1905.

Paployan, M. A. *Hay barperagan mamuli madenakidagan hamahavak' ts'uts'ag (1794–1980)*. Yerevan: Haygagan SSH Kidut'yunneri Agatemia Hradaragchut'yun, 1986.

Pehlivan, Zozan. "Abandoned Villages in Diyarbekir Province at the End of the 'Little Ice Age.'" In *The Ottoman East in the Nineteenth Century: Societies, Identities and Politics*, edited by Yaşar Tolga Cora, Dzovinar Derderian, and Ali Sipahi, 223–46. London: I. B. Tauris, 2016.

Petrov, Milen V. "Everyday Forms of Compliance: Subaltern Commentaries on Ottoman Reform, 1864–68." *Comparative Studies in Society and History* 46, no. 4 (2004): 730–59.

Pierce, Leslie. *Morality Tales*. Berkeley: Univ. of California Press, 2003.

Pjshgyan [Bıjışkyan], Minas. *Karadeniz kıyıları tarih ve coğrafyası*. Translated by Hrand Der Andreasyan. Istanbul: Istanbul Üniversitesi Edebiyat Fakültesi Yayınları, 1969. Originally published as *Badmut'iwn Bondosi vor ē Sew Dzov*. Venice: S. Ghazar, 1819.

Polatel, Mehmet. "Armenians and the Land Question in the Ottoman Empire, 1870–1915." PhD diss., Boğaziçi Univ., 2017.

Quataert, Donald. *Ottoman Manufacturing in the Age of the Industrial Revolution*. Cambridge: Cambridge Univ. Press, 1993.

Rosenthal, Steven T. *The Politics of Dependency: Urban Reform in Istanbul*. Westport, CT: Greenwood Press, 1980.

Rubin, Avi. *Ottoman Nizamiye Courts: Law and Modernity*. New York: Palgrave Macmillan, 2011.

Sack, Robert David. *Human Territoriality*. Cambridge: Cambridge Univ. Press, 1986.

Saraçoğlu, M. Safa. "Economic Interventionism, Islamic Law and Provincial Government in the Ottoman Empire." In *Law and Legality in the Ottoman Empire and Republic of Turkey*, edited by Kent F. Schull, M. Safa Saraçoğlu, and Robert Zens. Bloomington: Indiana Univ. Press, 2016.

Sasuni, Garō. *Badmut'iwn Darōni ashkharhi*. Beirut: Dbaran Sevan, 1956.

Schull, Kent F., M. Safa Saraçoğlu, and Robert Zens, eds. *Law and Legality in the Ottoman Empire and Republic of Turkey*. Bloomington: Indiana Univ. Press, 2016.

Sefer, Akın. "The Arsenal of Ottoman Modernity: Workers, Industry and the State in the Late Ottoman Istanbul." PhD diss., Northwestern Univ., 2018.

Shaw, Stanford. *The Jews of the Ottoman Empire and the Turkish Republic*. Hemshire: Macmillan Press, 1991.

Siruni, Hagop J. *Bolis ew ir terĕ*. Vol. 2. Beirut: Dbaran Mesrob, 1969.

———. *Bolis ew ir terĕ*. Vol. 3. Antilias: Catholicosate of Cilicia, 1987.

Stepanyan, Hasmik. *Ermeni harfli Türkçe kitaplar ve süreli yayınlar bibliyografyası*. Istanbul: Turkuaz Yay., 2005.

Strasser, Sabine. *Die Unreinheit ist Fruchtbar: Grenzüberschreitungen in einem türkischen Dorf am Schwarzen Meer*. Vienna: Wiener Frauenverlag, 1995.

Suciyan, Talin. *The Armenians in Modern Turkey: Post-genocide Society, Politics and History*. London: I. B. Tauris, 2016.

———. "Contesting the Authority of Armenian Administration at the Height of Tanzimat: A Case of Incest, Adultery and Abortion." *Reflektif* 2, no. 1 (2021): 29–47.

———. "Hagop Mnts'uri's *The Second Marriage*: Armenian Realities in the Pre- and Post-genocide Ottoman Empire and Turkey." *British Journal of Middle Eastern Studies* (2022): 1–17. https://doi.org/10.1080/13530194.2022.2069085.

———. "Kimsenin yüzünü görmedim: [Çocuk] dayımdandır: 1856'da Konya Akşehir'de Ermeni Kilisesi'nde çözülememiş bir dava." *Aurum* 2, no. 2 (2017): 33–42.

———. "Testifying Impotence, Annulling Marriage." In *Gender in Research and Politics: Development, Intersections and Perspectives*, ed. Sybille Lustenberger, Siran Hovannisyan, Andrea Boscoboinik, and Gohar Shahnazaryan, 157–70. Zurich: Lit Verlag, 2021.

Suciyan, Talin, with Harry Harootunian. "Abstracting the Peasant in Ottoman and Turkey's Historiography." In *The State of the Art of the Early Turkish Republic Period: Historiography, Sources and Future Directions*, ed. Barlow Der Mugrdechian, Ümit Kurt, and Ara Sarafian, 33–60. Fresno: California State Univ. Press, 2022.

Toledano, Ehud. *The Ottoman Slave Trade and Its Suppression: 1840–1890.* Princeton, NJ: Princeton Univ. Press, 1982.

Tomba, Massimiliano. *Insurgent Universality: An Alternative Legacy of Modernity.* Oxford: Oxford Univ. Press, 2019.

———. *Marx's Temporalities.* Translated by Peter D. Thomas and Sara L. Farris. Leiden: Brill. 2013.

Torlakyan, P. K. *Hay azkakrutyun ew panahyusutyun nyuter ew usumnasirutyunner 13, Hamshenahayeri azkakrutyunĕ.* Yerevan: HSSH KA, 1981.

Tuğ, Başak. "Ottoman Women as Legal and Marital Subject." In *The Ottoman World*, edited by Christine Woodhead and Artan Tülay, 362–77. London and New York: Routledge, 2012.

Ueno, Masayuki. "The First Draft of the Armenian Millet Constitution." *Annals of Japan Association for Middle East Studies* 23, no. 1 (2007): 213–51.

———. "Religious in Form, Political in Content? Privileges of Ottoman Non-Muslims in the Nineteenth Century." *Journal of the Economic and Social History of the Orient* 59 (2016): 408–41.

———. "Urban Politics in the 19th Century Istanbul: The Case of the Armenian Cemetery in Beyoğlu." In *Human Mobility and Multiethnic Coexistence in Middle Eastern Urban Societies: Tehran, Aleppo, Istanbul, and Beirut*, edited by Hidemitsu Kuroki, 85–102. Tokyo: ILCAA, 2015.

Vakalis, Anna. "Tanzimat in the Provinces: Nationalist Sedition (*fesat*), Banditry (*eşkıya*), and Local Councils in the Ottoman Southern Balkans." PhD diss., Univ. of Basel, 2019.

Wishnitzer, Avner. *Reading Clocks Alla Turca: The Time and Society in the Late Ottoman Empire.* Chicago: Univ. of Chicago Press, 2015.

Yavuz, Nuri. "Fırka-i Islahiye ordusunun özellikleri ve faaliyetleri." *Gazi Akademik Bakış* 5, no. 10 (2012): 113–27.

Yaycıoğlu, Ali. *Partners of the Empire: The Crisis of the Ottoman Order in the Age of Revolutions*. Stanford, CA: Stanford Univ. Press, 2016.

Zeevi, Dror. "The Use of Ottoman Sharia Court Records as a Source for Middle Eastern History." *Islamic Law and Society* 5, no. 1 (1998): 35–56.

Index

Talin Suciyan is associate professor (*privat dozentin*) of Turkish studies at Ludwig Maximilian University of Munich. She received her doctoral degree in 2015 with her book *The Armenians in Modern Turkey: Post-genocide Society, History and Politics* (I. B. Tauris, 2016), which has been translated into Turkish (Aras, 2018) and German (De Gruyter, 2021). In 2019 she received her *habilitation* with "'Ya derdimize derman, ya katlimize Ferman (Either save us from this misery or order our death)': Tanzimat of the Provinces." Her research focuses on Ottoman intercommunal relations and unevenness, noncontemporaneities, gender, peasantry, Armenian literature of the Ottoman provinces, and medical practices of the nineteenth- and twentieth-century Middle East. Among her recent publications are "Can the Survivor Speak?" (2022), "Hagop Mnts'uri's *The Second Marriage*: Armenian Realities in the Pre- and Post-genocide Ottoman Empire and Turkey" (2022), "An Armenian Woman's Appeal to Divorce: Kesedji Harutiwn's Testified Impotence" (2021), and "Contesting the Authority of Armenian Administration at the Height of Tanzimat: A Case of Incest, Adultery and Abortion" (2021).

Printed in the USA
CPSIA information can be obtained
at www.ICGtesting.com
LVHW101655121023
760930LV00003B/12

9 780815 638193